MIGHTY
IN
WORD
AND
DEED

MIGHTY
IN
WORD
AND
DEED

The Role of the Holy Spirit
in Luke–Acts

JAMES B. SHELTON

Wipf and Stock Publishers
EUGENE, OREGON

Wipf and Stock Publishers
199 West 8th Avenue, Suite 3
Eugene, Oregon 97401

Mighty in Word and Deed
The Role of the Holy Spirit in Luke-Acts
By Shelton, James
Copyright©1991by Shelton, James
ISBN: 1-57910-321-9
Publication date: January, 2000
Previously published by Hendrickson Publishers, 1991

Table of Contents

Preface

*F*OR MUCH OF THE twentieth century the church has been divided over the role of the Holy Spirit. Many valid issues have been raised, viz., What is the role of the Holy Spirit in Christian conversion? When does the Holy Spirit empower believers? How does one know if one has received the Spirit? Is there a difference between having the Spirit and being filled with or baptized in the Holy Spirit? What is the relationship between the Holy Spirit and miracles? Sadly, however valid these issues are, sometimes the debate over them has been conducted in a divisive, partisan way rather than in a genuine effort to understand and appreciate different perspectives within the body of Christ. At times the fruit of the Spirit has been shoved aside in the struggle to force the Holy Spirit into the box of each one's own set of theological presuppositions. Scholarship provides a solution to some of these misunderstandings. Redaction criticism can redirect New Testament study to look at the distinctive contributions and viewpoints of each writer separately rather than to assume that the theological agendas of the NT writers are basically the same and therefore interchangeable. The views of Luke on the Holy Spirit, for example, should not be indiscriminately interpreted in light of Paul's presentation of the Spirit (or vice versa), because often they are addressing different themes concerning the Holy Spirit. Ignoring the writers' individual perspectives on the Holy Spirit has resulted in much confusion. This is not to say that there is not a unified message about the Spirit in the scriptures, but at the same time there is a diversity in the witnesses to the Spirit which must not be overlooked in our attempts to harmonize NT pneumatology. When it is realized that each NT writer has a distinct solo to perform in the symphony of the Spirit, new and unique messages fall upon the readers' ears. When one listens to Luke as having a separate and distinct message, the theme of the Holy

Spirit is heard frequently throughout Luke–Acts. Luke presents the Spirit as the joy in the celebration of the gospel, the breath of prayer and praise, and the miraculous power behind bold and effective witness. In order to accomplish its mission, the church today needs to rediscover the joy and power contained in Luke's message of the Holy Spirit. It would be hoped that when the church realizes that there are different presentations of the Holy Spirit in the NT, division and misunderstandings will cease, and unity and power (yes, a new Pentecost) will occur. Then the church will be full of the Spirit to carry out its mission.

Special thanks is extended to Dr. John Drane, my doctoral advisor, since a good portion of the research for this book was done under his direction at the University of Stirling in Scotland. Thanks to Dr. I. Howard Marshall and Professor F. F. Bruce for graciously consenting to be the external readers of the original dissertation. I also would like to express appreciation to the faculty and administration of Oral Roberts University for their camaraderie and good will during the writing process and to Ms. Taylor Shepherd for help with the indices. Also, I would like to gratefully acknowledge the patience and help of Mr. Patrick Alexander, editor of Hendrickson Publishers, who made this opportunity possible. My enduring gratitude goes to Sally, my wife and co-laborer, who typed and helped edit the manuscript.

> And chiefly thou, O Spirit, that dost prefer
> Before all temples th'upright heart and pure
> Instruct me, for thou know'st; thou from the first
> Was present, and with mighty wings outspread
> Dovelike sat'st brooding on the vast abyss,
> And mad'st it pregnant: what in me is dark
> Illumine, what is low raise and support;
> That to the heighth of this great argument
> I may assert Eternal Providence,
> And justify the ways of God to men.
>
> —Milton, *Paradise Lost*, Book 1

James B. Shelton
Tulsa, Oklahoma

Selected Abbreviations

AB   Anchor Bible
Anbib   Analecta biblica
BAGD   Bauer, W., W. F. Arndt, F. W. Gingrich, and F. W. Danker. *A Greek-English Lexicon of the New Testament and Other Early Christian Literature*. Second edition; Chicago: University of Chicago Press, 1979.
BDF   Blass, F., A. Debrunner, and R. W. Funk. *A Greek Grammar of the New Testament and Other Early Christian Literature*. Chicago: University of Chicago Press, 1961.
Bib   *Biblica*
BNTC   Black's New Testament Commentaries
CBQ   *Catholic Biblical Quarterly*
CGTC   Cambridge Greek Testament Commentary
ExpT   *Expository Times*
FRLANT   Forschungen zur Religion und Literatur des Alten und Neuen Testaments
HTS   Harvard Theological Studies
ICC   International Critical Commentary
Int   *Interpretation*
JBL   *Journal of Biblical Literature*
JSNT   *Journal for the Study of the New Testament*
LXX   Septuagint
MSS   manuscripts
NASB   New American Standard Bible
NICNT   New International Commentary on the New Testament
NIDNTT   *New International Dictionary of New Testament Theology*. Edited by C. Brown, 3 vols. Exeter: Paternoster Press, 1978.
NIGTC   New International Greek Testament Commentary
NovT   *Novum Testamentum*
NT   New Testament
NTS   *New Testament Studies*
OT   Old Testament
OTP   *Old Testament Pseudepigrapha*. Edited by J. H. Charlesworth. New York: Doubleday, 1983.
RB   *Revue biblique*
Pss Sol   Psalms of Solomon
RevExp   *Review and Expositor*

RSV   Revised Standard Version
SBLMS   Society of Biblical Literature Monograph Series
Sir   Sirach (Ecclesiasticus)
SNTSMS   Society for New Testament Studies Monograph Series
Str-B   Strack, H. L. and P. Billerbeck. *Kommentar zum Neuen Testament aus Talmud und Midrasch.* 5 vols. Munich: C. H. Beck, 1926.
T 12 Patr   Testament of the Twelve Patriarchs
TDNT   *Theological Dictionary of the New Testament.* Edited by G. Kittel and G. Friedrich. 10 vols. Translated by G. Bromiley. Grand Rapids: Eerdmans, 1964–1976.
TNTC   Tyndale New Testament Commentaries
TynB   *Tyndale Bulletin*
UBS   United Bible Societies
VoxEv   *Vox Evangelica*
WMANT   Wissenschaftliche Monographien zum Alten und Neuen Testament
ZNW   *Zeitschrift für die neutestamentliche Wissenschaft*

1 | What Is the Role of the Holy Spirit in Luke–Acts?

RECENTLY THERE HAS been a renewed interest in the study of the Holy Spirit and Luke–Acts. Both church members and academicians have begun again to ask St. Luke questions about the Holy Spirit: Who is the Holy Spirit? What is the role of the Spirit? Does reception of the Spirit involve conversion or empowerment? What distinctive message does Luke provide concerning the Holy Spirit? Is Luke's message applicable to the church today? The rise of the Pentecostal and Charismatic movements has motivated the church as a whole to rediscover and redefine the Holy Spirit and the Spirit's significance for the church today. On one hand, the Holy Spirit's role in ecstatic worship and miracles has almost completely dominated the attention of some Christians; while, on the other hand, some have thoroughly rejected such a role. Sharp disagreement has arisen over the roles of the Holy Spirit in conversion, in empowerment, and in the nature of Christian experience with the Holy Spirit. Many non-charismatic groups assume that "filled with the Holy Spirit" and parallel phrases in Luke–Acts refer to conversion, while most Pentecostals assume that such phrases consistently indicate that some ecstatic experience, usually speaking in tongues, has occurred. Both groups are partially wrong because neither realizes or appreciates that there are different emphases on the role of the Holy Spirit among NT authors. Furthermore, biblical scholarship has shown a renewed interest in Luke–Acts over the past thirty years. During this time scholars have developed a new way of looking at the NT that respects each canonical writer's unique perspective and observations. This approach, called redaction criticism, offers a solution to the current debate about the Holy Spirit.

Traditionally the church has used Luke's Gospel mostly as a mere supplement to the Gospels of Matthew and John in "life of Christ" studies. Similarly, it has often pressed the book of Acts into service as a chronological and historical framework for courses on the life and teachings of Paul. Apart from this, Luke–Acts as a literary unit is often neglected. However, Luke wrote these two books as a single theological unit, and they deserve to be studied as such. In failing to treat them as a unit, we neglect the unique integrity and message of a work that comprises *one quarter* of the entire NT!

Luke's special view of the Holy Spirit suffers severe neglect under the traditional approach. Many of his distinctive and important messages are lost when bits and pieces of his work are frittered away in attempts to harmonize the NT message. This is especially true when his pneumatology, i.e., his view of the Spirit, is indiscriminately lumped together with the pneumatologies of Paul and John.

The Perils of Neglecting Luke's Unique Message: What Is At Stake?

To neglect the unique message of Luke–Acts imperils the church in several ways: misinterpreting scripture, causing division in the church, and denying the nature of Christian inspiration.

Scripture

First, a proper understanding of scripture falls into jeopardy when the unique messages of the Gospel writers are ignored. Each NT writer has distinctive reasons and unique occasions for writing, and therefore each work must be studied on its own. This is not to say that attempts to harmonize the NT material into one message are completely unwarranted; they can be fruitful exercises. Yet the distinctive message of each Gospel needs to be heard as well.

Listening to the common emphasis in the four Gospels is like listening to a symphony. The harmony they produce provides a strong message; yet the music often includes solos as well. It is during these solo performances that the unique message of each Gospel becomes evident. Each has distinct tones and emphases. For example, Matthew emphasizes Jesus' kingship and prophetic fulfillment; Mark speaks of action, conflict, and the role of servanthood; John speaks of the divinity of Jesus; Luke speaks of joy, praise, prayer, and the Holy Spirit. These unique messages are often missed when all the books are treated as one work. In fact, harmonization at the expense of the individual themes can in reality become (to change the metaphor) *homogenization.* The original contribution of each work is not respected, and a new product never intended by the writers is created; thus the cream of each Gospel is lost.

Unity

Second, a purely harmonistic approach to the pneumatologies of the various NT writers puts the unity of the church at risk. This is especially true when interpreters ignore that each NT writer does not address the same question when mentioning the Holy Spirit. As we will discuss in more detail later, Paul's pneumatology often addresses the question of ontology—what is the Holy Spirit's role in the conversion and maintenance of the life of a Christian—while John is more interested in the interrelationships between the Father, the Son, the Holy Spirit, and believers. Luke, however, is more interested in the role of the Holy Spirit in empowering believers to witness. When one tries to interpret Luke's pneumatology through Paul's or John's or vice versa, a doctrinal imbalance occurs. It is not surprising therefore that churches argue and divide over what should be their greatest asset and their indispensable common ground of being: the Holy Spirit. When one group tries to champion one NT pneumatology over another, misunderstandings, divisions, and pain ensue.

Inspiration

Third, the exclusively harmonistic approach to the NT's varied presentations of the Holy Spirit ignores the nature of Christian inspiration. The early church insisted on four Gospels. Tatian's attempt to harmonize them into a shorter version did not universally catch on. The church recognized that the object of the Gospels was not just to record facts about the life and teachings of Jesus. In addition, the church saw the Gospels as proclamations of good news written by different individuals with different perspectives and vocabularies. The Gospels are unique witnesses which, though inspired, reflect the distinct personality and concerns of each writer. The Christian view of inspiration does not eliminate the element of human participation. The writers did not come under a magical spell in which they were no longer under their own control. Even when God presented visions to the writers of scripture, he involved their will in recording the event. In Acts, when people like Peter and Paul are filled with the Holy Spirit and speak, they are still in possession of their own mental faculties even though the Holy Spirit is superintending their message and inspiring their words. Apparently the writing of scripture was not unlike prophecy in the early church. The Spirit-inspired speaker was still in control of his/her own spirit, mind, and vocal cords (1 Cor 14:31–32). Christian inspiration involved active human participation and not blank passivity.

Some Christians' view of inspiration resembles that of Islam, which teaches that Mohammed received a word-for-word revelation from Allah; Mohammed served merely as a recorder. This is why Moslems insist on only one Qur'an and criticize Christians for having four Gospels. For Christians, however, the ultimate revelation is the person of Jesus Christ, the Word of God. In a very real sense, the Gospels are the word of God, yet at the same time they remain the words of human witnesses. The Christian sees the Holy Spirit as being responsible not only for inspiring the content of the scripture but also for choosing the authors. Therefore, we can celebrate the differences in the Gospels as well as the similarities as part of the inspired message.

Luke's Perspective on the Holy Spirit: How Is It Unique?

The validity of differences in the NT canon is especially clear in the distinctive presentations of the Holy Spirit. Even though Luke was well acquainted with several written presentations of the gospel (Luke 1:1), he felt compelled to compose yet another gospel to emphasize, among other things, the work of the Holy Spirit. All of the Gospel writers referred to the Spirit, but Luke emphasized the Spirit's role by mentioning it in events where the other Gospel writers did not. Why did Luke do this? Our study will demonstrate that Luke was often pointing to the role of the Holy Spirit in effecting miracles and inspiring witness. This is one of the main reasons Luke wrote his Gospel and Acts: to add to the existing publications "those things which are most surely believed among us" (Luke 1:1, KJV).

Identifying Luke's Unique Perspective: What Method Will Be Used?

Luke Contrasted with the Synoptic Gospels. How can one identify Luke's distinctive interest in the Holy Spirit? A study of the Synoptic Gospels in a synopsis or harmony of the Gospels reveals significant differences in presentation and emphasis in the same passage. The discipline which tries to identify the reasons for these different emphases is called *redaction criticism*. By comparing and contrasting how the Gospel writers present the same events in the life of Jesus, we can identify their major reasons for writing their Gospels. Redaction criticism has tangible and measurable ways of identifying the distinctive theological agendas in each Gospel. These include the study of:

(1) the distinctive vocabulary and style of each evangelist (Gospel writer),

(2) the repetition of themes in the same Gospel,

(3) the comparison and contrast of the same passage in the different Gospels,

(4) how the evangelist handles his sources, and

(5) what the evangelist omits from his sources (particularly when Mark is used as the source).

(6) what the evangelist adds to the common gospel material.[1]

Thus we can see the distinctive emphases of power and witness in Luke's presentation of the Holy Spirit much more clearly when we contrast his Gospel with the other Gospels, as we will do in the next section.

Luke Contrasted with Paul. Also revealing is the contrast between Luke's presentation of the Holy Spirit and Paul's pneumatology. Paul, like Luke, connects fullness of the Spirit with inspired speech (Eph 5:18–20). Likewise, Paul links the Spirit with effectual prayer, even as Luke does (Rom 8:26–27). Yet there are some profound differences. Paul's pneumatology is pervasive and broad in its scope; the scope of the Spirit's influence encompasses nearly all aspects of life (Eph 5:18–6:9).[2] Although Paul discusses empowering in connection with the Holy Spirit, he often addresses the issue of ontology when he mentions the Holy Spirit. In Romans 8 Paul discusses the effects of Christian conversion and salvation in relation to "life in the Spirit" (8:2–8). He uses such phrases as "having the Spirit" (8:9) and being "led by the Spirit" (8:14) to describe Christian conversion and lifestyle.

Luke's presentation of the work of the Holy Spirit, by comparison, is much narrower. This is especially true of his use of "filled with the Holy Spirit" or "full of the Holy Spirit." For Luke, these two phrases usually indicate that *inspired witness is about to occur or has occurred.* The same is true for other expressions that Luke uses to describe the activity of the Holy Spirit. The most frequent and dominant function of pneumatology in Luke–Acts is witness and inspired speech. It is not surprising that Luke also describes the Holy Spirit as the prime source of praise and rejoicing. Luke shows that the Holy Spirit is responsible for miraculous deeds. Moreover, Luke inextricably connects the Spirit with the kingdom and with prayer. Where one of these activities exists the others often follow. Thus, in Luke–Acts the recipients of the Holy Spirit are, like Moses, "mighty in . . . words and deeds" (Acts 7:22), even as Jesus himself was "mighty in deed and word" (Luke 24:19). Luke does not show as much interest as Paul in the Spirit's role in conversion and who believers are in Christ; rather, power for mission catches the majority of Luke's attention.

Distinctives of the Holy Spirit in the Synoptics and Acts: A Summary

To recognize Luke's unique perceptions of the Holy Spirit, we will begin by summarizing the presentations of the Holy Spirit in the other Synoptic Gospels and then in Luke and Acts. Such a summary will provide a contrast that will allow us to more clearly see the theological intent of Luke. After we have viewed the pneumatologies in the various Gospels and Acts as separate theological systems, we will proceed with the comparisons and contrasts in specific texts in Luke (chs. 2–10) and in Acts (ch. 11). These similarities and differences will demonstrate that though the Gospel writers agree on the essentials of the good news of Jesus, the gospel message has many distinctives with many more unique applications to Christian life both then and now.

The Holy Spirit in Mark. Mark's pneumatology[3] includes the following components:

1. Jesus is described as the Baptizer in the Holy Spirit to indicate that the ministry of Jesus is greater than the ministry of John. The writer of Mark undoubtedly is aware of the charismatic phenomena attributed to the Holy Spirit during the apostolic era. Furthermore, in the final version of Mark tongues and miracles appear in the longer ending (16:17–18). However, Mark does not explicitly present John's prophecy concerning Jesus, the Spirit-Baptizer, as fulfilled at Pentecost. It appears that the reference to the Holy Spirit (Mark 1:4–11) mainly shows the superiority of the ministry of Jesus over John's and identifies Jesus as the Son of God. The reference's primary function is not to assert that the Holy Spirit empowered Jesus at his baptism. Furthermore, the manifestations in 16:17–18 are not specifically ascribed to the Holy Spirit. Thus, Mark is content to present the Holy Spirit prophecy concerning Jesus through John the Baptist's temporally limited perspective, and he does not anticipate the church's understanding of the prophecy after Pentecost.

2. Jesus was to some degree subordinate to the Holy Spirit. After the baptism the Spirit thrust Jesus into a confrontation with the tempter (Mark 1:12–13).

3. The works of Jesus were the works of the Holy Spirit, for those who spoke against exorcisms performed by Jesus were blaspheming against the Holy Spirit (Mark 3:22–30). In v. 30 Mark implies that the Holy Spirit was in Jesus; however, this is parenthetical and does not appear to be one of his major interests.

4. Prophecy of old was uttered by means of the Holy Spirit, especially prophecies concerning Jesus (Mark 12:35–36).

5. The Holy Spirit specially spoke through believers when they were confronted by the authorities (Mark 13:11).

6. The blasphemy of the Holy Spirit saying, in conjunction with the Holy Spirit's leading Jesus to the scene of the temptation, may indicate a special function of the Spirit, i.e., the ability to confront the devil successfully, but this is at best implied.

The material on the Holy Spirit in Mark is minimal compared to the other Gospels. Mark's audience and objectives may not have required notations on the relationship of the Holy Spirit with Jesus and believers, but still by comparison with what Matthew, Luke, John, and Paul explicitly say about the Spirit, Mark is indeed impoverished. When Mark does mention the Holy Spirit, he does so primarily to identify Jesus as the Messiah, the Son of God.

The Holy Spirit in Matthew. Matthew's pneumatology is much more extensive than Mark's and contains the following elements:

1. The Holy Spirit was the agent of Jesus' conception (1:18).

2. The baptism in the Holy Spirit and fire distinguishes the ministry of Jesus from that of John the Baptist (ch. 3). Fire appears to be primarily a baptism of judgment. For Matthew the reference to Jesus as the Baptizer is primarily used to warn the Pharisees and Sadducees that Jesus would execute justice in the immediate context: Matthew, however, indicates here and elsewhere (28:19) that the baptism in the Holy Spirit and the baptism in fire are two different baptisms. Two groups were addressed in the preaching of John the Baptist in Matthew: (1) the truly repentant and (2) the Pharisees and Sadducees. The fire is for the trees that do not bear fruit (3:8–10). That the baptism with the Holy Spirit is for the believers is implied in the baptismal formula in 28:19.

3. As in Mark, the baptism scene identifies Jesus as the one associated with the Holy Spirit and therefore as the great Baptizer. This provides an occasion for the voice from heaven to identify Jesus as Messiah (3:16–17).

4. The Holy Spirit leads Jesus (4:1).

5. The Holy Spirit (the Spirit of God) enables Jesus to proclaim judgment and lead justice to victory. Matthew considers this as fulfillment of prophecy concerning Jesus' ability to heal and/or his overt avoidance of conflict with the Pharisees. Matthew sees the Spirit as greater at least in a hierarchical sense (12:15–21).

6. The Spirit, the Holy Spirit, and the Spirit of God are synonymous (ch. 12).

7. The Spirit of the Father speaks through believers when confronted by the authorities (Matt 10:19–20).

8. To speak against the works of Jesus is to speak against the Holy Spirit, which is the capital sin (12:22–32).

9. As implied in Mark, performing exorcisms and confronting the devil are associated with the Holy Spirit and his power (12:28).

10. The prophets spoke by the Holy Spirit (22:43).

11. Baptisms performed by the disciples are to occur in the name of the Father, the Son, and the Holy Spirit. All authority is given to Jesus. Apparently, prior to the resurrection, Jesus operates by the authority of the Holy Spirit. Jesus dispenses power (implied) to the disciples in the commission (28:18–20).

The material in Matthew is more detailed than that in Mark. This could well indicate an expansion of the Spirit traditions in the church. But this is not a necessary conclusion. To assume this, Marcan material would have to be identified as one of the most ancient sources available for Christian pneumatology in the extant texts. Mark's interest in Christology and the passion may have minimized his interest in the relationship of the Spirit with Jesus and the church. The understanding of the work of the Holy Spirit common to Pauline and Johannine material and to Luke and Matthew indicates a widespread and basic pneumatology that exceeds the content presented in Mark.

Matthew's material on the Holy Spirit serves two of his distinct interests well: the role of the church (ecclesiology) and the identification of Jesus (Christology). Matthew often speaks of the affairs of the church when other writers do not (e.g., Matt 16:17–19; 18:15–20; 20:1–16; 28:18–20). Matthew views the Holy Spirit as the source of inspiration and authority for the church (10:19–20; 28:18–20). Following Mark's lead, Matthew also emphasizes Jesus' link with the Holy Spirit to demonstrate his sonship. Matthew demonstrates that although Jesus humbled himself by accepting baptism at the hands of John, Jesus is greater than the Baptist. The descent of the Holy Spirit as a result of Jesus' baptism proves John's prophecy: The one who would come after him would be his superior in the Holy Spirit. This is an important point that Matthew makes to his decidedly Jewish audience.

The Holy Spirit in Luke. Like the other Gospel writers, Luke uses the Holy Spirit material to make distinctive theological points. His material on the Spirit can be summarized as follows:

1. John the son of Zechariah is filled with the Holy Spirit from his mother's womb. He is therefore great before the Lord. He is filled with the Holy Spirit apparently to be enabled both to perform the task of proclaiming the kingdom and the gospel and to witness to the Messiah (1:15, 17, 41; 3:2).

2. The Holy Spirit is responsible for the conception of Jesus. Thus Jesus is holy. In addition, because of the Holy Spirit's activity, Jesus is called the Son of God (1:35). It can also be said that the Holy Spirit is the means whereby the Messiah comes, and all the ministry of Jesus described in 1:32–33 can be ascribed, at least initially, to the agency of the Holy Spirit (i.e., called the Son of the Most High, accession to the throne of David, the reign over the house of Jacob with a kingdom that would have no end).

3. The Holy Spirit reveals things to people and enables them to speak authoritatively in prophecy, in both forthtelling and foretelling. This often occurs when the author notes that the Holy Spirit comes upon or fills people such as Elizabeth, Zechariah, Simeon, John, and even Jesus (1:15, 17, 41f.; 2:25ff.; 3:2, 22; 4:1, 14, 18).

4. The filling of the Holy Spirit and his abiding upon someone function in two ways. First, the filling might be seen as an abiding state, e.g., John, Jesus, and possibly Simeon (1:15 with 1:41, and 3:2; 4:1, 14; 2:25ff.). Second, Luke also uses it to express a specific endowment by the Holy Spirit for a specific occasion. This endowment usually enables the recipient to witness authoritatively concerning Jesus or salvation history, to properly interpret the scriptures, to speak of the nature of the Messiah's kingdom, or to confront and defeat the enemies of the true Israel. This usage seems to be the dominant theme even in the passages where "fullness" as an abiding state may be inferred.

5. Though Jesus has a special relationship with the Holy Spirit as indicated in the annunciation to Mary, he receives power from the Holy Spirit at his baptism to begin his ministry (4:1, 14, 18).

6. Jesus is associated with the Holy Spirit in John's prophecy about the Baptizer in the Holy Spirit (3:16).

7. In Luke the baptism in the Holy Spirit is not primarily a baptism of judgment but is a baptism of empowerment (3:16 with Acts 2:3f.; note also the lack of reference to vengeance or to repentance in Luke 4:18f.).

8. The Holy Spirit guides people from one place to another, as in the case of Simeon in the temple and Jesus in the wilderness of temptation (Luke 2:27; 4:1). (This may be somewhat parallel to the account in Acts of Philip's supernatural transportation to Gaza, 8:39.)

9. According to Luke's introduction of Jesus' ministry in Galilee at the Nazareth synagogue, the Holy Spirit rests upon and anoints Jesus to proclaim fulfillment of scripture, to exegete authoritatively, to recount the salvation history of Israel, to release the captives of the evil one, to confront and defeat the devil, to heal, to preach the good news, and to do wonders in general (4:14, 18f.).

10. Blasphemy against the Holy Spirit is failing to provide a witness to Jesus when the Holy Spirit provides the ability to do so (12:10–12).

11. Jesus gives the power of the Holy Spirit to his disciples (9:1 implied and 24:49). The source of the power to do wonders is ascribed to the Lord (5:17), to the name of Jesus (in Acts 3:6, 16; 4:7, 10, 17–18, 30), and to the Holy Spirit (4:18f.). This overlapping continues in Acts.

12. The activity of the Holy Spirit is seen as an event in Israel's salvation history. The Holy Spirit is the source of and direction for the salvation history, and to some extent the advent of the Holy Spirit is the fulfillment of the eschaton (Luke 3:16 with Acts 2:3ff.; Luke 11:2 [variant]; Luke 24:49 with Acts 1:6–8).

Although the work of the Holy Spirit and the ministry of Jesus sometimes overlap in the book of Luke (as elsewhere), the Holy Spirit has an extensive work separate from the work of Christ. I. H. Marshall is correct in identifying the central theme of the writing of Luke as "Jesus offers salvation to men" (Luke 19:10; Acts 4:12).[4] For Luke, however, this is revealed principally by the acts of the Holy Spirit in and around the church (Acts 5:32). The works of the Holy Spirit, though varied, serve one primary function in Luke–Acts: to witness to the ministry of Jesus and to bring about the working of salvation in the church. The primary function of the Holy Spirit in Luke–Acts is to witness concerning Jesus.

The Holy Spirit in Acts. The activity of the Holy Spirit as presented in Acts can be summarized in five main categories: the Spirit and Jesus, the Spirit and the scriptures, the Spirit and believers, Luke's specialized use of the phrase, "filled with the Holy Spirit," and the Holy Spirit as an "event."

The Spirit and Jesus. 1. The Holy Spirit empowers Jesus to give orders to his apostles (Acts 1:2).

2. God anoints Jesus with the Holy Spirit and power at his baptism, enabling him to do good, to heal, and to confront and overpower evil. Jesus, through whom peace is preached to all, who is Lord

of all, who through his death and resurrection (implied) becomes judge of all, and who made available forgiveness of sins to all, is anointed with the Holy Spirit and power. He in turn dispenses the Spirit and subsequent power to his disciples and followers (2:33; 10:36–38). Jesus' works attest to God's power working through him (2:22).

The Spirit and the Scriptures. The Holy Spirit inspires and speaks through the writers of old (4:25; 28:25). The Holy Spirit, or the state of being filled with the Holy Spirit, apparently enables proper interpretation of the scriptures. Being filled with the Holy Spirit is related to the recounting of salvation history. (See sermons of Peter and Stephen—2:14, 4:8; 6:10ff.)

The Spirit and Believers. 1. The Holy Spirit guides and empowers the believer in a manner similar to the way he guides and empowers Jesus (1:5, 8; 2:33, 38ff.; 10:37ff.; and passim in Luke–Acts).

2. The Holy Spirit speaks to believers (13:2; 20:23; 21:11; 28:25).

3. The Holy Spirit miraculously transports people (8:39).

4. There is a relationship between signs, wonders, healing, and the Holy Spirit (10:38; 5:32; 13:9–10); however, signs and wonders are also done in the name of Jesus (3:6; 4:10, 30).

5. The power received after the Holy Spirit comes upon the believer is primarily for witnessing of Jesus (2:4ff.; 4:8, 31; 6:5ff.; 9:17ff.; 13:9, 48–49, 52; and passim).

6. Baptism of believers and reception of the Holy Spirit are closely associated, if not synonymous (2:38ff.; 8:39 [variant]; 19:2ff.).

7. The Spirit is the source of prophecy and discernment to the believers (2:17ff.; 16:6; 13:9–10; 20:23; 21:10ff.).

"Filled with the Holy Spirit." 1. The phrase is used in conjunction with the reception of the Holy Spirit as in 2:4ff. and 10:44ff. (In the last citation, though the phrase is not specifically used, the context identifies it as synonymous with the Acts 2:4ff. account.)

2. Luke employs this phrase when a special dispensation of the Spirit is manifested or when the readers are to be reminded of the power behind the person who was speaking with authority (e.g., Acts 4:8, 31; 6:3, 5; 7:55; 13:9). The use of the phrase in connection with definitive statements, interpretation of scripture, acts of discernment, visions, and revelations shows that Luke understands these utterances and perceptions to have come directly from the Holy Spirit; therefore, these acts proclaim divine truths. Luke believes that he is describing utterances, interpretations, and insights inspired by the Holy Spirit.

In the sermons in Acts that are addressed to Jews and to the household of Cornelius, the speaker is often noted to be full of the Holy Spirit, or filled with the Holy Spirit, at the time he speaks. Furthermore, these speeches usually contain some form of recounting the salvation history of the OT in relation to Jesus and/or the early church. By reconstructing the speeches in this manner, Luke is declaring that the Spirit who prompted the writers of old and caused the wonders of God in the OT is the same Spirit who now speaks through the church. Luke makes a conscious effort to link the events of the church with the events of God's redemption in the past. By the same Spirit who had inspired the prophets of old the church recognizes these events both past and present to be parts of one and the same plan of God.

The Holy Spirit as an "Event." At times Luke treats the Holy Spirit as an "event" that validates the claims of Jesus and his church. Thus the advent of the Holy Spirit in the life of the church is seen as an act of the salvation history, and according to the sermon at Pentecost it is, to some extent, the fulfillment of salvation history.

Thus the Holy Spirit speaks to, guides, and edifies the church as well as having spoken through the prophets of old. He also enables the church, but here Luke identifies the work of the Spirit and the name of Jesus together as the source of power for believers in Acts. The Holy Spirit is not only a name for divinity, but he is also an event—an act in salvation history. Manifestations of the Holy Spirit witness to Jesus and the church. However, in Acts the most frequent function of the Holy Spirit is to witness to Jesus by empowering believers to speak authoritatively concerning Jesus. In Acts Luke maintains the pneumatology that he presents in his Gospel. Inspired by the Holy Spirit, believers relate the salvation history of old to Jesus, fulfill prophecy, correctly interpret scripture, and confront the powers of Satan. Thus the speeches (or the references to speeches) in Acts are often prefaced with some comment on the relationship of the speaker with the Holy Spirit. This usually is an explanation indicating that the speaker is specially empowered to speak on that occasion (usually signalled by "filled" or "was filled with the Holy Spirit"), or that the speaker is full of the Holy Spirit in a continual sense, or both. This is not the exclusive use of "filled with" or "full of the Holy Spirit," but it is the dominant and consistent one (Acts 2:4ff.; 4:8, 31; 6:3, 5; 7:54ff.; 11:24; 13:9; 19:6).

This special function of the Holy Spirit in Acts serves the overall purpose of Acts. To be filled with the Holy Spirit means primarily to be a witness to Jesus and his works. The Spirit who caused the ancient events of deliverance and who spoke through the prophets is the same Spirit who empowers Jesus and who causes the apostles and disciples to proclaim the true salvation history and to work the wonders that Luke reported to Theophilus.

It is not surprising that the pneumatology in the Gospel of Luke is very similar to that in Acts, but what is of more particular interest is that Luke adjusts the synoptic material to conform to the concepts of the Holy Spirit which he and his community have experienced. Thus the pneumatology of Acts is superimposed upon the Gospel of Luke. Fortunately Luke does not totally eliminate the pneumatology of his sources. This is not necessary, since he is really expanding, applying, and clarifying the traditions he received. When Luke is compared and contrasted with the other synoptists, differences in pneumatology become apparent. In chapters 2–10, an analysis of the material in Luke in comparison and contrast to the other Synoptic Gospels will demonstrate this.

Plan of Study

This study of Luke–Acts will demonstrate that Luke emphasizes the Holy Spirit's role both in miracles and in the proclamation of the church. The role that seizes Luke's attention the most, however, is that of Spirit-inspired witness. First, we will examine Luke's references to the Holy Spirit in his Gospel. By comparing and contrasting the way the Gospel writers handle passages that they have in common, we will note Luke's distinct interest in the Holy Spirit. When we analyze the passages that only Luke has (what is called the L material), we will see that the Holy Spirit and witness are at the heart of Luke's theology. Identifying the distinguishing vocabulary of Luke will show how Luke adjusted his Gospel sources to emphasize the role of the Holy Spirit. Finally, we will see Luke's pneumatology blossom and proliferate in the Acts of the Apostles where he is no longer dependent upon the Synoptic Gospel sources that he treats so deferentially. We will see that in Luke's hand, Spirit-inspired witness dominates the one quarter of the NT that we call Luke–Acts. I hope that through this study the church will more clearly hear the message that Luke proclaimed nearly 2000 years ago: "Filled with the Holy Spirit . . . speak the word of God with boldness."

Notes to Chapter 1

1. This "new" material does not mean that it is spurious; it too could have apostolic origin. No Gospel writer told us everything that could be told about Jesus (John 20:30; 21:25).

2. Note that grammatically Eph 5:18–6:9 is one unit. Paul describes what it means to be filled with the Spirit by modifying the phrase with a string

of participles: "speaking . . . singing and making melody . . . giving thanks," and "be[ing] subject to one another in the fear of Christ" (NASB). This description of the Spirit-filled life involves corporate worship, family life, and employment.

3. For a treatment of Marcan pneumatology see M. Robert Mansfield, *Spirit & Gospel in Mark* (Peabody, Mass.: Hendrickson, 1987), 18–19, 164–65.

4. I. H. Marshall, *Luke: Historian and Theologian* (Grand Rapids: Zondervan, 1970), 116 and passim.

2 The Holy Spirit and the Infancy Witnesses

*F*ROM THE VERY BEGINNING of his Gospel, Luke's major emphasis is the Holy Spirit's inspiring human beings to witness concerning Jesus. In the infancy stories of John the Baptist and Jesus, Luke makes the first of many deliberate associations of the Holy Spirit with inspired speaking. This pattern continues throughout his Gospel and Acts. In contrast to Mark and John, who do not record the nativity, Luke discusses the events surrounding the births of John the Baptist and Jesus. In contrast to Matthew, who also records the birth and early life of Jesus (Matt 1–2), Luke introduces events and personalities that Matthew does not even mention. Matthew concentrates on events that emphasize Jesus' messianic royalty and the fulfillment of prophecy, while Luke highlights the major themes of salvation, praise, joy, and the Holy Spirit.[1] Through his presentation of the earliest witnesses to Jesus and the gospel, Luke continually emphasizes inspired witness.

In his first two chapters, Luke records the Holy Spirit-inspired responses of Mary, John, Elizabeth, Zechariah, Simeon, and Anna to the advent of salvation. Luke 1–2 is a veritable litany of Spirit-inspired witnesses to Jesus. Luke describes the characters' enablement to witness in the same terms ("filled with the Holy Spirit" or "the Holy Spirit came upon") that he uses for the empowerment for witness in the early church (e.g., Acts 1:8; 2:4; 4:8, 31). Apparently Luke considers the witness of the pre-Pentecost believers equally as inspired and valid as those he presents in Acts after Pentecost. As mentioned in chapter 1, some scholars feel the necessity of forcing Luke's concept of the Holy Spirit into a Pauline mold and thereby assume that these references to being filled with the Holy Spirit are indications of conversion in Luke–Acts. While Luke is not averse to associating the Holy Spirit with conversion, he does not usually do so, and certainly he does not in the case of the infancy narrative witnesses. These are "filled with the Holy Spirit" to pray, to praise, and to witness to the Christ, not as a sign of conversion. It is of special interest to note that Luke describes these witnesses to Jesus as righteous, faithful, devout people of God who are looking forward to the coming of the Messiah (e.g., Luke 1:6; 2:25–26; 2:37). In their case conversion does not appear to be the major issue; but their witness to Jesus is.

The way Luke presents the work of the Holy Spirit sheds light on still another interpretation of Luke–Acts. Conzelmann has asserted that Luke divides his Gospel material into three epochs of time: (1) the era of the old age or covenant, (2) the era of Jesus, otherwise known as the "middle time"; and (3) the era of the new age or new covenant, often called the era of the church or the era of the Holy Spirit.[2] It is generally acknowledged that the other Gospel writers recognize two eras—that of the old covenant and that of the new. According to Conzelmann, Luke supposedly creates the concept of a middle time, the Jesus era.

However, while it may be generally true that such divisions of time appear in early Christian theology, Luke does not consistently respect these conventions, especially when it comes to the Holy Spirit. Whether speaking of the witnesses of the nativity, or of Jesus, or of the early church, Luke suggests that the same Holy Spirit inspired all of them.[3]

For Luke, the difference between the experiences with the Holy Spirit for the pre- and post-Pentecost faithful is *not* primarily qualitative but quantitative (Acts 2:17; see chapter 11 on Acts). Luke does not portray the early witnesses' experience with the Holy Spirit as being inferior to that of the later ones—the witness of Mary, John, Elizabeth, Zechariah, Simeon, and Anna has a powerful effect upon his audience. Therefore, when it comes to pneumatology, he blurs the epochs. Luke's interest is in the witness that the Holy Spirit inspires regardless of the epoch.

The Spirit and the Conception of Jesus

And the angel said to her,

The Holy Spirit will come upon you, and the power of the Most High will overshadow you; therefore the child to be born will be called holy, the Son of God.

—Luke 1:35

While not the first reference to the Holy Spirit in Luke's Gospel, this reference to the conception of Jesus is crucial to our understanding of the role of the Holy Spirit. From the outset, the church has focused its attention in gratitude, wonder, and amazement on this event (John 1:14; Phil 2:5–11). Reminiscent of the Hebrew understanding of the Spirit as creator (Gen 1:2), the angel declares that the Holy Spirit is responsible for the conception of Jesus. Jesus' advent, the ultimate witness of God's salvation, is initiated by the Holy Spirit. The angel Gabriel states that the Holy Spirit is the reason (*dio*) Jesus would be called holy (v. 35). In addition, the Spirit is also the agent of Jesus' messiahship and Sonship, not of his birth and holiness alone (vv. 32, 33, 35).

The presence of the Holy Spirit at Jesus' conception does more than bring him into the world; Luke sees the Holy Spirit as the source of Jesus' development and activity as a child. He points out, for example, that as a young man approximately twelve years old, Jesus astounds the teachers in the temple with his understanding (2:41–50). Also Luke twice refers to Jesus' growing up in Nazareth, increasing "in wisdom and stature, and in favor with God and man" (2:52; also 2:40). Despite this early unique relationship with the Holy Spirit, Jesus is dependent upon a subsequent empowering by the Holy Spirit to fulfill his mission as the Christ (Luke 3:21–22; 4:1, 14, 18; Acts 10:38).

The Spirit and the Witness of John

The babe leaped in her womb.

—Luke 1:41

Immediately after the angel Gabriel announced the conception of Jesus (1:26–39), Mary hurried from her home in Nazareth of Galilee to the hill country of Judah to see the sign that would confirm the angel's message to her: her aged kinswoman Elizabeth, after years of infertility, was six-months pregnant. As Mary entered the door of her relative's house, there began a Spirit-inspired progression of response and counter-response of joyous witness to Jesus' messiahship (1:39–56).

John

When Mary entered the house of Elizabeth, the unborn John leaped for joy at the sound of Mary's greeting. Elizabeth, filled with the Holy Spirit, interprets the significance of John's movement in the womb: Elizabeth and John are in the presence of the mother of the Lord and the Lord himself in Mary's womb. John's leaping acknowledges the presence of the Lord. It is no accident that Luke previously described John as "*filled with the Holy Spirit* even from his mother's womb" (1:15, my ital.).[4] The angel Gabriel and Zechariah both explain why John received the power of the Spirit: to call the people to repentance, to go before the Lord as his precursor and herald (1:17, 76–79).

Usually Luke notes one is filled with the Holy Spirit just prior to an inspired utterance or other miraculous work (e.g., 1:41, 67; 4:1; Acts 2:4; 4:8, 31; 9:17–20; 13:9). If John does not fulfil this role until his debut as an adult in chapter three, then why does Luke refer to an infilling of the Spirit in the womb? It is quite plausible that Luke does so because he wishes to show that John was empowered to witness to Jesus *before* his adult ministry, while yet in his mother's womb, by jumping for joy. Perhaps this is why John is described as "filled" so early in the account. Whether Luke understands that John was filled with the Spirit at the moment of Mary's visit or that the endowment had a durative character lasting through his adult ministry cannot be settled. What is significant is that the first reference to "filled with the Holy Spirit" in Luke's Gospel is followed by inspired witness to Jesus which is the usual context Luke provides for the phrase.

John "in the Spirit and Power of Elijah"

In the angel Gabriel's prophecy concerning the Spirit-filled John, he also predicted that John would minister "in the spirit and power of Elijah" (1:17). Luke includes this mention of Elijah in reference to John here, but elsewhere he avoids equating John with Elijah (e.g., Luke 7:24–28 contra Matt 11:7–19; 17:10–13; Mark 9:13). Instead, Luke prefers to emphasize that *Jesus* is the new Elijah; Luke makes numerous allusions and parallels to the miracles of Elijah and Elisha in relation to Jesus' ministry (e.g., Luke 4:24–27 with 1 Kings 17 and 2 Kings 5; Luke 7:11–17 with 1 Kings 17:17–24; Luke 24:49 and Acts 1:4 with 2 Kings 2;[5] Luke does this because he wishes to present Jesus as the Spirit-anointed miracle worker (Luke 4:18; Acts 10:38) like Elijah. Luke prefers the Elijah-Messiah parallels over the Elijah-precursor parallels. Luke's middle position of allowing both views of the end-time Elijah to stand reflects the varied first-century identifications of Elijah as a type both of the Messiah and of the herald of the Messiah (Matt 11:13, 14; 17:10–13; Mark 9:11–13; Luke 1:15; 4:25–27; John 1:6–8, 19–23).[6]

Luke allows this reference to John as Elijah to stand in Gabriel's prophecy because the angel's words carefully define the role of John as a type of Elijah:

> And he will turn [*epistrephō*] many of the sons of Israel to the Lord their God, and he will go before him in the spirit and power of

Elijah, to turn the hearts of the fathers to the children, and the disobedient to the wisdom of the just, to make ready for the Lord a people prepared.

—Luke 1:16–17

The prophecy of Zechariah also described John's role as a herald of forgiveness and repentance (1:76–79). In this role, Luke allows John to be identified as Elijah because he sees John as a Holy Spirit-motivated witness to Jesus' messiahship and the true nature of repentance. This same role dominates Luke's presentation of the adult ministry of John in the third chapter of his Gospel, where he emphasizes John's preaching more than his baptizing. Luke reserves the Spirit-wrought miracles so dominant in the Elijah cycle of stories for Jesus' ministry.[7]

The Spirit and the Witness of Elizabeth

After John leaped in his mother's womb when Mary and the unborn Jesus entered the house, Elizabeth, "filled with the Holy Spirit" (1:41), explained why her son moved:

Blessed are you among women, and blessed is the fruit of your womb! And why is this granted to me, that the mother of my Lord should come to me? For behold, when the voice of your greeting came to my ears, the babe in my womb leaped for joy.

—Luke 1:42–44

Here as elsewhere in Luke–Acts, "filled with the Holy Spirit" indicates that inspired witness is about to take place. Luke provides a double witness to the prophetic role of the Holy Spirit: John, filled with the Holy Spirit, joyfully leaped, acknowledging the presence of Jesus and Mary. Elizabeth, filled with the Holy Spirit, interpreted the significance of John's actions. Again, we do not have a reference to conversion here but rather a simple yet powerful statement of the divine origin of the witness of John and Elizabeth.

Nevertheless, Elizabeth is not just giving a mere "Amen" to her son's apparent witness; she serves two other crucial functions. She gives important information to Luke's readers concerning the nature of the Messiah and his mother; furthermore, she confirms Mary's earlier encounter with the Holy Spirit (1:35). Elizabeth does both, enlightened by the Holy Spirit. The angel gave Mary only one sign that she had not imagined her angelic and divine encounter: Her "kinswoman Elizabeth in her old age has also conceived a son; and this is the sixth month with her who was called barren"(1:36). Expecting only one sign, she is given more: First, the unborn John rejoices at the coming of Jesus and his mother (vv. 41, 44). Second, John's mother realizes Mary is pregnant (v. 42). Third, Elizabeth knows that Mary is carrying the Messiah (v. 43). Fourth, Elizabeth tells Mary that she has indeed received a message "from the Lord," and that she is blessed because she believed "what was spoken to her" (v. 45). In giving these comforting confirmations to Mary, Elizabeth utters inspired witness from the same Holy Spirit who had "overshadowed" the mother of Jesus a few days earlier. Thus, through the witness of Elizabeth, the same Spirit responsible for the conception of Jesus provided the mother of Jesus the confirming word of that conception.

The Spirit and the Witness of Mary

When Mary receives Elizabeth's inspired greeting, she responds with praise and joy:

> My soul magnifies the Lord, and my spirit rejoices in God my Savior, for he has regarded the low estate of his handmaiden. For behold, henceforth all generations will call me blessed; for he who is mighty has done great things for me, and holy is his name.
> —Luke 1:46–49

Was Mary Filled with the Holy Spirit?

Luke does not explicitly tell his readers that at this moment Mary was speaking under the influence of the Holy Spirit. But why should Luke feel compelled to preface every inspired witness with a reference to the Holy Spirit? Often throughout Luke–Acts, one previous reference to Spirit-endowment suffices. Some students of the Bible are quick to point out that Mary is not referred to as being filled with the Holy Spirit until Pentecost (Acts 1:14; 2:4). They conclude either that Mary was not converted until the Christian Pentecost or that she lacked the Holy Spirit's empowering prior to Pentecost. Both conclusions err in that they do not take into account Luke's understanding of fullness of the Holy Spirit. They both assume that Mary as a post-Pentecost Christian could not have had a qualitative relationship with the Holy Spirit prior to Pentecost.

In light of this one must ask: How is it that Mary, the mother of the Lord, is seen as less under the influence and guidance of the Holy Spirit than John, Elizabeth, Zechariah, or Simeon? Luke has clearly ignored the so-called epoch of the Holy Spirit and the church when he describes the experience of these four in terms of the post-Pentecost church. So too in the experience of Mary and the Holy Spirit, the division between the old covenant era and that of the new is not clear-cut. But even if one insists that Mary's filling with the Holy Spirit be exclusively joined with the Pentecost event, the observation is still correct that in both Acts 2:4 and Luke 1 Luke's preferred meaning for the phrase, "filled with the Holy Spirit," is primarily divine empowerment to speak.

It is significant that after the angel announces to Mary that the Holy Spirit will come upon her and that she will be overshadowed by the "power of the Most High" (1:35), she later utters the Magnificat (1:46–55). From the time of the annunciation until she delivers the holy child, Mary is under the influence of the Holy Spirit. It is true that the stated effect of the Holy Spirit was to cause Jesus to be called holy. For Luke, however, the Spirit probably has a double effect, influencing both the mother and the child. Furthermore, given the parallel structure of Mary's words and those of Zechariah, Elizabeth, and Simeon—all of whom spoke under the direction of the Holy Spirit—there is little doubt that Mary's Magnificat is inspired by the Holy Spirit. It is perhaps significant that the verb used here in 1:35, *eperchomai* ("come upon"), is the same one used to describe the predicted Pentecost events in Acts 1:8. In both instances "power" (*dynamis*) is mentioned. Luke is probably responsible for the parallels here between the applications of divine power in the case of Mary and in that of the disciples. The verb *eperchomai* occurs seven times in Luke–Acts and only twice elsewhere (Eph 2:7; James 5:1). Its presence on the lips of the angel may be due to Luke's conscious attempt to create parallels between the infancy narrative and the post-Pentecost church.[8]

Mary and Grace

Hail, O favored [graced] one, the Lord is with you!

—Luke 1:28

Traditionally the church has understood Gabriel's description of Mary as having been favored or "graced" by God (1:28) as an indication of the presence of the Holy Spirit's gifts.[9] This understanding is not without biblical justification. In the Greek text Gabriel used the imperative of *chairō* to greet Mary. Usually this is translated as "hail," but it more accurately means "rejoice."[10] Next Luke uses the perfect participle of *charitoō* to describe Mary as the woman favored or "graced" by God (*kecharitōmenē*). He then uses *charis* in 1:30 to note that she had "found favor with God" (*heures gar charin para tō theō*). These words belong to the *chara-charien-charis-charitoō-charisma* word family which can mean "joy," "to rejoice," "grace," "to bestow favor or grace," and "gift."[11] Luke is responsible for the play on words and intends it to convey special meaning.[12] In this instance, the three references to the gracious visitation result from the favor or grace of the Lord.[13] Luke probably intends multiple meanings here, for he uses "grace" (*charis*) to describe the power of God that the Holy Spirit works in the Acts of the Apostles (6:8; 11:23–24; 14:26; 15:40; 18:27).[14]

Luke's description of Stephen provides a helpful parallel to the experience of Mary. Stephen is described as "full of grace and power," "full of the Holy Spirit and wisdom," and "full of faith and of the Holy Spirit" (Acts 6:8, 3, 5). As a result of this fullness he gives inspired witness (6:10; 7:55–56). Likewise, after Mary is visited with God's grace, she too utters an inspired message. Under the influence of the Holy Spirit (Luke 4:1, 14, 18), Jesus also speaks "words of grace" which amaze the Nazareth synagogue (*euthaumazon epi tois logois tēs charitos*) (4:22).[15] Luke has already associated Jesus with God's favor (*charis*) in 2:40, 52. Thus Luke's references to grace and the Holy Spirit in relation to Mary show not only how she would give birth to the "Son of the Most High," but also how the enduring grace of the Holy Spirit will influence her child and her tongue. Luke apparently wants his readers to understand that Mary's utterances are not devoid of guidance, for "God was with her," as with her Spirit-anointed Son (cf., Luke 1:28 with Acts 10:38).

Mary's experience with the Holy Spirit is not inferior to the other witnesses described as Spirit-filled, nor does she have to wait for Pentecost for Spirit-endowment. The realization that Mary was overshadowed by the Holy Spirit and that her womb bore the infant Christ has a profound effect in Luke's thought. Granted, Mary's experience with the Holy Spirit did not assure perfect understanding (2:48–50); however, being filled with the Holy Spirit did not perfect John's understanding either (7:19). In the case of the pregnant Mary, the very locus of divine creativity—the ultimate expression of the Holy Spirit—was within her. She therefore is inspired to reveal the revolutionary character of God's kingdom in her Magnificat hymn. She also speaks of God's visitation to the destitute which Luke frequently reiterates. Along with John and Elizabeth and the other early witnesses, Mary gives inspired witness and praise after her experience with the Holy Spirit.

The Spirit and the Witness of Zechariah

Luke describes the witness of Zechariah in the same way as he presents the testimony of Zechariah's wife and son, for he too witnesses after he is "filled with the Holy Spirit" (1:67). Because he did not believe the angel's announcement that his wife would conceive, Zechariah is struck silent until after the child is conceived and delivered (1:20–24, 57–64). Luke relates that after Zechariah confirmed on a writing tablet Elizabeth's assertion that the child's name was to be John, Zechariah's "mouth was opened and his tongue loosed, and he spoke, blessing God" (1:64). Then two verses later Luke repeats himself, "And his father Zechariah was filled with the Holy Spirit, and prophesied saying, 'Blessed be the God of Israel' " (1:67–68a). This repetition is not a mere redundancy nor is it merely superfluous stylistic variation. Luke wishes to make it clear that the words of Zechariah are directed by the Holy Spirit and are not mere human gratitude or relief. Even though Luke has already said that Zechariah blessed God in general terms, the repetition is well founded since it affords Luke an opportunity to record the content of the old priest's prophetic utterance and to impress on his reader that the Holy Spirit is superintending Zechariah's words.

The Spirit and the Witness of Simeon and Anna

Luke's pattern of Spirit-directed witness to Jesus continues in the case of Simeon, the fourth person in the infancy narrative to be specifically designated as giving a testimony via the Holy Spirit. Notice that Simeon is linked with the Holy Spirit three times:

> Now there was a man in Jerusalem, whose name was Simeon . . . and the *Holy Spirit* was upon him. And it had been revealed to him by the *Holy Spirit* that he should not see death before he had seen the Lord's Christ. And inspired by the *Spirit* [or "in the Spirit," literal trans.] he came into the temple.
> —Luke 2:25–27, my ital.

This makes three important points about the Holy Spirit's influence upon Simeon. First, it is significant that:

> the Holy Spirit was continually upon Simeon (*ēn*, imperfect tense). Rarely in the Old Testament were individuals noted to be continually endowed with the Holy Spirit (Genesis 41:38; Daniel 4:8; Numbers 11:17). That the Holy Spirit was continually on Simeon is an indication not only of his prophetic empowerment but also of his ongoing devout character.[16]

Second, the Holy Spirit had revealed to Simeon that before his own death he would see the Messiah. The word for "revealed" (*kechrēmatismenon*) usually expresses divine admonition or instruction in its biblical use. We are not told what specific form this instruction took, whether it was a dream, voice, or insight, but we are told that the Holy Spirit provided the revelation.

Third, while he was "in the Spirit," Simeon went into the temple where he uttered an inspired witness concerning the infant Jesus. The phrase, "in the Spirit," indicates both direction and inspired speaking by the Holy Spirit. First, Simeon was led by the Spirit to the temple and arrived there at the moment the holy family came in (*en tō eisagagein*). Luke provides other incidents in his Gospel and in Acts where the Spirit leads people to particular locations or situations: Jesus to the wilderness (Luke 4:1); Philip to the Ethiopian chariot on the road to Gaza and then mysteriously to Azotus (Acts 8:29, 39); Peter to Caesarea (Acts 11:12); Paul and Barnabas to missions (Acts 13:2); Paul not to Asia but to Macedonia (Acts 16:6–10), and Paul again, this time to Jerusalem (Acts 20:22). Here in Simeon's case, not only is he led into the temple by the Holy Spirit, but he is also inspired by the Spirit to witness concerning Jesus. This appears to be the major interest for Luke. Furthermore, in Luke–Acts the reason the Holy Spirit directs a person from one place to another is usually to provide a witness for Jesus. In this case, Simeon is led to the temple not only to see the Savior but to prophesy over him and his mother.

Anna, the aged widow of the temple, confirms Simeon's identification of Jesus as Messiah. She, like Simeon, is described as a devout person. The timing of her arrival was also supernaturally arranged (*kai autē tē hōra*): "And coming up at that very hour she gave thanks to God, and spoke of him to all who were looking for the redemption of Jerusalem" (2:38).

Although Luke does not specifically identify Anna as having been directed by the Holy Spirit, he does describe her as a prophetess (v. 36). Luke has already established that the Holy Spirit and genuine prophecy are inseparable (1:67), and he considers Anna's prophecy to be equally as inspired as Simeon's.

The Lucan Agenda in the Infancy Narrative

When Luke presents his pneumatology in Luke 1–2 he ignores distinctions between the old and new age; from his perspective these temporal divisions do not qualitatively affect the work of the Holy Spirit. Clearly, Luke has anticipated Pentecost with this "little Pentecost" presented in the infancy narrative and in the preaching of John, the son of Zechariah.

Luke has not kept separate the old and new epochs that the Gospel and kerygmatic traditions present him (Mark 1:9–11; Matt 11:11–12; Luke 16:16; Acts 10:37ff.). Luke is not responsible for making these clear-cut divisions in salvation history. Rather, he sets them aside here when he describes the activity of the Holy Spirit in the infancy narrative in the same terms he uses to express the post-Pentecostal church's experience of the Holy Spirit. Here as elsewhere in his work, Luke has superimposed the structure of the early church pneumatology upon the synoptic material. This results in what appears to be an anachronism, a temporal incongruity. John, whose ministry is not normally associated with the Holy Spirit (Matt 3:11; Mark 1:8; Luke 3:16; Acts 1:5; 19:2ff.), is characterized in Luke's birth stories as being "filled with the Holy Spirit." Luke is comfortable with this because he is not so much interested in defining epochs as in identifying the work of the Holy Spirit in the Gospel in terms of the church's experience.[17] This incongruity is due to the fact that Luke is viewing John in hindsight. He sees John and other participants in the infancy narrative as speaking by means of the Holy Spirit in identical terms used in Acts and in the church era.[18]

It is not adequate merely to ascribe the activities of Mary, Elizabeth, Zechariah, John, Simeon, and Anna to OT prophecy. Only Anna and John are explicitly identified as prophets (1:76; 2:36), although Luke does describe Zechariah's utterance in 1:67–79 as "prophesying" (1:67). The language Luke uses to describe these anointed utterances closely parallels the language he uses later in his Gospel to describe Jesus' ministry and in Acts to describe the inspired speeches of the church. The activity of the Holy Spirit in the infancy narrative cannot be seen as limited to OT prophecy, because Luke uses the same pneumatological terms in Luke 1–2 as he does in Acts 1–13.[19] If Luke wishes the pneumatological events in his first two chapters to be considered distinct from the Holy Spirit in the rest of his work, especially in Acts, he would not use the phrase, "filled with the Holy Spirit."

This goes back to Luke's tendency to blur the epochs of salvation history. To him, salvation history is progressive, something like slowly turning up the volume on a radio. Just as it difficult to pinpoint the precise moment that the radio gets loud, so it is hard to pinpoint the precise moment of the arrival of the new age. Luke does not even try. He simply starts at the beginning of the Gospel: the birth story of Jesus and the witnesses to that story who are a part of it.

From Luke's perspective, John, Zechariah, Elizabeth, and Mary are not just heralds of the new age of Jesus; they do not just advertise the future event—rather they themselves are a part of it. As witnesses they participate in the new era of salvation. For Luke, the birth of Jesus and the activity of the Holy Spirit in it and around it are not a mere prelude or preparation for salvation; they are part of the event of salvation of which Jesus' ministry, death, resurrection, and ascension are also a part. For Luke, the advent of the Holy Spirit in the birth narratives is an advent of salvation, and the witnesses to salvation's beginning are guided by the Holy Spirit as much as those who followed them. These are full members of the Kingdom and bearers of the Spirit.

If one insists that a difference must be maintained between the experience of the infancy narrative witnesses with the Holy Spirit and that of the disciples at Pentecost, it must be seen not as a qualitative difference but as a *quantitative* one. The apostles were promised not a new spirit but the Holy Spirit. Peter, "filled with the Holy Spirit," described Pentecost as unique not in character but in scope:

> This is what was spoken by the prophet Joel: "And in the last days it shall be, God declares, that I will pour out my Spirit upon all flesh."
> —Acts 2:16–17a

This does not mean that Luke has completely abandoned epochal divisions in salvation history. The spiritual predecessors to Jesus' apostles and disciples—that is, the nativity witnesses—spoke by the inspiration of the Holy Spirit (Luke 1–2); while before Pentecost, the apostles who preached and performed wonders did not explicitly do these things by the Holy Spirit—at least not in Luke's commentary on the events. The focus of the Holy Spirit's work in the ministries of the apostles and disciples was at Pentecost and afterwards (Luke 24:49; Acts 1:8). Thus, Luke maintains the traditional divisions of salvation history in the different epochs up to a point. He sets aside these divisions, however, when he talks about the activity of the Holy Spirit, particularly in recording the infancy narrative, the ministry of John, and the ministry of Jesus. Such divisions would tend to obscure the Spirit's role as an expeditor of salvation, and in some respects, as the event of salvation itself. Luke presents the Spirit-inspired witnesses of Mary, Elizabeth, John, Zechariah, Simeon, and Anna in 1–2:38 in affirmation and anticipation of the inspired ministry of Jesus, the Anointed One, and the outpouring of the Spirit upon his followers as a result of his ascension. Luke finds it necessary to describe the witnesses of the Lord's birth not only in terms analogous to the prophets of the old covenant but also in the same pneumatological terms which explain the birth of the church and the witness it bears to its Lord. Luke continues this emphasis of Spirit-witness throughout much of his work.

Notes to Chapter 2

1. For example, Matthew includes Jesus' genealogy; the question of the wise men, "Where is he who has been born king of the Jews?"; the star; the prophecy of Bethlehem; and the evil king Herod. In all of these Matthew emphasizes Jesus as the true messianic King. Matthew also exults in the fulfillment of messianic prophecy in his frequent announcements that scripture is fulfilled in Jesus (1:23; 2:6, 15, 18, 23). Instead of wise men, Luke presents poor shepherds; instead of Joseph as the key character, he listens to the daughters of Israel—Mary, Elizabeth, and Anna—proclaim the salvation of Israel. In Zechariah, Simeon, and Anna he presents the "Amen" to Jesus from the ministers at the temple who in Matthew are at the beck and call of evil king Herod (Matt. 2:4–6).

2. H. Conzelmann, *The Theology of St. Luke*, trans. G. Buswell (New York: Harper and Row, 1961).

3. Conzelmann's "three-fold division of history into three distinct periods is too artificial, and few would concede that this basic outline was really present in the mind of the author of Luke–Acts. It rests mainly on the interpretation of one verse of Luke (16:16) plus the fact of Acts"; see W. Gasque, *A History of the Criticism of the Acts of Apostles*, 2d ed. (Peabody, Mass.: Hendrickson, 1989), 294. Conzelmann's interpretation of 16:16 maintains a division between John, Jesus, and the church which is not so clear. Luke does not exclusively associate John with the old era. Neither in 7:28 nor in 16:16 does he explicitly associate John with the OT prophets as does Matthew (11:13–14; 17:10–13) and apparently Mark (9:11–13). In Luke's statement, "The law and prophets were until [*mechri*] John; since then the good news of the kingdom of God is preached, and every one enters it violently" (16:16), it is not clear whether John was in the old age or the new. This contrasts with Matthew's presentation (11:11–12).

Contrary to Conzelmann's suggestion, Luke is not presenting a "third age" in Acts to explain the delay of the Parousia. Luke is writing history—what he is recording has already happened. Since he knows the second coming of Jesus has not occurred in the time frame with which he is dealing, he is not preoccupied with it. When one is writing history, the future is for the moment held at bay. This does not mean, though, that Luke does not hold to an imminent Parousia (Luke 3:9, 17; 10:9–12; 13:6–9; 18:7–8; 21:32). However, his task in Acts is not to create a new era to explain the delay of the "day of the Lord"; rather, Luke's purpose in Acts is to look at the past in which the acts of Jesus are continued in the lives of his apostles through the power of the Holy Spirit.

P. S. Minear asserts that it is only by ignoring the birth narrative that Conzelmann is able to impose his threefold chronology on Luke–Acts. In the infancy narrative themes like Holy Spirit-endowment and universal salvation abound which are characteristic of the new era; see "Luke's Use of the Birth Stories," in *Studies in Luke–Acts. Essays Presented in Honor of Paul Schubert*, ed. L. E. Keck, J. L. Martyn (London: SPCK, 1966), 111–30. For a detailed critique of Conzelmann's thesis see Marshall, *Luke: Historian and Theologian*.

4. This statement stands in the middle of traditional material, but "filled" (*pimplēmi*), especially with the Holy Spirit, is characteristically Lucan

(in Luke 13x; in Acts 10x; with "Holy Spirit," Luke 1:15, 41, 67; Acts 2:4; 4:8, 31; 9:17; 13:9). "Filled" (*pimplēmi* or *pleroō*) followed by various words in the genitive is also characteristic of Luke. While "filled with the Holy Spirit" is definitely a Lucan expression, especially when it appears in Luke's own commentary on events, here it occurs in a speech containing many elements which can be identified as traditional. Therefore, the phrase in this case may not be a Lucan insertion; in fact, Luke's source for the infancy narrative may well be the origin of the phrase. To be sure, Luke quickly appropriates it and uses it as his own; cf. J. Jeremias, *Die Sprache des Lukasevangeliums* (Göttingen: Vandenhoeck and Ruprecht, 1980), 35–36, and J. Fitzmyer, *The Gospel According to Luke I–IX,* AB 28 (New York: Doubleday, 1981), 1.319, who both identify the phrase as Lucan, while the latter doubts it stood in traditional material. Luke's use of this phrase centers around the infancy narrative and his account of the early church in Acts. The infancy narrative and the first half of the book of Acts contain links to the early Palestinian church, both in content and in language. In the immediate text isolated from the rest of Luke–Acts, "filled with the Holy Spirit" may be seen as a contrast to the negative influence of wine and strong drink which is reflected elsewhere in the literature of the early church (Acts 2:15–17; Eph. 5:18), J. A. Bengel, *Gnomen of the New Testament,* trans. A. Fausset (Edinburgh: T. & T. Clark, 1858), 12; F. Godet, *A Commentary on the Gospel of St. Luke,* trans. E. W. Shalders (Edinburgh: T. & T. Clark, 1879), 78; A. Plummer, *A Critical and Exegetical Commentary on the Gospel According to St. Luke,* ICC, ed. S. R. Driver, A. Plummer, and C. A. Briggs (Edinburgh: T. & T. Clark, 1901), 14; J. M. Creed, *The Gospel According to St. Luke* (London: Macmillan, 1942), 10; A. R. C. Leaney, *A Commentary on the Gospel According to St. Luke,* BNTC, ed. H. Chadwick (London: Adam and Charles Black, 1966), 38; E. E. Ellis, *The Gospel of Luke,* NCB, rev. ed. (London: Oliphant, 1966), 70. Luke may not object to the antithetical comparison, but he is attracted to the phrase mainly because it coincides so well with his general program. The parallelism in 1:15, 17 has the structure of a traditional saying which Luke has appropriated largely intact, and is similar to the parallelism he preserves in 3:7–9, 17; 3:16; 4:1–13. It is possible that the phrase originates from the wealth of material from the Palestinian community which Luke apparently utilizes and which influences his thinking, see P. Winter, "On Luke and Lucan Sources," *ZNW* 47 (1956): 217–42. Though Luke may have found the phrase in various sources, he uses it to serve his overall objectives so effectively that it appears to be of Lucan origin. Luke may well have prefaced the traditional reference to "the spirit and power of Elijah" with "filled with the Holy Spirit" to make it clear that this aspect of Elijah's ministry is primarily inspired speaking! The place of the filling, "in his mother's womb," links the Spirit-filled John with his prenatal witness to the Messiah (1:41–45). See Jeremias for the traditional and redactional character of vv. 15–17 in *Die Sprache,* 35–38.

5. Parallels between the ministries of Jesus and Elijah/Elisha are:

Luke 4:25ff.   Jesus ministered to those beyond his home country as did Elijah and Elisha (1 Kings 17; 2 Kings 5).

7:11–17   Jesus raised a widow's son as did Elijah (1 Kings 17:24).

9:54 Jesus refused to call down fire from heaven on those who mistreated him as Elijah did (2 Kings 1:9–12).

12:49 Jesus claimed that he came to cast fire upon the earth (1 Kings 18:20–40; 2 Kings 1:9ff.).

12:50–53 Jesus did *not* see his ministry akin to Elijah's work of reconciliation as described in Mal 4:5–6.

12:54–56 Jesus spoke of a "cloud rising in the west" (1 Kings 18:44).

24:50–53; Acts 1:9 Jesus ascended to heaven (2 Kings 2:11).

Acts 1:9 A cloud took Jesus from sight (2 Kings 2:11–12).

Acts 1:10–11 Jesus' disciples stood gazing into heaven after the ascension as Elisha did (2 Kings 2:11–12).

Luke 9:51 *Analēmpsis* refers to the ascensions of both Jesus and Elijah (2 Kings 2:9, 11).

Luke 9:61f. Jesus' call of a disciple uses language similar to Elijah's call to Elisha (1 Kings 19:19–21).

Luke 24:49; Acts 1:4 The disciples of Jesus were instructed to wait until they were "clothed with power from on high." Elijah instructed Elisha to wait, and he received the mantle of Elijah (2 Kings 2).

Luke 12:24 "Consider the ravens" (1 Kings 17:1–7). (This reference in Luke is omitted by several old texts.)

Luke 3:21; 9:18, 28f.; 11:1; 22:32; etc. Jesus was portrayed as a man of prayer as was Elijah (1 Kings 17:20–22; 18:36f., 42; cf. Jas 5:17f.).

Luke 24:46–53 (Acts 1:1–11) The disciples' witnessing the ascension of Jesus is related to their subsequent reception of power. This is parallel to Elisha's experience whose empowering was contingent upon seeing Elijah ascend into heaven (2 Kings 2:10). Compiled from P. Dabeck, "Siehe, es erschienen Moses und Elias," *Bib* 23 (1942): 175–89. Wink, *John the Baptist*, 44. Hinnebusch, *Jesus the New Elijah*, 5ff. Jeremias suggests that the Lucan material in the Gethsemane account is reminiscent of the flight of Elijah in 1 Kings 19:1ff. (cf. Luke 22:43; 1 Kings 19:5–7). See "*Elias*," *TDNT* 2:928–41.

6. E.g., J. A. T. Robinson, "Elijah, John, and Jesus," *Twelve New Testament Studies* (London: SCM Press, 1962), 28–52. S. H. Lee, "John the Baptist and Elijah in Lucan Theology" (Ph.D. diss., Boston University, 1972), 34–38. J. A. Fitzmyer, "The Aramaic 'Elect of God' Text from Qumran Cave 4," in *Essays on the Semitic Background of the New Testament* (Missoula, Mont.: Scholars Press, 1974), 127–60, 137. M. McNamara, *Targum and Testament* (Grand Rapids: Eerdmans, 1972), 48. M. M. Faierstein, "Why Do the Scribes Say that Elijah Must Come First?" *JBL* 100 (March 1981): 77. Apparently by the time of the writing of Mark, Mal 3:1 had been applied to John the precursor unless Mark 1:2 was really describing Jesus in v. 1. For more on Luke's redactional work on Elijah see T. L. Brodie, *Luke, the Literary Interpreter: Luke-Acts as a Systematic Rewriting and Updating of the Elijah/Elisha*

Narrative in I and II Kings (Rome: Angelicum, 1981). Scholars who argue that Elijah as forerunner was a common idea contemporaneous with the NT are: J. Jeremias, *"Elias," TDNT* 2:928–41, 931; G. F. Moore, *Judaism in the First Centuries of the Christian Era,* 3 vols. (Cambridge, Mass.: Harvard University Press, 1928), 358 n. 2; J. Klausner, *The Messianic Idea in Israel* (New York: Macmillan, 1955), 257; S. Mowinckel, *He That Cometh* (Nashville: Abingdon, 1954), 299.

7. By allowing the reference to John in relation to Elijah to stand in 1:17, "Luke is voicing a synoptic theme in his infancy narrative," R. E. Brown, *The Birth of the Messiah* (Garden City, N.J.: Image, 1977), 276. However, Luke is not responsible for the insertion of the phrase, "in the spirit and power of Elijah."

The phrase connotes the whole range of Elijah's ministry and not his call for repentance or his office of forerunner alone. The phrase may owe its existence to a tradition which saw John as the Elijah-Messiah figure or which saw that the parallels of John with Elijah included wonder-working. The association of *pneuma* (Spirit) and *dynamis* (power) with miracles is frequent in Luke–Acts (e.g., 4:36; 5:17; 6:19; 8:46; 9:1ff.; 10:13, 19; Acts 1:8; 2:22; 3:12ff.; 8:13; 10:38; 19:11). Mark also has a pattern with *dynamis* and miracle (e.g., 5:30; 6:2, 5, 14; 9:39). See C. K. Barrett, *The Holy Spirit and the Gospel Tradition* (London: SPCK, 1966), 75ff. Luke avoids the association of miracles with John the Baptist in Luke 9:7–9, in contrast to Matt 14:1–2 and Mark 6:14–16 which identify it as a mistaken belief of the crowd. We have already noted the usual absence of associations between John and the Holy Spirit in the synoptic tradition and in Luke–Acts (Luke 3:16 and parallels, and Acts 19:1ff.). In all probability, Luke would not have used this word association of Spirit and power to describe John's ministry if it had not been in his source. However, he is willing to let the phrase stand because he views John as fulfilling Elijah's office in that he spoke authoritatively under the direction of the Holy Spirit in his call to repentance which is the synoptic view of the forerunner's ministry. Luke is usually careful to reserve for Jesus any allusions to Elijah associated with the working of miracles. Since Luke is able to weave John the infant into his presentation of John's preaching, he lets the phrase stand. Jeremias also sees the expression and similar word associations as traditional (*Die Sprache,* 38). There are, therefore, linguistic and theological grounds for considering this reference to Elijah's spirit and power as a tradition Luke drew from an earlier source (contra Brown, *The Birth of the Messiah,* 279).

8. The word may be Lucan, but the concept's origin is from the OT (e.g., 1 Sam 16:13 and Isa 32:15 LXX). The latter reference uses *eperchomai* ("come upon"), and the concept is used throughout. As in the case of the phrase, "filled with the Holy Spirit," the presence of *eperchomai* here may indicate Luke's Christian source for its use in relation to the Holy Spirit. G. Montague elaborates: "It sounds as if the small circle around Mary have already experienced Pentecost! How explain this [*sic*]? Clearly, the infancy narrative which originated out of post-Pentecostal meditation on the earliest beginnings is meant to be in some way both the Gospel and the Acts in foreshadowing and anticipation. The result is not only a prologue to the Christology of the Gospel but a prologue to the ecclesiology of Acts" (*The Holy Spirit: Growth of a Biblical Tradition* [New York: Paulist Press, 1976],

268). P. Alexander suggests that Mary's praise and rejoicing in the Magnificat (vv. 46–55) came from "the realization of the promise of the angel in verse 35 that the Spirit would come upon [her]" ("Jesus Christ and the Spirit," *Dictionary of Pentecostal and Charismatic Movements*, ed. S. Burgess, G. McGee [Grand Rapids: Zondervan, 1988], 489).

9. This view has been encouraged by the Vulgate version of 1:28, *gratia plena*, "full of grace," especially among scholastic theologians. J. Fitzmyer, *Luke* 1.246. Pope Paul VI summarized the contemplation of the church fathers on this passage in his "Marialis Cultus" (Feb 2, 1974). They "called Mary the 'Sanctuary of the Holy Spirit,' an expression that emphasized the sacredness of the Virgin who became the permanent dwelling of the Spirit of God. Moreover, in exploring the doctrine of the Paraclete, they recognized that he was the spring from which flowed the fullness of grace (cf. Luke 1:28) and abundance of gifts that adorned her. Hence, they attributed to the Spirit the faith, hope, and charity that animated the Virgin's heart, the strength that maintained her obedience to God's will, and the fortitude that upheld her as she suffered at the foot of the cross. In Mary's prophetic canticle (cf. Luke 1:46–55), they saw a special working of that same Spirit who formerly had spoken through the mouths of the prophets" (E. O'Connor, *Pope Paul and the Spirit: Charisms and Church Renewal in the Teaching of Paul VI* [Notre Dame: Ave Maria, 1978], 202).

10. For the possibility that the literal "rejoice" is intended, see Fitzmyer's discussion of the alternative in *Luke*, 1.344–45, J. Navone, *Themes of St. Luke* (Rome: Gregorian University, 1970), 58 and S. Lyonnet, "*Chaire, kecharitōmenō*," *Bib* 20 (1939): 131–41, esp. 131.

11. Although Luke does not use *charisma* for gift of the Holy Spirit but *dōron*, Luke does use *charis* in close association with the Holy Spirit (e.g., Luke 4:18 with 4:22; Acts 4:31–33; 6:3–10; 11:23–24).

12. A. Plummer, *Luke*, 21–22 and Fitzmyer, *Luke* 1.345.

13. The phrase, "found favor," is semitic in origin, and the LXX translates the Hebrew *ḥēn* as *charis* "grace" (e.g., Gen 6:8; Exod 33:12–13; Esth 8:5).

14. For more on the Lucan concept of grace, see H.-H. Esser, "Grace, Spiritual Gifts," *NIDNTT* (1976), 2:115–24, 118–19.

15. Given Luke's use of *charis* elsewhere, he is not just saying that Jesus had a way with words. He uses the word "grace" to describe the content of the gospel (e.g., Acts 13:43; 20:24).

16. J. B. Shelton, "Luke 2:18–4:13," *The New Testament Study Bible: Luke* (Springfield, Mo.: Complete Biblical Library, 1986), 69–119, esp. 73.

Both "filled with the Holy Spirit" and "the Spirit came upon" are OT expressions; however, the latter is more frequent there than the former. Luke uses fullness in relation to the Spirit much more frequently than it is used in the OT. The phrase "filled with the *Holy* Spirit" is not common in the OT (Sir 34:12 exception). "The Spirit of the Lord" or "filled with spirit/Spirit" plus an attribute occurs in the OT (e.g., Exod 28:3; 31:3; 35:31; Deut 34:9; Isa 61:1–2).

Although the dominant theme of filled with/full of the Holy Spirit involves inspired speech, it also involves other operations of the Holy Spirit. Apparently in the case of John, Simeon, and Jesus, they were in a durative relationship with the Holy Spirit. The reference to Jesus being "full of the Holy Spirit" in 4:1 prefaces the temptation account where Jesus overcame temptation by speaking effectively against the devil's suggestions. In 4:14 he came "in the power of the Spirit" to proclaim the nature of his ministry by interpreting Isa 61:1ff. in terms of his work. Acts 4:8ff. provides not only witness to Jesus but also authoritative indictment of the enemies of Jesus. In Acts 13:9ff. Paul was filled with the Holy Spirit to speak authoritatively against the evil magician Elymas and to effect a curse on him. The phrase is also used to denote the character of individuals (Acts 6:3, 5; 11:24). Yet even in these instances inspired speech is the means whereby these acts are accomplished. Further, in every instance where an individual is characterized as "full of the Holy Spirit," inspired speaking results in the immediate context. For Luke, both "full of the Holy Spirit" and "filled with the Holy Spirit" cause inspired utterances.

17. This is probably why Luke presents a different view from Matthew's, "For all the prophets and the law prophesied until John" (Matt 11:13). The context in Matthew clearly places John in the OT era. Luke's version is more obscure when delineating eras; it can be seen as associating John with the new era of the "gospel of the kingdom."

18. The general consensus among scholars is that Luke's Gospel originally began at ch. 3 and that chs. 1–2 were added as a preface to the earlier work; see H. J. Cadbury, *The Making of Luke–Acts* (London: SPCK, 1961), 204–9; B. H. Streeter, *The Four Gospels* (London: Macmillan, 1924), 209; V. Taylor, *Behind the Third Gospel: A Study of the Proto-Luke Hypothesis* (Oxford: Clarendon, 1926), 165ff., et al. R. Brown also observes the affinities the infancy narrative has for Acts in relation to its nature as a later preface to the Gospel: "If Luke composed the infancy narrative last of all (and thus after Acts) and if he intended a certain parallelism between the two transitional sections (Luke 1–2; Acts 1–2), it is not surprising that in many ways the infancy narrative is closer in spirit to the stories in Acts than to the gospel material which Luke took from Mark and Q" (*Birth of the Messiah*, 243).

19. Nor is it adequate to make a distinction here between the Holy Spirit of prophecy in the old covenant and the Holy Spirit, or the "Spirit of Jesus," in the new covenant given at Pentecost. These titles overlap in their functions and to a certain degree are synonymous. The Spirit of Jesus is the same Holy Spirit who empowered the characters in Luke 1–2, Jesus himself, and the church. Contra Brown, *Birth of the Messiah*, 274ff. For a more exhaustive presentation of John as part of the new era see chapter 3. *Pneuma tou Iēsou* (Spirit of Jesus) should not be seen as a genitive of apposition or as exclusively genitive of possession. Jesus is associated with the Holy Spirit in this construct because for Luke, Jesus was brought into the world via the Holy Spirit (1:35). The Spirit anointed and empowered Jesus (3:21ff.; 4:18; Acts 10:37ff.), and Jesus poured out this same Spirit upon his followers (Acts 2:33). Thus, Spirit of Jesus and the Holy Spirit are synonymous in Luke's mind.

3 | *The Holy Spirit and John the Son of Zechariah*

A MOST IMPORTANT passage for understanding the role of the Holy Spirit in the Gospel of Luke is the ministry of John the Baptist—or as Luke has called him, "John the son of Zechariah" (Luke 3:1–22). Here Luke continues his emphasis on Spirit-inspired witness that he began in the infancy narrative. A comparison of Luke's presentation of the Baptist material with that of the other Gospel writers will help to reveal Luke's distinctive emphases (Matt 3:1–17; Mark 1:1–11; John 1:19–36). In looking at the specific passages regarding John, we will pay particular attention to the titles used for him and to the references to his speaking—preaching, teaching, and answering questions. We will see that Luke's tendency to avoid the Baptist title for John and his frequent references to John's speaking point to his interest in John's repentance-preaching ministry rather than in his baptizing. Furthermore, we will see that the deemphasis of John's role as baptizer in water is paired with an emphasis of Jesus' role as baptizer in the Holy Spirit.

The Baptist Material in the Other Gospels

The accounts of John's preaching and baptizing in the other Gospels vary considerably from Luke's. The way each Gospel writer presents these events shows what he thinks are the important lessons about the role of John. By observing how the Gospel writers present the ministry of John and his baptism of Jesus, we will find that while Luke's attention is often focused on the role of the Holy Spirit in John's ministry, the other Gospel writers exhibit other specialized interests, Christology in particular.

Mark 1:1–11

Mark includes the material on John the Baptist in his Gospel primarily to establish who Jesus is. This christological function appears to be the earliest reason for the preservation of the Baptist material in the Gospels, for it is universally present in all four Gospels and in Acts. Christology appears to be the dominant interest in the Baptist traditions.[1] Mark makes his interest in Christology clear from the very first verse of his book, "The beginning of the gospel of Jesus Christ, the Son of God" (1:1).[2] In effect, this christological statement is Mark's preface to the ministry of "John the Baptizer" since his account of John immediately follows (1:2–11). Mark's main purpose in recounting the ministry of John and Jesus' baptism by John is to state that Jesus Christ is the Son of God. Further, Christology is also Mark's primary motive for making the rest of his references to John (Mark 1:18; 6:14–32; 8:27–30; 11:27–33).

The preaching of John in Mark 1:2–11 serves two purposes: (1) to identify the baptism for repentance as the preparation of the "way of the Lord" described in vv. 2–3, and (2) to identify Jesus as the Son of God. The first purpose is reduced to an observation made by Mark, "John the baptizer appeared in the wilderness, preaching a baptism of repentance for the forgiveness of sins" (v. 4); the second purpose is found in the quotation of John that Mark provides here, "After me comes he who is mightier than I, the thong of whose sandals I am not worthy to stoop down and untie" (v. 8).[3]

Here Mark is characteristically brief in his description of John and his ministry. It seems apparent that Mark's primary interest in using the Baptist material is to point to Jesus and to establish who Jesus is. Mark does not relate that John said, "Repent, for the kingdom of heaven is at hand," as Matthew does (3:2). Rather, Mark presents the messianic prediction, "I have baptized you in water; but he will baptize you with the Holy Spirit" (1:8). This for Mark is primarily a christological statement, a way of identifying the recipient and subsequent dispenser of the Spirit as the Son of God.

In Mark's presentation of John's prophecy, he shows a special interest in what it says about Jesus, i.e., the one mightier than John (*ho ischyroteros*) who performs the greater baptism and is therefore Messiah. Here Mark is interested in the office of Jesus; he is not immediately concerned about the results of Jesus' Spirit baptism. Only later, in the longer ending of Mark, do we see an interest in the activities of believers that Luke would ascribe to the baptism that Jesus would pour out upon his church (16:17).[4] The inclusion of the divine voice from heaven in 1:11, proclaiming Jesus as Son, indicates that Mark's primary interest is in the office of Jesus. (This is a frequent Marcan interest, cf. 1:1; 3:11; 5:7; 9:7; 14:61; 15:39.)

Matthew 3:1–17

Matthew follows Mark's example in that he too uses the Baptist material to make christological statements. Yet he uses the occasion of John's preaching and baptism to make a more pronounced and specific statement about Jesus. Matthew's concern is to assert to his Jewish-oriented audience that Jesus is greater than John the Baptist even though Jesus submitted to baptism at the hands of John. Only Matthew informs his readers that Jesus and John disagreed over who should baptize whom (3:13–15). Matthew's account makes it emphatically clear that John considered himself unworthy to baptize Jesus and, moreover, that it would be more appropriate for Jesus to baptize him. Apparently John's disclaimer that he was unworthy to untie the Messiah's sandals, which is found in all four Gospels (Matt 3:11; Mark 1:7; Luke 3:16; John 1:27), is not strong enough for Matthew, who wants to put a greater emphasis on Jesus' superiority. Matthew follows the common motive for discussing John in the Gospels and Acts; he uses other references to John in his Gospel to state that Jesus is the Messiah (Matt 3; 11:1–19; 14:1–12; 16:13–20; 21:23–27).

In addition to this common christological interest, Matthew presents another distinctive between John and Jesus in the incident of the imprisoned John's inquiry to Jesus, "Are you he who is to come, or shall we look for another?" (Matt 11:3). Here Matthew quotes a statement by Jesus which clearly classifies John as part of the old era and Jesus as part of the new:

> Truly, I say to you, among those born of women there has risen no one greater than John the Baptist; yet he who is least in the kingdom of heaven is greater than he. From the days of John the Baptist until now the kingdom of heaven has suffered violence, and men of violence take it by force. For all the prophets and the law prophesied until John; and if you are willing to accept it, he is Elijah who is to come.
>
> —Matthew 11:11–14

Matthew notes that Jesus used John's questions to clarify his relationship with John. Matthew emphatically records that John marked the end of the old era and identifies him as the Forerunner-Elijah (Matt 11–14 with Mark 9:1–13 and Luke 7:18–35). As we have seen in the previous chapter, Luke does not stringently maintain the division of the epochs between John and Jesus. (See Appendix.)

Christology is Matthew's primary motive in presenting the preaching of John in 3:2–12. Yet even here he continues to expand his presentation of Christ. Of all the Gospel writers only Matthew identifies the Pharisees and Sadducees as the recipients of John's scathing rebuke, "you brood of vipers," and of his warnings of impending judgment (3:7). Thus in Matthew's mind, John's prediction concerning the Holy Spirit Baptizer serves to identify Jesus not only as God's Son but also as the end-time judge. Matthew preserves the emphasis on judgment that the Baptist originally asserted. There are good trees and bad trees, the wheat and the chaff, which will be separated in the end-time harvest involving the winnowing wind (*pneuma*) and the destructive fire (3:7–12). This is not unusual since instances of judgment frequently occur in the teaching of Jesus that only Matthew preserves (13:24–30, 36–43, 47–50; 18:23–35; 22:1–14; 25:1–13, 31–46). We will see, however, that in contrast to Matthew, who places the prophecy concerning the Holy Spirit in terms of judgment, Luke emphasizes the role of the Spirit in empowerment for witness and ministry.

John 1:19–36

Although John's Gospel includes Baptist material which parallels the presentations in Matthew, Mark, and Luke, John presents his own distinct view of John the Baptist. Like the synoptists, he presents both the descent of the dove and John's prophecy which links the Holy Spirit with Jesus as evidence that Jesus is the Son of God. However, his view is decidedly different in that he omits John the Baptist's call for a baptism of repentance and includes his declarations both that Jesus is the Lamb of God and that Jesus is preexistent God (1:29, 36; 1:15). Though John presents a different version of the Baptist traditions, he maintains two common themes found in all the synoptic sources: John the Baptist's being the precursor of Jesus, and the primary christological function of the Baptist traditions. In John's Gospel, John the Baptist predominantly witnesses concerning Jesus and presents his own subordination to Jesus (especially 3:22–30). Again, as in Matthew and Mark, the Baptist material answers the question of who Jesus is.

Luke's Primary Interests in the Baptist Material

Christology

Like the other evangelists, Luke maintains the basic reason for preserving the Baptist material: John's ministry identifies Jesus as the

Christ. Luke's references to John and his ministry usually tell who Jesus is: Messiah—1:13–17; Lord—1:41–44; horn of salvation—1:60–80; baptizer in the Holy Spirit—3:1–18; Acts 1:5; 11:16–17; God's beloved Son—3:21–22; bridegroom—5:33–39; the coming one, the miracle worker, and friend of sinners—7:18–35; preacher and healer—9:6–9; the Christ of God—9:18–27; the founder of the kingdom—16:16; the one with authority—20:1–8; the resurrected one—Acts 1:22; the Anointed One—Acts 10:37–38; the Christ—Acts 18:25–28; the one who was to come after John—Acts 13:25; 19:4.

The Baptism in the Holy Spirit as Empowerment to Witness

Though Luke's understanding of Jesus as the Christ—the Messiah—is like that of the other Gospel writers, his understanding of how this messianic identification is carried out is distinctive. To him it *requires an emphasis on the work of the Holy Spirit.* Luke does not consider this a maverick or novel imposition of his own genius on the Gospel tradition; rather, he claims that the emphasis on the role of the Holy Spirit in the Baptist material comes from Jesus' own interpretation of John's ministry. Twice in Acts, Luke records Jesus' version of John's prophecy: "John baptized with water, but before many days you shall be baptized with the Holy Spirit" (Acts 1:5; also 11:16.) Jesus was reinterpreting John's prophecy in terms of empowerment to witness (Acts 1:8). (We will discuss this further later in the chapter.) Luke presents the Baptist material in conformity to the pneumatology he presents in the infancy narrative, in the ministry of Jesus, and in the book of Acts. Thus Luke presents the witness of John as a Spirit-filled, prophetic announcement that the Spirit-filled witness would continue in Jesus and his followers.

The Baptism of Repentance

Luke is attracted to John's ministry because, in addition to providing material on Christology and the Holy Spirit, it emphasizes repentance. Luke sees baptism primarily as a symbol of John's message of repentance. Following Mark, Luke describes John as "preaching a baptism of repentance for the forgiveness of sins" (Luke 3:3 with Mark 1:4). He utilizes the expression "preached a baptism of repentance" in Acts 13:24 and "the baptism which John preached" in Acts 10:37. In the account of the "Ephesian Pentecost" he uses the expression, "John baptized with the baptism of repentance" (Acts 19:4).

In Luke 7:28–30 and 20:1–8 he mentions the baptism of John in the context of repentant and unrepentant groups of people. In the first passage, only Luke of all the Gospel writers mentions the acceptance of John's *baptism* by repentant sinners and its rejection by the elite enemies of Jesus (contrast 7:28–30 with Matt 21:31–32). Clearly Luke is more interested in the message of repentance which John preached and less interested in John's performing the rite of water baptism. The act of baptism is for Luke a metonymy for John's message of repentance.

Luke stresses repentance in addition to the Holy Spirit in the Baptist material because of its indispensable role in the preaching of Jesus and the early church (e.g., Luke 5:32; 13:3–5; 15:7–10; 16:30; 17:3–4; 24:47; Acts 2:38; 5:31; 8:22; 11:18; 17:30; 19:4; 20:21; 26:20). He is presenting the *raison d'être* for "those things which are most surely believed" and preached by the early church (Luke 1:1, KJV). He is also attracted to the Baptist material because it defines the true nature of repentance.[5]

Evidence of Luke's Distinctive Message in the Preaching of John (Luke 3:1–18)

Several unique elements appear in Luke's presentation of the common synoptic material. In his version of the ministry of John, Luke emphasizes the role of the Holy Spirit and John's repentance-preaching at the expense of his role as baptizer.

"John the Son of Zechariah"

Luke immediately begins adjusting the Baptist material in chapter three by deliberately avoiding the title "Baptist" for John: "the word of God came to John *the son of Zechariah* in the wilderness" (3:2, my ital.).

Mark's Gospel describes John as "John the Baptizer" (*Iōannēs ho Baptizōn*, Mark 1:4), and Matthew calls him "John the Baptist" (*Iōannēs ho Baptistēs*, Matt 3:1); however, Luke calls him "John the son of Zechariah" (*Iōannēn ton Zachariou hyion*). Luke reminds his readers that John is the son over whom his father Zechariah prophesied in Luke 1. Luke previously noted that both the father and son were "filled with the Holy Spirit" to provide inspired witness to Jesus (1:15–17, 41, 67–79). Luke is interested in John not as a baptizer primarily, but as a witness. As a result, he links the chapter concerning John's adult preaching to the infancy narrative which has already carefully circumscribed his role in the Gospel, particularly through the prophecies of Gabriel and Zechariah.

The prophecy of Gabriel to Zechariah concerning John speaks specifically of the role of the Holy Spirit in inspiring John's witness not only as an unborn child as we have seen in the previous chapter, but as an adult. John was "filled with the Holy Spirit, even from his mother's womb" not only to jump with joy at his initial encounter with the Messiah, but in the later years when he went "before him in the spirit and power of Elijah . . . to make ready for the Lord a people prepared" (1:17).

The prophecy of Zechariah (1:67–79) goes on to define John's role in greater detail, carefully distinguishing between the Messiah and the one who would prepare the way for the Messiah. John clearly was not the Messiah since the "horn of salvation" was to be raised up in the house of David (v. 69). Neither here nor elsewhere in the NT is there any reference to a Messiah from the tribe of Levi. Zechariah made it clear that John was the one who would "go before the Lord to prepare his ways" (v. 76), i.e., to give knowledge of salvation by the forgiveness of sins, to give light to those in darkness and in the shadow of death, and to guide the faithful in the way of peace (vv. 77–79). Zechariah recognized that the salvation history of old anticipated the advent of the ministries of John and Jesus as its own fulfillment (vv. 68–73). In his prophecy Zechariah promised salvation and deliverance through the Messiah ben David who would enable Israel to serve God without fear in holiness and righteousness (vv. 74–75). Zechariah portrayed John as "the prophet of the Most High" (v. 76), who, like the prophets of old (v. 70), not only announced the coming of God's kingdom, but also called for a return to God and his ways.

Thus John's ministry and the prophecy of his father are inseparable. When the word of God came to John in the desert (3:2), he spoke by the same means his father uttered prophecy concerning himself and the Anointed One—by being filled with the Holy Spirit (1:67). Having been filled with the Holy Spirit in his mother's womb (1:15), John was empowered for mission. The same Spirit-endowed John who bore witness to Jesus before either of them were born now continued his witness as an adult. He fulfilled his father's prophecy by prophesying through the inspiration of the Holy Spirit concerning the forgiveness of sins, the nature of the coming kingdom, and the arrival of the Savior-Messiah. Luke sees John as his father saw him, not so much as a baptizer, but as a prophet of the culmination of salvation history. For Luke, the primary work of "John the Zechariah son" was to bear witness to the Messiah.

The Spirit and "the Word of God"

Luke does not say whether John's experience with the Holy Spirit was durative or iterative; nevertheless, Raymond Brown notes that the association between "the word of God" in 3:2 and the Holy Spirit in 1:15 is undeniable.

> In the Gospel account of the ministry, John the Baptist is presented as a prophet, indeed greater than any other prophet (Luke 7:28; 20:6), and so it would follow logically that John the Baptist was filled with the prophetic Holy Spirit. If one compares the OT passages where the *Spirit* of the Lord is said to come upon a prophet to enable him to speak God's message (Isa 61:1; Ezek 11:5; Joel 3:1 [RSV 2:28]) with the passages where the *word* of God is said to come to a prophet for the same purpose (Isa 2:1; Jer 1:2; Joel 1:1), it becomes clear that when Luke 1:15c says that John the Baptist "will be filled with the Holy *Spirit* even from his mother's womb," he is saying exactly the same thing as he says in 3:1–2: "In the fifteenth year of the reign of Tiberius Caesar . . . the *word* of God came to John, the son of Zechariah, in the desert." These are simply alternate ways of describing the beginning of the career of a prophet. In the former Lucan statement, when the career is traced to infancy, the dominating model is that of a prophet like Samson ("a Nazirite to God from my mother's womb," Judg 16:17; 13:7) or Jeremiah ("Before I formed you in the womb, I knew you . . . I appointed you a prophet to the nations," Jer 1:14). In the latter Lucan statement, when the career is traced to the beginning of a preaching ministry, the dominating model is the standard opening of several prophetic books, e.g., "In the second year of Darius, the word of the Lord came to Zechariah, the son of Berechiah" (Zech 1:1).[6]

Luke employs traditional language to express the divine origin of John's ministry. The phrase, "the word of God came," is not Lucan in origin, but rather from a semitic and ultimately OT origin.[7]

Luke's Avoidance of the Baptist Title

A piece of evidence that leads to the conclusion that Luke is emphasizing John's role as witness rather than baptizer is his tendency to avoid the Baptist title for John. This is true not only in his first reference to John in 3:2 but elsewhere in Luke–Acts. In fact, he seldom uses the title even when his source does. Luke's omissions of the Baptist title are not only statistically striking but also programmatically significant and are not due to stylistic variation or accident. Luke is more interested in Jesus' role as the baptizer in the Holy Spirit and less interested in John's role as a baptizer in water.[8]

Furthermore, in the instances where Luke does allow the Baptist appellation, he sometimes modifies it by emphasizing the repentance ministry of John and/or the pneumatic ministry of Jesus. For example, the reference to the Baptist in 7:20 is immediately followed by a description of Jesus' wonder-working ministry, "In that hour he cured many of diseases and plagues and evil spirits, and on many that were blind he bestowed sight" (v. 21). By phrasing it this way, Luke comments on John's earlier prophecy concerning Jesus and his anointing by the Holy Spirit. Luke stresses that John's emissaries actually witnessed—they saw with their own eyes—the pneumatic activity of Jesus, because he records Jesus' saying to them, "Go and tell John *what you have seen and heard*: the blind receive their sight, the lame walk, lepers are cleansed, and the deaf hear, the dead are raised up, the poor have good news preached to them" (7:22, my ital.). Luke is reiterating the point because this is a major reason that he includes the account: the agent of the Spirit does the works of the Spirit.

Following this reference to the Baptist in 7:20 is a reference to John's ministry to the tax collectors (7:29–30) whom he called to repentance and to whom he defined repentance (3:12ff.). Luke underlines repentance in John's preaching earlier. The reference to the Baptist in Peter's confession (9:19) highlights the identification of Jesus as the Anointed One ("the Christ of God"), which, for Luke, means anointed by the Holy Spirit (4:18). Here Luke retains the traditional Baptist title because the identification of Jesus as the Christ overshadows the reference to John. In these instances, he does not directly use "Baptist" or "baptism" to refer to the water rite, but rather, he often uses them as a symbol for John's message of repentance or as an occasion to present Jesus as the Anointed One of God.

Emphasis on Repentance and the Holy Spirit rather than Water Baptism

In addition to reminding his readers that John was a Spirit-inspired witness of Jesus as prophesied by his father, the Spirit-filled Zechariah, Luke avoids references to the Baptist title or the act of baptism for another reason. John's preaching is a treasure trove for material on repentance. We have already seen that this is a major interest for all of Luke–Acts. Luke, therefore, follows Mark's description of John as "preaching a baptism of repentance for forgiveness of sins" (Mark 1:4 with Luke 3:3). Only Luke presents the people's questions concerning the true nature of repentance (3:10–14). A clear definition of repentance is important for Luke's presentation of the gospel.

The act of baptism recedes into the background in Luke. The first instance of the verb "to baptize" occurs in 3:7, where it appears as an infinitive (*baptisthēnai;* see also 3:12), indicating the time frame of the more important act—John's repentance-preaching. "He said therefore to the multitudes that came out to be baptized by him, 'You brood of vipers! . . . Bear fruits that befit repentance' " (3:7–8). Contrast this with Mark's references to John as baptizer and the use of the verb *baptizō* in main clauses in Mark 1:4, 5, 8 and Matthew 3:1, 6, 7, 11. In Luke 3:7 the verb, "to be baptized" is in a subordinate clause introducing a call to repentance. The crowds came out for baptism, and they received a sermon on repentance.

Next, Luke mentions the verb "baptize" in John's prophecy concerning water and Spirit baptism, "I baptize you with water; but . . . he will baptize you with the Holy Spirit" (3:16). Yet even here water baptism takes a back seat to the Holy Spirit's endowment.

Luke's deemphasis of John's role as baptizer is even more remarkable, however, in his description of the baptism of Jesus at the Jordan. He records Herod's arrest of John (3:19–20) *before* mentioning Jesus' baptism (3:21–22). When he does say that Jesus was baptized, he does not say that John was the one performing the baptism. Further, the reference to Jesus' baptism is in an introductory clause that tells the timing of the more important event—the descent of the Holy Spirit upon Jesus. Luke appears not to have been too concerned that John baptized Jesus or that Jesus was baptized in water. More crucial for him is that Jesus was baptized *in the Holy Spirit.*

Jesus' Reinterpretation of the Spirit Baptism Prophecy

In the prophecy concerning Spirit baptism (3:16–17), Luke shifts his accent from repentance to the Holy Spirit empowerment. In doing so he is following the pattern of the preaching of the early church, "Repent, and be baptized every one of you in the name of Jesus Christ for the forgiveness of your sins; and you shall receive the gift of the Holy Spirit" (Acts 2:38). Although Luke imposes the preaching outline of the early church on the synoptic material, he does not ignore the original message of the tradition. Luke brilliantly weaves together the christological import of John as the prophetic witness to the Christ (3:15) and the stern rebuke and warning of judgment (3:7–9, 17) with the priority of a Holy Spirit baptism of power.

As mentioned earlier, Luke quotes Jesus as the source of the empowerment interpretation of John's prophecy (Acts 1:5; 11:16). Apparently John the Baptist interpreted the prophecy of the Spirit baptism in terms of judgment and restoration of Israel's political autonomy, which was the traditional Jewish concept of messiahship. However, Jesus saw a greater significance in John's prophecy, i.e., a *sensus plenior*, in a fuller sense. For Jesus, Spirit baptism was the power of God present in strength.[9]

When John sent his emissaries to Jesus inquiring, "Are you he who is to come, or shall we look for another?" (7:19), he was apparently asking if Jesus was the Messiah in the traditional sense. While both Luke and Matthew record this incident of John's second thoughts (7:18–23; Matt 11:2–19), only Luke notes that at the very moment John's disciples arrived Jesus was performing healings and exorcisms (7:21). Jesus sent a message back to John telling him of the healings and miracles. Both Jesus' actions and words served as a corrective to John's limited view of messiahship. Jesus revealed himself to John not as a military deliverer or as an eschatological judge, but as the Anointed One, the one empowered by the Spirit to minister. Jesus' response to John here is similar to his correction of the disciples' messianic expectations, "Lord, will you at this time restore the kingdom to Israel?" (Acts 1:6). The disciples asked this question after the resurrection when Jesus was reminding them of John's prophecy that they would be baptized in the Holy Spirit (Acts 1:5). Jesus' response was not in terms of judgment; neither was it in terms of the political restoration of Israel. Rather, he responds, "It is not for you to know times or seasons which the Father has fixed by his own authority. But *you shall receive power when the Holy Spirit has come upon you; and you shall be my witnesses*" (Acts 1:7–8). Just as Jesus corrected his disciples' understanding of John's prophecy, so too he corrected John's, emphasizing to him that the true nature of the Spirit baptism is empowerment to witness through word and deed.

John and Speaking

Luke's specialized interest in inspired speaking is further corroborated by the number of times he refers to the speaking ministry of John in contrast with the other synoptists.[10] All of the references to John's preaching peculiar to Luke are conscious insertions for effect. The whole of John's ministry, as presented by Luke, is framed and interlaced with the references to speaking beginning with the "word of God came to John" in the wilderness, and concluding with: "So, with many other exhortations, he preached good news to the people" (3:18). The constant references to speaking appear to be Luke's deliberate attempt to give examples of the "word of God" which introduces the teachings of John. Luke alone of the Gospel writers shows an interest in John as inspired teacher (3:10–16). Only in Luke is John referred to as *didaskale* (v. 12; see also 11:1). Luke is compelled to present John's ministry not only because of its concern for repentance, but also because it describes Jesus' mission in terms of Spirit empowering. First, John's prophecy identifies Jesus as the *Christos*, the one anointed by the Spirit (3:15–16 with 4:18 and Acts 10:38). Second, it shows that Jesus himself witnessed and ministered by the Holy Spirit. Third, Jesus saw John's prophecy as a promise that the same Spirit who empowered him would empower his believers as well (Luke 24:49; Acts 1:5, 8; 2:33). Finally, John's prophecy allows Luke to show that even John uttered his prophecy about the Holy Spirit by the power of the Holy Spirit.

Notes to Chapter 3

1. E.g., the ministry of John and the baptism of Jesus (Matt 3:1–17; Mark 1:1–11; Luke 3:1–22; John 1:19–36); the questions of John's emissaries to Jesus (Matt 11:2–19; Luke 7:18–35); the death of John the Baptist (Matt 14:1–2; Mark 6:14–32; Luke 9:7–9); the Petrine confession (Matt 16:13–16; Mark 8:27–29; Luke 9:18–20); the questioning of the chief priests, scribes and elders concerning the authority of Jesus (Matt 21:23–27; Mark 11:27–32; Luke 20:1–8); and John's baptism and preaching as the beginning of the gospel of Jesus (Mark 1:1; John 1:6–8, 15; Acts 1:22; 10:37; 13:24).

In John's Gospel John the Baptist was asked, "Are you Elijah?" As in the synoptic Petrine confession, he used the question of Elijah's identity to proclaim who Jesus is (1:19–36). All of these passages provide occasions to reveal the identity of Jesus. Thus, even without the longer reading of Mark 1:1, Christology is the dominant function of the Marcan Baptist material.

2. "Son of God" should be included on the basis of strong textual attestation. Furthermore, Mark uses the sonship of Jesus as a christological reference frequently. See V. Taylor, *The Gospel According to Mark* (2d ed.; London: Macmillan, 1966), 152; B. Metzger, *A Textual Commentary on the Greek New Testament* (New York: UBS, 1971), 73.

3. The only other quotation of John which Mark employs is his denunciation of Herod, "It is not lawful for you to have your brother's wife" (6:18). Mark mentions the quotation, along with the account of John's death, only because Herod mistook the works of Jesus for evidence that John had been resurrected. In ch. 6, Mark wishes to show the pervasive impact of the miracles of Jesus in Palestine. The quotation in chapter one shows who Jesus is.

4. In the longer ending of Mark, the writer relates the experiences of the early church in that he records phenomena which occur in the early church as a result of Jesus' pouring out the Holy Spirit (see the Acts of the Apostles). While it would seem obvious that Mark or his redactor would be aware of the significance of the prophecy, "he will baptize you with the Holy Spirit," for the post-ascension church, he is content to let it serve the basic reason for

being of all the Baptist synoptic tradition: to proclaim who Jesus is—which is quite justifiable since in his title for his gospel he makes it clear that he is writing the "beginning of the gospel of Jesus Christ, the Son of God" (1:1). Unlike Luke, Mark makes no attempt to give Spirit baptism a second meaning of empowering. So regardless of the question of Mark's responsibility for the longer ending of ch. 16, the primary function of John's prophecy in Mark is christological.

5. Luke often emphasizes repentance when the other Gospel writers do not. It is a major interest of his.

6. R. Brown, *Birth of the Messiah*, 274–75.

7. Jeremias especially notes that the use of the phrase *rhēma theou* without articles is semitic and that it is not one Luke uses elsewhere: "Luke himself writes with two articles: *to rhēma tou kyriou* (Lk 22, 61 P[69,75] B א.)" Luke does not follow Mark in the parallel Mark provides (14:72). Furthermore in Acts 11:16 where Luke is not dependent upon his synoptic sources he uses the two articles: "*the* word of *the* Lord" (my ital.; *Die Sprache*, 103).

8. J. B. Shelton, "Filled with the Holy Spirit: Redactional Motif in Luke's Gospel" (Ph.D. thesis, University of Stirling, Scotland, 1982).

9. B. D. Chilton, *God in Strength: Jesus' Announcement of the Kingdom*, Studien zum Neuen Testament und seiner Umwelt, ed. A. Fuchs and F. Linz (Freistadt: Verlag F. Plöchl, 1979).

10. See Shelton, "Filled," 85.

4 | *The Holy Spirit and Jesus' Baptism*

W HAT IS THE SIGNIFICANCE of Jesus' baptism for Luke? In all of the Gospels, the baptismal experience of Jesus at the Jordan confirms him as the fulfillment of the messianic prophecy of John, "He who is mightier than I is coming, the thong of whose sandals I am not worthy to untie; he will baptize you with the Holy Spirit" (Luke 3:16). In Matthew and Mark, and implicitly in John, Jesus identifies with humanity through water baptism, and then the descent of the dove and the accompanying divine voice identify him as the divine Son (Matt 3:13–17; Mark 1:9–11; John 1:29–34). While Luke also identifies Jesus as such in his account of Jesus' baptism (Luke 3:21–22), he also stresses the significance of the Holy Spirit in the life and work of Jesus, and of those whom Jesus would later anoint. In comparing and contrasting the synoptic accounts, it becomes apparent that Luke associates the Holy Spirit with Jesus for reasons beyond messianic and divine identification. His purpose is clear: to show that the divine acts of Jesus which follow his baptism are a result of the Holy Spirit coming upon him. Luke is proclaiming: When the dove descended, he anointed Jesus with power from on high.

Matt 3:13–17	Mark 1:9–11	Luke 3:21–22
Then Jesus came from Galilee to the Jordan to John, to be baptized by him. John would have prevented him, saying, "I need to be baptized by you, and do you come to me?" But Jesus answered him, "Let it be so now;	In those days Jesus came from Nazareth of Galilee and was baptized by John in the Jordan. And when he came up out of the water, immediately he saw the heavens opened and the Spirit descending upon him	Now when all the people were baptized, and when Jesus also had been baptized and was praying, the heaven was opened, and the Holy Spirit descended upon him in bodily form, as a dove, and a voice came from

for thus it is fitting for us to fulfil all righteousness." Then he consented. And when Jesus was baptized, he went up immediately from the water, and behold, the heavens were opened and he saw the Spirit of God descending like a dove, and alighting on him; and lo, a voice from heaven, saying, "This is my beloved Son, with whom I am well pleased."

like a dove; and a voice came from heaven, "Thou art my beloved Son; with thee I am well pleased."

heaven, "Thou art my beloved Son; with thee I am well pleased."

Absence of John at the Baptism

While Matthew and Mark say that John baptized Jesus and often refer to John's activity as baptizer, Luke minimizes John's baptism as a religious rite and concentrates on the *message* of baptism, i.e., repentance and the empowerment of Jesus. Oddly, Luke reads against his source(s) (Mark and Q), which depict John as the agent of Jesus' baptism. As well, in light of the previous context, it is implied by Luke in the temporal phrase, "when all the people were baptized" (*en tō baptisthēnai hapanta ton laon*, v. 21). Yet Luke records the imprisonment of John before the account of Jesus' baptism (3:19–20). Matthew and Mark include the imprisonment much later, when Herod began inquiring about the activities of Jesus and his disciples (Matt 14:3–4; Mark 6:17–18). This detailed account of Herod's politically expedient sacrifice of John is conspicuously absent in Luke's account of Herod's inquiries.

In all probability, Luke does not wish to associate John with the mighty works of the Holy Spirit that Jesus would perform. As Luke sees it, John fulfills the role of Elijah primarily as a preacher of repentance and as the prophetic herald of Jesus. Jesus himself corresponds to Elijah as miracle worker (Luke 9:7–9 contra Matt 14:2; Mark 6:15–16). When John finished preaching in Luke, his job was completed for the most part. Thus Luke's early reference to John's imprisonment removes John from the scene.

In Luke's Gospel, John completes his primary theological function by preaching repentance and proclaiming Jesus as the one who would baptize in the Holy Spirit. Luke's use of the aorist of *baptisthēnai* ("to be baptized") in v. 21 indicates that John's ministry ends with this baptism. Here the baptism of Jesus is not one of John's primary functions as it is in Mark and Matthew. Furthermore, Jesus is the primary baptizer in the mind of the writer of Luke–Acts. John's baptism in water, at this point, is merely an attendant circumstance to the empowering of Jesus—and later his church—by the Holy Spirit.[1]

Grammatical Deemphasis of Jesus' Baptism

Not only does Luke minimize John's role as baptizer, but he sees Jesus' baptism as a temporal circumstance, an indication of a more important event, for he deemphasizes it both grammatically and thematically. Mark says that Jesus "was baptized by John" (v. 9). Matthew specifically states the purpose of Jesus coming to John was "to be baptized by him" (v. 13), that John permitted it (v. 15), and that after Jesus was baptized the Spirit of God came upon him.[2] In contrast, Luke sees the descent of the Holy Spirit on Jesus as the main event, and the reference to the baptisms of Jesus and the people[3] he expresses as an introductory clause, telling the reader when and where the event occurs. (Note the aorist infinitive and participle of *baptizō* in the clause). On the heels of the baptism comes the principal event recorded in the main clause (21b–22): the opening of heaven, the divine voice, and the descent of the dove. Luke is *not* describing baptism and anointing as two simultaneous events, although they are related as is evident in the baptismal formula in Acts: "Repent, and be baptized every one of you in the name of Jesus Christ for the forgiveness of your sins; and you shall receive the gift of the Holy Spirit" (2:38).

Empowering or Divine Attestation?

Luke, like the other evangelists, sees the descent of the dove as a messianic sign. Immediately after the divine announcement of Jesus' sonship at the Jordan, Luke reiterates the sonship concept in the genealogy which concludes that Jesus was "the son of Adam, the son of God" (3:23–38). Also, two of the temptations of Jesus in Luke 4 are prefaced with Satan's query, "If you are the Son of God . . ." (vv. 3, 9). Thus Luke maintains the traditional significance of the descent of the Spirit found in all four Gospels. But in addition to the declarations that Jesus is the Son of God, Luke frequently and overtly declares that after the descent of the dove, Jesus was full of the Holy Spirit and empowered to do mighty works. Furthermore, of all the Gospel writers only Luke notes this (4:1,

14, 18; 10:21; 24:19; Acts 1:2; 2:22; 10:38). Three of these Lucan references to empowerment immediately follow the descent of the dove.

A Baptism in the Holy Spirit for Jesus?

At this point a crucial question arises: Does Jesus' pneumatic experience compare to the believers' experience in the Holy Spirit as recorded in the infancy narratives and Acts? How similar or dissimilar are they?

Although it is impossible to *equate* the empowering of Jesus at the Jordan with the baptism of believers in the Holy Spirit,[4] similarities do exist which would justify viewing this experience of Jesus and the Holy Spirit baptism of his followers in the same light. It is true in the case of the believers' baptism in the Holy Spirit that tongues of fire, rather than the dove, rested on them, a sound like a mighty rushing wind, rather than the voice, came from heaven, and the believers were *not* declared the Son of God as Jesus was (cf. Acts 2:2–4). But as a dispensing of divine power, the two experiences are congruent if not equal. In this aspect the difference is quantitative and not qualitative, for the Holy Spirit is the agent of both anointings. (The qualitative difference in Jesus' experience with the Spirit in contrast to the believers' experience is in his conception, 1:35.) That Jesus saw his experience at baptism in terms of anointing (*chriō*) is evident in 4:18, and Luke says in Acts that Jesus poured out (*ekcheō*) the same Spirit upon the believers. Note that Luke often uses the terms "anointing," "baptism," and "pouring out" synonymously to indicate empowering. He prefers to reserve "anointing" for Jesus' experience; nevertheless, the effect of these terms is the same: power for ministry.[5] James Dunn observes:

> We may legitimately speak of the descent of the Spirit on Jesus at Jordan as a baptism in the Spirit; and we certainly cannot deny that it was this anointing with the Spirit which equipped Jesus with power and authority for his mission to follow (Acts 10:38).[6]

Jesus, the Spirit, and the New Age

It has been suggested that the descent of the Holy Spirit on Jesus in some sense marks the beginning of the age of the new covenant[7] or Luke's so-called middle era (*die Mitte der Zeit*).[8] The idea is that Jesus' experience with the Holy Spirit at the Jordan is unique in that it inaugurates a new age; therefore, the experience of Jesus with the Holy Spirit is not analogous to that of the believers. Luke is not trying to place an unbridgeable chasm between Jesus' experience with the Spirit and that of his followers in the new age of the Spirit after Pentecost. While Luke sees Jesus as uniquely the Christ, the anointed man of God, he often uses the same terms for Jesus' experience with the Holy Spirit that he uses to describe the experience of others. For example, the Holy Spirit descends upon (*katabainai epi*) Jesus, while the Holy Spirit falls upon (*epipiptō*) believers (Acts 8:16; 10:44; 11:15; 19:6 with similar usage for Simeon in Luke 2:25). Luke follows the synoptic tradition in the use of *katabainō* for the descent of the Spirit on Jesus (Mark 1:10 and Matt 3:16). Jesus, Stephen, and Barnabas are described as "full of the Holy Spirit" (Luke 4:1; Acts 6:3, 5; 11:24). Jesus "returned in [*en*] the power of the Spirit;" Simeon in [*en*] the Spirit came into the temple (4:14; 2:27). Jesus says, "The Spirit of the Lord was upon [*epi*] me" (4:18), while the "Holy Spirit is upon [*epi*]" Simeon (2:25). Jesus is anointed with the Holy Spirit (*chriō*, 4:18; Acts 10:38), and the Holy Spirit is poured out on believers (Acts 2:17, 33). Although the dove does not appear above the disciples, these other parallels are no accident. Luke sees the believers functioning in like manner to the Spirit-filled Messiah. If Luke had wished to emphasize the difference between Jesus and the believers, would he have created so many parallels?

To maintain that Luke views the baptism of Jesus as the beginning of the new age can be done only by ignoring the salvific activity of the Holy Spirit in the infancy narrative. Previously in the infancy accounts, Luke shows that the Holy Spirit is responsible for Jesus' conception and for the witnesses to his birth. The questions and answers of the boy Jesus in the temple apparently occur as a result of the inspiration of the Holy Spirit. The later followers of Jesus in Acts give witness even as Jesus and the infancy witnesses did. Apparently the coming of the new age is an era, a process in itself. When it comes to the activity of the Holy Spirit, Luke blurs the so-called epoch that he has allegedly created. Clearly Jesus' experience with the empowering Spirit is exemplary for believers. While the experience of believers is not the same as that of Jesus, it is certainly congruent with and parallel to Jesus' experience (see Appendix).

The Divine Voice

"Thou art my beloved Son; with thee I am well pleased."
—Luke 3:23

In keeping with his general program, Luke associates the empowering of Jesus with the divine announcement of his sonship at the descent of the dove. This association is at best only implicit in the other Gospels. In Mark the voice affirms the divine sonship of Jesus in keeping with the title Mark gives to his Gospel (1:1). Furthermore, in Mark the Baptist's prophecy concerning the Baptizer in the Holy Spirit is underdeveloped, and its ramifications for the church are largely ignored (but cf. the longer ending, 16:17–18).

Matthew follows the pattern of Mark by acknowledging that the events surrounding the baptism of Jesus primarily affirm that Jesus is the Son of God. The prophecy predicting the coming of the Baptizer in the Spirit in Matthew also links Jesus with the descent of the Spirit of God and the divine voice which follows. For Matthew, the voice not only points to the sonship of Jesus, but it also reiterates Jesus' supremacy over John, which is one of Matthew's particular concerns.

The Q tradition presents a different concept for the opening of the heavens. Mark reads *schizomenous* ("were torn or split") while Matthew and Luke use a form of *anoigō* ("were opened"). *Anoigō* often describes acts of divine revelation.[9] The context in Luke, however, reveals more.

The Descent of the Spirit as Confirmation of John's Prophecy of the "Spirit-Baptizer"

As noted, Luke maintains the traditional understanding of the baptism of Jesus by using it to proclaim Jesus as the Son of God. However, he primarily sees the event as the divine empowering of Jesus. This is probably Luke's observation and not Q's, since the frequent references to the empowering of Jesus subsequent to his baptism are exclusively Lucan.[10] Unlike the other Gospel writers, Luke does not consider the identification of the Son of God as the only function of John's prediction of the Holy Spirit Baptizer (Matt 3:11, 16–17; Mark 1:8, 10–11; John 1:33–34). For Luke, the prophecy of John identifies Jesus as the Anointed One; but in identifying him as such the prophecy is primarily understood in terms of empowering, which Luke portrays as the manner in which Jesus himself viewed the prophecy (Acts 1:4–5, 8; 11:16–17). Here the spiritual experiences of Jesus and his followers converge. The title, the Christ—the Anointed One—is more than just a Greek equivalent of the Hebrew title Messiah. Like those anointed in the OT (e.g., 1 Sam 10:1–10; 16:13), Jesus too was empowered for ministry. Elsewhere, Luke maintains that the anointing of Jesus empowered him for ministry (4:18; Acts 10:38). Luke has anointing for ministry in mind when he alone notes that the Holy Spirit came upon Jesus bodily (3:22).

Relationship between the Holy Spirit and Sonship

In the passages following the account of Jesus' baptism, the empowering of Jesus and his sonship are dominant themes. In the temptation account (4:1) and in two references to Jesus' exorcizing demons (4:33–35, 41), the empowering of Jesus and attestation of his sonship are interrelated. Even the forces of evil acknowledge his divine sonship as a result of witnessing his power. Luke expresses Jesus' sonship in terms of the Holy Spirit's activity (4:1, 14, 18; with 5:17). It is then not surprising that Luke makes his references to the descent of the Holy Spirit upon Jesus and the divine announcement of sonship grammatically parallel and equal to one another. The sonship of Jesus is attested by the Holy Spirit: "The Holy Spirit will come upon you, and the power of the Most High will overshadow you; therefore the child to be born will be called holy, the Son of God" (1:35). The attestation of his sonship and messiahship in the resurrection is also accompanied by the Holy Spirit (Acts 2:32–36; 13:33).

Adoptionistic Christology

Although Luke links the empowerment of the Holy Spirit to Jesus' messianic ministry, he does not subscribe to an adoptionistic Christology. He does not view Jesus as a man who became the Christ as a result of the descent of the dove. A variant reading is Luke 3:22 for, "You are my beloved son, in you I am well pleased" seems to lend weight to adoptionism: "Thou art my beloved son; *today I have begotten thee.*" While this reading occurs in some church fathers and might be interpreted as the *lectio difficilior potior,* its textual support is late, rare, and in less dependable manuscripts.

Even if the "begotten" reading is original with Luke, it should not lead to the conclusion that Luke held to an adoptionistic Christology. First, the reading comes from Psalm 2:7, a messianic enthronement psalm. "Begotten" refers to the accession of the new king to the throne. In this sense the king fills the office of the son of God, or king. This event was accompanied by anointing with oil which was to invoke the power of the Holy Spirit for the royal task (1 Sam 10:1–10; 16:13). Begottenness in this context simply means inauguration. Second, the infancy narratives rule out any adoptionistic notion. Jesus is first declared Son of God as a result of the Holy Spirit's work at his conception (1:35), not at his baptism. Furthermore, for Jesus the contact with the Holy Spirit at conception enabled him to converse brilliantly in the temple as a mere lad (2:40–52). It is not necessary to hold to an adoptionistic Christology to maintain that as a human, albeit a unique one, Jesus was specially equipped by the Holy Spirit to fulfill his mission as Messiah. The experience of Jesus at the Jordan, Luke asserts, does *not* constitute his becoming the Son of God (cf. 1:35), but it does mark the point when he is, as Messiah, publicly enabled to perform mighty deeds.

Conclusion

The Holy Spirit's Relationship with Jesus Compared with His Relationship with Believers

The Holy Spirit equips witnesses in the infancy narrative to bear witness to the Messiah. The same Holy Spirit empowers believers to witness concerning Christ in the church era (Acts 2:33ff.). In his description of the role of the Holy Spirit in inspiring the witnesses of Luke–Acts, we see Luke as a theologian who realizes that the work of the Holy Spirit in Jesus' ministry and in the lives of his followers is often analogous, and in many instances identical. Thus, the baptism of Jesus, and particularly the descent of the dove, held great import for the early church's understanding of its experience with the Holy Spirit. The anointing of Jesus at the Jordan and his subsequent ministry became an example for the believers.

Yet, Luke also insists on the uniqueness of Jesus' relationship with the Father, his redemptive work in the passion-resurrection, and his supreme position with God as the one who pours out the Holy Spirit after his ascension. Luke may not always delineate between the roles of the Holy Spirit and Jesus, but he certainly makes it clear that in principle, the experiences of believers with the Holy Spirit can *not* be equivalent to Jesus' relationship with the Spirit. The conception of Jesus by the Holy Spirit is unmistakably unique (Luke 1:35). However, Luke often notes the similarities between the relationship of Jesus and the Spirit, and those of the believers and the Spirit. In fact, he observes the similarities more than the differences. Luke holds the two in a dynamic tension, not omitting one or the other.

Jesus, the Spirit-Anointed Son of God

Luke's Gospel deliberately avoids saying that John baptized Jesus. Luke minimizes water baptism in the ministry of John and in the experience of Jesus at the Jordan while he centers on equipping for ministry. Further, in the context that follows, Luke emphasizes the power and guidance of the Spirit in the ministry of Jesus that resulted from the descent of the dove. He inserts references to the Holy Spirit in the synoptic tradition and replaces the synoptic account of Jesus' Nazareth ministry with another version that emphasizes the role of the Holy Spirit. Furthermore, he ignores the usual chronological order of the ministry of Jesus found in Matthew and Mark to place references to Jesus' Spirit-enablement at the beginning of Jesus' ministry.

Luke is not making these assertions about the role of the Holy Spirit in empowering Jesus simply on the basis of his own opinion. Rather, he is bearing witness to the truth: Jesus was indeed empowered by the Holy Spirit at the Jordan. Furthermore, just as the Holy Spirit inspired the early witnesses of Christ's birth in Luke and the early church witnesses in Acts, the Holy Spirit has inspired Luke's own witness to Jesus. The Holy Spirit has given Luke a mandate—he is to tell his readers that, yes, Jesus was indeed empowered by the Holy Spirit. Later he informs us that Jesus will pour out the same Holy Spirit upon all who believe in him and empower them for witness as well. In the next chapter we will explore Luke's presentation of Jesus' Spirit-filled ministry.

Notes to Chapter 4

1. I. H. Marshall, *The Gospel of Luke: A Commentary on the Greek Text*, NIGTC (Exeter: Paternoster Press, 1978), 150, 152.

2. Both Matthew and Luke place the reference to the act of Jesus' baptism as a temporal phrase (*baptistheis de ho Iēsous*, Matt 3:16; *kai Iēsou baptisthentos*, Luke 3:21) before the descent of the Holy Spirit upon Jesus. This may indicate that Q placed more emphasis on the descent of the Holy Spirit than Mark did.

3. Luke alone notes the presence of both Jesus and the baptized penitents at the descent of the Holy Spirit. This probably serves two functions. First, the people are witnesses to the divine visitation. This fits in well with Luke's frequent witness motif, "that which you see and hear," which is often associated with the works of the Holy Spirit. Luke's use of *su* instead of *houtos* for the divine address does not demand that Jesus alone was aware of the supernatural events at the Jordan. The omission of John from the baptismal scene may be a conscious effort to say that the people, the baptized penitents, were witnesses of the Holy Spirit, not just John. If the people were witnesses of the divine events at the Jordan, then the reference to their presence and John's "absence" can best be explained. They were there to see the dove in *bodily form* and to hear the divine voice. Second, Luke notes their presence to associate the baptized believers with the power of the Holy Spirit which comes through Jesus as he expressly does in the preaching of Acts.

4. Marshall, *Gospel of Luke*, 150.

5. In the LXX *epicheō* is used to describe the acts of anointing and in context is used interchangeably with *chriō* (e.g., Exod 29:7; Lev 8:12; 21:10; 1 Sam 10:1ff.). *Epicheō* can be used to describe pouring in general like the Hebrew word it translates (*yṣq;* but both *epicheō* and *yṣq* consistently are used to describe the act of anointing (*chrisma* and *mišḥah*). Being familiar with the LXX, Luke also notes the association of the act of anointing with the Holy Spirit's coming upon (*epi*) the one anointed (1 Sam 10:6, 10; 16:13).

In Acts, Luke does not use *epicheō* to describe the Holy Spirit being poured upon people; rather, he employs *ekcheō* (2:17, 18, 33; 10:45). It is apparent that the intention of Luke here is basically the same as the use of *epicheō* in the LXX. Luke uses *epi* in context with *ekcheō* in Acts 2:17, 18; 10:45; and also 2:33 since it refers back to the previous context with *epi* in 2:3. Luke may prefer *ekcheō* instead of *epicheō* since the former is used in the prophecy of Joel which serves as the backbone for Peter's Pentecost address.

Another possible reason for the preference of *ekcheō* may be that he is aware that the uses of *epicheō* in 1 Samuel are royal anointings. At this point Luke wishes to distinguish between the royal anointing of Jesus, the Son, and the Christ of God (Luke 9:20), and the Holy Spirit coming upon his followers. In this restricted sense, only Jesus can be anointed; hence only Luke explicitly says that Jesus was anointed (*echrisen*). In Luke Jesus' followers are not expressly described as anointed (i.e., using *chriō* or *chrisma* which occurs only in reference to believers in the NT; 2 Cor 1:22 and 1 John 2:20, 27). The royal significance is reserved for Jesus, but Luke readily appropriates the rest of the parallels to express the relationship of believers and the Holy Spirit.

Another more apparent reason for Luke's use of *ekcheō* for believers' experiencing the Holy Spirit is that the verb emphasizes the act of God/Jesus pouring out the Holy Spirit rather than underscoring the result of the outpouring. (Luke often uses "filled with/full of the Holy Spirit" to emphasize results.) The verb is particularly suited to describe the event of Pentecost. The Holy Spirit was poured out without restriction as a container being emptied. The believers who previously had limited access to the Holy Spirit were filled. The kingdom as the advent of the Holy Spirit was consummated. This was as much an act of God as an experience of believers.

Any explanation of Luke's preference for *ekcheō* over *epicheō* must be presented with caution in light of the increased frequency of use of prepositional prefixes with verbs and their interchangeability in hellenistic Greek. Yet superfluous use of prepositional prefixes is not the explanation here; for the presence of *ekcheō* is from the quotation of Joel and the absence of specific references to anointing (*chriō*) of believers appears to have governed Luke's use of the term. It is also apparent that Luke sees the terms as at least congruent if not equal since he uses *epi* in context with *ekcheō*. Because he uses *epi* with *cheō*, the image of anointing is inescapable when viewing the relationship of believers and the Holy Spirit.

6. Dunn, *Baptism in the Holy Spirit* (London: SCM Press, 1970), 24. He concedes that one could "argue that the theme of *imitatio Christi* is here," but he suggests that "there is no real exegetical basis for this inference."

7. Ibid., 24–33.

8. Conzelmann, *Theology*, 22–23.

9. Concerning the use of *anoigō*, Marshall states, "The opening of the heavens is an indication that divine revelation is about to take place" (*Gospel of Luke*, 152). C. H. Peisker and C. Brown note Luke's special use of *anoigō* ("open") in expressing the revelation of truth (Luke 3:21; 4:17; 11:9–13; 12:36; 13:25): "The references in Lk. suggest that the time to open and the authority to open ultimately rest with God." They also note a use of *anoigō* parallel to the use in 3:21 in Peter's vision of the clean and unclean beasts. "The fact that heaven is opened in order to let down the sheet (Acts 10:11) signifies the divine origin and authority of the vision"; "Open," *NIDNTT* (1976), 2:726–27. The use of *anoigō* in relation to apocalyptic revelations is in keeping with OT usage. (See Marshall, *Gospel of Luke*.)

10. Luke's hand is boldly present in his account of the baptism of Jesus. The use of *en* with the articular infinitive is typically Lucan as Plummer notes in his list of such uses (*Luke*, 98, many of which are preceded by *egeneto*). The epexegetical uses of *egeneto*, which Plummer recognizes as being semitic in character, are used by Luke more frequently than by any other Gospel writer. Plummer also notes, however, that Luke also adjusts the constructions used with *egeneto* to fit classical structures as well, as in the case with 3:21–22 (ibid., 45; see also Jeremias, *Die Sprache*, 112–13). Several of these uses occur in exclusively Lucan material, and it also appears that Luke has adjusted his sources to fit into this structure as is apparent in the text at hand. Notice Matthew and Mark have *phōnē ek tōn ouranōn* (3:17 and 1:11 respectively) while Luke has *phōnēn ex ouranou genesthai*. (Also contrast the synoptic parallels with 5:1; 9:33.) The grammatical deemphasis of the baptism of Jesus was Luke's work, which makes the parallel structure of the descent of the Holy Spirit and the divine voice more striking (*Egeneto de . . . aneōchthēnai ton ouranon kai katabēnai to pneuma to hagion . . . kai phōnēn . . . genesthai*).

Jeremias also notes that this construction is Lucan since it occurs twenty-two times in Luke–Acts and only once in Matthew and once in Mark (*Die Sprache*, 113). Note also the characteristically Lucan *hapas*. References to prayer in Jesus' ministry are frequently inserted by Luke as in 3:21. The singular of *ho ouranos* is probably Luke's correction of the more semitic "heavens" with which he was confronted in Mark and Q.

5 | The Holy Spirit and Jesus' Temptation

> And Jesus, full of the Holy Spirit, returned from the Jordan, and was led by the Spirit for forty days in the wilderness, tempted by the devil.
>
> —Luke 4:1–2

"In the Power of the Spirit"

Following Luke's account of the Holy Spirit's empowering of Jesus at the Jordan, he continues the same theme in the account of Jesus' temptation in the wilderness. Luke mentions the Holy Spirit and his influence upon Jesus on four occasions in chapter 4 (twice in 4:1 immediately before the temptation in the wilderness, once in 4:14 immediately before Jesus' public ministry, and once in 4:18 at the inauguration of his ministry in Nazareth). Thus he frames the temptation account with references to the Holy Spirit. In contrast, the corresponding synoptic parallels in Mark and Matthew mention the Holy Spirit only once (Mark 1:12; Matt 4:1). Although Luke uses the same basic account of the temptations as Matthew, there is some variation in their order, and Luke inserts some of his own unique comments. Luke's presentation of Jesus' temptation is similar to his handling of the Baptist material: he underlines the role of the Holy Spirit. Yet while emphasizing the Holy Spirit, Luke maintains the common synoptic theme of sonship by declaring that Jesus was able to fulfill his office of sonship because he was anointed by the Spirit. In our analysis of the references to the Holy Spirit in the temptation account, we will see that (1) Luke is primarily interested in recording the empowering of Jesus, (2) this empowering enabled Jesus to speak authoritatively, in this case particularly against Satan, (3) empowerment to speak is in harmony with the preceding and following context, and (4) the way Jesus overcame temptation is a paradigm, or pattern, for the way his followers would overcome temptation.

After Jesus' reception of the Holy Spirit at the Jordan, Luke presents the genealogy of Jesus, then returns to the outline of Matthew and Mark in presenting the temptation account. By doing so Luke continues the Son of God theme inaugurated by the voice from heaven at the Jordan. Even the devil presupposed Jesus' sonship in the temptations when he said, "if [or since] you are the Son of God . . ." (in Greek a first class conditional clause which assumes the presupposition is a fact). Although Luke is quick to affirm Jesus' sonship by making repeated references to it, he points out that Jesus fulfills his mission by the power of the Holy Spirit (1:35; 4:14, 18; Acts 4:27; 10:38).[1]

Matt 4:1	Mark 1:12	Luke 4 :1–2
Then Jesus was led up by the Spirit into the wilderness to be tempted by the devil.	The Spirit immediately drove him out into the wilderness.	And Jesus, full of the Holy Spirit, returned from the Jordan, and was led by the Spirit for forty days in the wilderness, tempted by the devil.

Lucan Adjustment of the Temptation Account

Luke uniquely molds the account of Jesus' temptation that he receives in Mark and Q: first he avoids Mark's emphatic expression, "the Spirit immediately drove Jesus into the wilderness" (cf. Mark 1:12 with Luke 4:1). Luke often omits Mark's redundant use of "immediately" (*euthys eutheōs*, used 42 times in Mark; e.g., Mark 1:10 with Luke 1:22; Mark 1:21 with Luke 4:31; 1:23 with 4:33; 1:29 with 4:38; 1:30 with 4:38 and passim). Luke, along with Matthew, avoids Mark's verb "drove out" or "cast out" (*ekballō*) to describe the guidance of the Holy Spirit, preferring the milder "led" (*agō* in Luke; *anagō* in Matthew). Luke avoids Mark's strong language elsewhere as well.[2]

"Full of the Holy Spirit"/"Led by the Spirit"

More significant for our study is Luke's inclusion of the phrase "full of the Holy Spirit" and Luke's retention of the synoptic "led by the Spirit." Luke includes both expressions in the same introductory statement. One must ask, "Would not one reference to the Spirit suffice?" For Luke the answer is no. Luke is not being redundant or pleonastic, nor is he being effusive or sloppy. Elsewhere when Luke describes some-

one as "filled with" or "full of the Holy Spirit" the phrase has a specialized function in the text. Its use in 4:1 is not an exception; here as
elsewhere, "fullness" results in *inspired speech* (Acts 6:3, 5, 8 with 6:10;
7:55; 11:23–24). It is not enough for Luke to say that Jesus was led by
the Spirit into the wilderness to be tempted. Luke implies that he was
filled to conquer temptation.[3]

Luke's exclusive use of the phrase, "returned from the Jordan," also
shows that he intends his readers to associate the pneumatic fullness of Jesus
with the descent of the Spirit upon Jesus at the Jordan. Furthermore, Luke
drops Mark's reference to the wild beasts (1:13) as well as the mention of
angels which is included in both Matthew and Mark. Luke is anxious to
show that Jesus conquered the devil by relying on the Holy Spirit.

Inspired Witness against the Devil

Luke is attracted to the temptation account for several reasons.
First, Jesus overcomes the suggestions of the devil *not* by performing a
miracle (4:3), but by the words given to him by the Holy Spirit. This is
why Luke describes the activity of the Spirit in Jesus' life here as "full of
the Holy Spirit." This is not to preclude other meanings for the phrase;
Luke is not averse to associating the fullness of the Spirit with wisdom,
power, joy, miracles, faith, and revelation, as is evident throughout
Luke–Acts (Acts 6:3, 5, 8, 10; 7:55; 11:23–24). However, the dominant
role of "filled" and "full" in Luke–Acts is inspired speech. Words from
the Holy Spirit are adequate to squelch the temptation of the devil.

Not Magical Power but a Lifestyle

It should not be assumed, however, that the words of Jesus are
mere magical formulas that enable him automatically to render the
temptations ineffective. The responses of Jesus reveal that the power of
his words is predicated upon his existing relationship with God. All of
his words in the temptations underscore that relationship (4:4, 8, 12).
Luke makes it clear that the Holy Spirit's power is not a neutral magical
power for any to use; he gives Ananias, Sapphira, and Simon the magician as examples of the follies of such presumption (Acts 5:1–11; 8:9–
24). Although Luke does not object to Jesus' experience as "full of the
Holy Spirit" as durative and indicative of an ongoing relationship with
God, he uses it here to explain how Jesus is able to speak effectively
against temptation.[4]

Luke also tells us that witness, even when it correctly identifies
Jesus as God's Son, will not be tolerated if it is not from God's Spirit.

"And demons also came out of many, crying, 'You are the Son of God!' But he rebuked them, and would not allow them to speak because they knew he was the Christ" (Luke 4:41; see also 4:35; 8:28; Acts 16:16–18). Thus speaking "full of the Holy Spirit" is not an exercise in gnostic incantation or magic, but an empowerment which requires a righteous relationship with God.

Jesus as a Spirit-Led Human

Luke's unique presentation of the temptation makes a strong statement about Jesus' nature and that of his followers. Jesus is described in the same terms as other human beings: empowered by the Holy Spirit. Jesus relies on God's resources to overcome temptation. Drawing from other texts in the canon, some have assumed that since Jesus was divine it was impossible for him to fall to temptation. Luke's use of "full of the Holy Spirit" and "led by the Spirit" makes it doubly clear that Jesus' temptations were real and that he was truly human. He relied not on his own power and resources but on God's. Otherwise the temptations would have been a pre-arranged drama, a mere sham.[5]

Jesus and Temptation as an Example

While Luke maintains that Jesus' experience as God's Son through the work of the Holy Spirit is unique, he also shows that in his humanity Jesus is dependent upon the Holy Spirit to overcome temptation and carry out his ministry.[6] This is why Luke uses the same terms to express Jesus' relationship with the Holy Spirit and that of believers. This is good news to Luke's readers. The temptations of Jesus are real, as real as anyone else's dilemmas. Jesus does not rely on the uniqueness of his Spirit-generated birth (1:35) or his office of Messiah to win over temptation. He overcomes evil as God expects all people to triumph—through the power of the Holy Spirit. The inspired words that enable Jesus to overcome originate from his experience with God's Spirit of power.

Inspired Speech Against Opponents

The same Spirit who empowered Jesus will enable his followers to speak against opposition, just as he had predicted: "And when they bring you before the synagogues and the rulers and authorities, do not be anxious how or what you are to answer or what you are to say; for the Holy Spirit will teach you in that very hour what you ought to say" (Luke 12:11–12). This prophecy is important for Luke since he shows its fulfillment several times in Acts (4:11–23; 5:25–41; 6:10–7:60; 22:30–26:32) and gives *two* versions of it on the lips of Jesus (Luke 12:11–12; 21:12–15). In the latter version, Luke says Jesus will give the witness "a mouth and *wisdom*, which none of your adversaries will be able to withstand or contradict," (21:15). Linked with 12:11–12, Luke sees the Holy Spirit as the origin of the witness and its impeccable wisdom. In Acts Luke gives us an example of a fulfillment of Jesus' prophecy: Stephen was "full of the Holy Spirit" (Acts 6:3, 5); as a result, his opponents "could not withstand the *wisdom* and the Spirit with which he spoke" (Acts 6:10, my ital.).

Elsewhere Luke relates that Elymas the magician tried to dissuade the proconsul Sergius Paulus from Barnabas' and Paul's testimony. Paul, "filled with the Holy Spirit, looked intently at him and said, 'You son of the devil, you enemy of all righteousness, full of all deceit and villainy, will you not stop making crooked the straight paths of the Lord? And now, behold, the hand of the Lord is upon you, and you shall be blind and unable to see the sun from a time.' Immediately mist and darkness fell upon him . . ." (Acts 13:9–11). Filled with the Holy Spirit, Paul witnessed against one who was full of fraud. The same Spirit that speaks for the Son of God speaks against the sons of the devil. Thus for Luke the experience of Jesus in the wilderness temptations is very similar to the experiences of his followers.

A Lifestyle of Dependency on the Holy Spirit

Luke, alone among the Gospel writers, suggests that for Jesus the wilderness temptation experience was not a one-time confrontation with the devil, for Luke says the devil "departed from him until an opportune time" (4:13). Luke recognizes that the temptations of embracing popular views of righteousness, taking short cuts, and condoning evil to do good dogged the heels of Jesus all the way to the cross. Thus for Luke enduring the temptations is not merely a *staged act* by a divine being incapable of being tempted, but it is a *lifestyle* of a human being endowed by and dependent upon the Holy Spirit. Luke's emphasis on the Spirit in the temptation narrative is simultaneously sobering and encouraging for the followers of Jesus in their struggle with evil.

Notes to Chapter 5

1. "On the one hand, the story demonstrates how the Spirit, who had come upon Jesus, guided and empowered him in his new task; on the

other hand, it shows how Jesus, as the Son of God, was obedient to God" (Marshall, *Gospel of Luke*, 165–66).

2. For example, Mark says that the heavens were "torn asunder" (*schizō*, Mark 1:10), while Luke and Matthew prefer a milder verb (*anoigō*, Luke 3:21 and Matt 3:16).

3. For the Lucan nature of "full of the Holy Spirit" see Jeremias, *Die Sprache*, 114–15. "The phrase obviously refers to the descent of the Spirit on Jesus at baptism." Fitzmyer says the phrase is Lucan redaction(*Luke* 1.507). "These words connect the Temptation closely with the Baptism" (Plummer, *Luke*, 107).

4. In some brands of theology in the charismatic movement, "the power of the spoken word" is emphasized. It is assumed that positive confession as a "spiritual law" will create something out of nothing, bringing into being things that are not. For an analysis of this doctrine see D. McConnell, *A Different Gospel* (Peabody, Mass.: Hendrickson, 1988). This is not what Jesus did in the wilderness. Jesus did not merely "confess" more scriptures than the enemy. On the contrary, the three OT quotations spoken by Jesus did not create something new but reminded Jesus of his already existing relationship with his Father. Jesus did not get into a shouting match with the devil; what Jesus said centered his attention on God. The power was predicated on a relationship with God (1:35; 2:49; 3:21–22, 38). Simon Peter made it clear to Simon the magician that the power comes only in the context of a relationship with God (Acts 8:9–24). Jesus was not practicing magic, applying gnostic formulas, or relying on the resources of his own genius for manipulating "spiritual laws;" he overcame the devil because he was empowered by the Holy Spirit which he received from his Father. Even the man Jesus relied on the grace of God (Shelton, "Luke 4:1–13," 111–19).

5. This does not mean that Luke or the present writer would be averse to acknowledging Jesus as divine. Any claims to divinity do not diminish Jesus' humanity. Jesus as a man subject to human passions precludes any gnostic imbalance that would weaken the reality of Jesus as an earthly Savior as well as a divine spiritual being.

6. John Navone correctly asserts that "the temptation of Christ (Lk 4:1–13) has a unique sense." He observes that Luke does not call Satan "the tempter" as does Matthew; thus the experience of Jesus is unique "indicating that the devil is not exercising here his typical function which he also exercises with regard to the faithful (1 Thess 3:5). This temptation does not have any counterpart in the life of the Christian; rather, it is the unique experience of the Son of God (Lk 4:3)" (*Themes*, 179). It is true that the messianic experiences of Jesus as the Son of God are unique. But the absence of the term tempter (*ho peirazōn*) is not significant because Luke says that Jesus was "being tempted (*peirazomenos*) by the devil" (4:2). The experience of Jesus in temptation was not exactly the same as that of Christians in that his messiahship was being attacked. Nevertheless, his experience *is* congruent to the experience of his followers, and his example *is* paradigmatic for them. When one takes into account the redactional significance of "full of the Holy Spirit" in Luke–Acts, the parallels between Jesus' experience and that of believers are inescapable.

6 | *The Holy Spirit and the Inauguration of Jesus' Public Ministry*

As IN THE TEMPTATION account, the Holy Spirit is a central feature of Luke's description of the inauguration of Jesus' public ministry in Nazareth (Luke 4:14–30). In both his introduction to the beginning of Jesus' public ministry (vv. 14–15) and his version of Jesus' ministry at Nazareth (vv. 16–30), Luke tells of the activity of the Holy Spirit. Mark and Matthew, though, say nothing of the Spirit in their versions of the same events. Only Luke mentions that following the wilderness experience Jesus returned to Galilee in the "power of the Spirit" (4:14) and that he read from the Isaiah scroll in the Nazareth synagogue, "The Spirit of the Lord is upon me" (4:18–19; Isa 61:1).

Luke's Adjustment of the Synoptic Account

Luke consciously digresses from Mark's version of the beginning of Jesus' ministry: (1) He edits and reorders the Marcan material, often differing from the content, chronology, and order of Matthew as well as Mark. (2) He inserts his own observations using his vocabulary and style to make his overriding interests known. (3) Also, he prefers a version from an early tradition rather than the Marcan account. As earlier in the Gospel, his purpose is to show the centrality of the Holy Spirit in Jesus' ministry.

Lucan Creativity?

Earlier in this century, some scholars asserted that Luke created a new version of the beginning of Jesus' ministry and the rejection at Nazareth by extensively reworking and expanding Mark's version into a longer propaganda piece. In this reconstruction of the history of the synoptic tradition, Luke was often seen as *creating* new events in the story of Jesus. Luke did so, it was argued, to make a theological point not made by Mark. To attribute the variations on the theme in the Nazareth rejection account to Lucan creativity has proved attractive. Bultmann, Creed, Dibelius, Leaney, and others[1] hold to extensive Lucan creativity. Leaney, however, makes modifications in his evaluation and considers Luke 4:16–22a, 23a, 25–30 as possibly having been derived from a non-Marcan tradition;[2] nevertheless, he maintains that the essence of Luke's account, whether created by him or by a predecessor, comes from Mark.[3]

The main reasons for considering the passage a work of Lucan creativity are: (1) Luke records the contents of Jesus' speech while Matthew and Mark do not; (2) the theme of the speech fits Luke's purpose; (3) the parenthetical reference to Capernaum without an explicit antecedent implies a reverse in chronology (v. 23);[4] (4) there is an apparent contradiction between the crowd's praise of Jesus and their animosity toward him (vv. 22ff., 28);[5] (5) the universalistic tone of the references to the Gentiles which dominates Luke's attention later (vv. 25–27) has parallels to the mission of the church which seem strange at this early period in Jesus' ministry; and (6) in Matthew and Mark, Jesus' visit to Nazareth results in rejection and limited effectiveness, whereas in Luke it results in attempted murder on the part of the crowd.

An Alternate Tradition

Other scholars, however, have a different theory to explain the differences in Luke's version of the introduction of Jesus' ministry (4:14–15) and the ministry at Nazareth (4:16–30). On the basis of Luke's vocabulary preferences, they have identified an alternate tradition behind Luke's version.[6]

While it must be admitted that some elaboration and addition occur in the Lucan account,[7] the objections to an alternate tradition as the source can be answered. All of the synoptic versions note that Jesus taught in Nazareth. Only Luke gives an account of what was said, but Jesus "must have said *something*, and it is not unlikely that Mark has omitted details, as he often does."[8] Luke's interest in pneumatology is obvious before and after this passage, but this does not necessarily demand that Luke created the speech of Jesus which declared his spiritual anointing. The presence of the references to the Holy Spirit may have indeed attracted Luke to the non-Marcan source.[9]

Joachim Jeremias has made a carefully studied statistical case that much of the language in Luke 4:14–30 is pre-Lucan. Words that Luke usually avoids in Mark appear in this passage; in fact he seldom uses these words even in Acts. Jeremias considers this as evidence that Luke is utilizing non-Marcan traditions.[10] Furthermore, the presence of semitic structures tends to confirm the passage's pre-Lucan character.[11] Of several examples of this evidence, the spelling used for Jesus' hometown is striking. In 4:16 Nazareth is spelled "Nazara." This spelling never occurs in Mark's Gospel, and Luke prefers "Nazareth" elsewhere. It is probable that Luke gets this spelling from his non-Marcan source.[12] Since this spelling occurs only here and in Matthew 4:13, which also describes the beginning of Jesus' ministry, Schürmann and Streeter suggest that Q might be Luke's alternate tradition here.[13]

The Preeminence of Lucan Redaction

Regardless of the final verdict on the origins of Luke's presentation of the inauguration of Jesus' ministry, his redactional and theological agenda stand in stark contrast to that of the other Gospel writers. Fortunately, these are identifiable and immutable whether the passage is seen (1) as primarily Luke creating a new gospel event or (2) as the result of Luke's careful balance of traditions connected with his distinctive vocabulary. Recent research which reveals pre-Lucan tradition behind our passage does not obscure Luke's redactional emphasis.

In the first case, downplaying references to repentance, Luke transforms the Marcan tradition into a new story of Jesus to present the role of the Holy Spirit and power in Jesus' early ministry. In the second case, Luke prefers a non-Marcan tradition because it provides him an opportunity to emphasize the Holy Spirit and power instead of the repentance motif found in Mark's version of Jesus' first public words (1:14–15). Either way, Luke's message and motives remain clear: Jesus is the Spirit-led man *par excellence*.

It is not possible here to identify exhaustively the traditional or redactional character of the vocabulary of Luke 4:14–30; neither is it directly crucial to identify the pedigree of these words to isolate Lucan redactional interests. This is not to say, however, that the history of the Gospel traditions is unimportant, for Christian belief rises or falls on witnesses within history. These witnesses relate both supernatural and natural events that occurred in the time-space continuum of earthly history and not in some mythical nether world. In this case Luke is apparently using another tradition as the source for 4:14–30 and is *not* creating a new legend. Luke is being careful to transmit his source faithfully, yet does not hesitate to use it to make a theological point.[14]

Although the passage does indeed possess some Lucan characteristics,[15] many items appear to have a traditional coloring, some of them with affinities and parallels to passages which have been ascribed to Q. The instances of non-Lucan terminology make it more probable that Luke is primarily dependent upon a non-Marcan tradition.[16]

Fortunately for our investigation, neither a source reconstruction relying heavily on Mark nor a non-Marcan variant tradition would significantly affect our observations of the Lucan handling of the inaugural address at Nazareth. In either case, Luke is responsible for the final product either by his conscious selection of one tradition over the other or by his literary creativity, and it must be significant for his program to engage in either activity.[17] As is often the case in Luke, source reconstruction does not hinder our discernment of Lucan intent.

The First Public Words of Jesus in Luke

Luke's interest in Jesus' Spirit empowerment becomes quite clear when one contrasts the first public words of Jesus presented in Matthew, Mark, and Luke.

Matt 4:12–17	Mark 1:14–15	Luke 4:14–19
Now when he heard that John had been arrested, he withdrew into Galilee; and leaving Nazareth he went and dwelt in Capernaum by the sea, in the territory of Zebulun and Naphtali; that what was spoken by the prophet Isaiah might be fulfilled: "The land of Zebulun and the land of Naphtali, toward the sea, across the Jordan, Galilee of the Gentiles—the people who sat in darkness have seen a great light, and for those who sat in the region and shadow of death light has dawned."	Now after John was arrested, Jesus came into Galilee, preaching the gospel of God, and saying, "The time is fulfilled, and the kingdom of God is at hand; repent, and believe in the gospel."	And Jesus returned in the power of the Spirit into Galilee, and a report concerning him went out through all the surrounding country. And he taught in their synagogues, being glorified by all. And he came to Nazareth, where he had been brought up; and he went to the synagogue, as his custom was, on the sabbath day. And he stood up to read; and there was given to him the book of the prophet Isaiah. He opened the book and found the place where it was written,

From that time Jesus began to preach, saying, "Repent, for the kingdom of heaven is at hand."	"The Spirit of the Lord is upon me, because he has anointed me to preach good news to the poor. He has sent me to proclaim release to the captives and recovering of sight to the blind, to set at liberty those who are oppressed, to proclaim the acceptable year of the Lord."

The first words of Jesus that Mark presents say that Jesus ushered in God's kingdom and continued John the Baptist's call for repentance and for people to trust God's announcement of good will. Matthew follows Mark, his source, and presents essentially the same message. However, Matthew sees it as an opportunity to elaborate on his frequent theme of the geographical fulfillment of prophecy (e.g., Bethlehem 2:5–6; Egypt 2:14–15; Ramah 2:16–18; Nazareth 2:23; wilderness of Judah 3:1–3; Jerusalem 21:5; the temple 21:12–13; the potter's field 27:7–10).

Luke, however, prefers to follow a different tradition of the beginning of Jesus' ministry. While primarily associating repentance with the ministry of John, he prefers to associate the empowerment of the Holy Spirit with the ministry of Jesus. As has already been pointed out, the role of the Holy Spirit in empowering Jesus is so important for Luke that he mentions it twice in his version (4:14, 18–19). This pattern is a continuation of the double emphasis of the Holy Spirit's influence upon Jesus that he established in the temptation (4:1 "full of the Holy Spirit" and "led by the Spirit"). Clearly Luke is responsible for this positioning of references to the Spirit.

Later in Acts, Luke again presents his Spirit emphasis in Jesus' ministry when he recounts the early apostolic preaching. Peter, for example, associates Jesus with spiritual power (2:22; 4:27; 10:38) while John the Baptist is associated with repentance (10:37; 19:4).[18] No doubt at least a part of the reason that Luke feels justified in making this pneumatic emphasis, especially in the early part of his presentation of Jesus' ministry, is that the early preaching of the church includes this emphasis. (Note, however, that later in the Gospel he makes several references to repentance in connection with Jesus: e.g., Luke 5:32; 13:3, 5, 15:7; 17:3, 4; 24:47.) The parallels between Luke 4 and Luke's presentation of the early church's proclamation of Jesus in Acts are striking:

Luke 4:14a, 18–19	Acts 2:22
And Jesus returned in the power of the Spirit into Galilee ... "The Spirit of the Lord is upon me, because he has anointed me to preach good news to the poor. He has sent me to proclaim release to the captives and recovering of sight to the blind, to set at liberty those who are oppressed, to proclaim the acceptable year of the Lord.	"Men of Israel, hear these words: Jesus of Nazareth, a man attested to you by God with mighty works and wonders and signs which God did through him in your midst, as you yourselves know—"

Acts 10:38
"How God anointed Jesus of Nazareth with the Holy Spirit and power; how he went about doing good and healing all who were oppressed by the devil, for God was with him."

As Chilton observes, "The Jesus of Lk's special tradition preaches, not the proximity of the kingdom, but precisely what the Church preaches (cf. Acts 3, 20; 4, 27; 10, 38): his own anointing."[19]

Luke's Adjustment of the Gospel Chronology

To strategically position the references to the Holy Spirit in chapter 4 (verses 1a, 1b, 14, 18), Luke moves the Nazareth ministry forward chronologically. In Matthew and Mark the rejection at Nazareth occurs much later in Jesus' Galilee campaign (Matt 13:53–58; Mark 6:1–6). Luke's version exhibits evidence that Luke himself knows it is out of sequence and purposely allows it to stand that way: In anticipation of the audience's objections, Jesus said, "Doubtless you will quote to me this proverb, 'Physician, heal yourself; *what we heard you did at Capernaum,* do here also in your own country' " (4:23, ital. mine). Like Mark and Matthew, Luke is aware that Jesus ministered *first* in Capernaum and actually makes a reference to Jesus' ministry there in his Nazareth account.

Thus Luke ignores chronology in order to group events and sayings together to make a theological point. Obviously for Luke, chronology is not as important as theology. We have already seen another example of this when Luke records John's imprisonment *before* Jesus' baptism. Since Mark is one of his sources, Luke knows quite well that John baptized Jesus (3:19–22). Apparently Luke is in a hurry to announce Jesus' endowment with the Holy Spirit at the Jordan; therefore what he sees as minor details, such as John as the agent of Jesus' water baptism, must give way. Likewise, Luke is in a hurry to have Jesus read the Isaiah 61 passage at Nazareth: Jesus is anointed by the Holy Spirit to perform his mission. Only after Luke has made this point does he focus his attention on Jesus' ministry in Capernaum (4:31–41).

Luke is attracted to the Nazareth passage and feels compelled to present it at the *beginning* of Jesus' ministry because he sees it as programmatic for all of Jesus' ministry. Jesus is not the only one Luke has in mind here, however. Chilton remarks, "Luke introduces the pericope in a manner which makes it paradigmatic for the mission of his own church."[20] Like Jesus, the church depends on the Holy Spirit. Only through the power of the Holy Spirit does the church continue the works and words of Jesus.

The Spirit and Inspired Speech in Jesus' Ministry

The presence of the Holy Spirit at the beginning of Jesus' ministry has a dual function: to enable Jesus "to heal and reveal," both to perform wonders and to speak authoritatively.[21] It would appear that Luke is interested in inspired speaking more than wonder-working, but the two are inextricably connected in Luke–Acts. In the first half of Luke 4, and in the summary statement of verses 14–15, however, speaking has the dominant role. Luke reports here that Jesus returned in the power (*dynamis*) of the Spirit. Elsewhere *dynamis* is associated with healing and miracles. The major result of this *dynamis* is the teaching of Jesus. Granted, Luke later associates the message of Jesus with his ability to perform miracles (4:36), yet even in the previous event—the temptation—Jesus was empowered by the Spirit not to perform a miracle— not to turn stones into bread—but to effectively withstand temptation through the word of God. Also in Luke's summary of the beginning of Jesus' ministry (4:14–15), the first thing he mentions about Jesus is that "he taught in the synagogues." In the Nazareth passage Jesus primarily functions as a prophet with Spirit-filled words. Inspired by the Holy Spirit, Jesus reads from Isaiah[22] about his Spirit-anointing and declares the prophecy to be fulfilled. Luke notes here "the gracious words which proceeded out of his mouth" (v. 22). Jesus anticipates the audience's reservations and utters more inspired words which cut them to the quick and lead to a murderous riot.

Jesus alludes to his Capernaum miracles and compares his miracle ministry to Elijah and Elisha (4:23–27), saying that no miracles would occur in Nazareth. His Spirit-anointing at Nazareth is for speaking. In contrast to Matthew's and Mark's Nazareth accounts, Luke gives the impression that Jesus *would not* perform miracles there rather than *could not* because of unbelief (Mark 6:5–6; Matt 13:58). He *refuses* not only because of their unbelief, but also because he wants to make a theological point: from the beginning his ministry is extended to the Gentiles, a theme repeated throughout Luke–Acts.[23]

When one analyzes the prophecy from Isaiah that Jesus reads, speaking appears to be the dominant role. Jesus is anointed "to *preach* good news to the poor," "to *proclaim* release to the captives," and "to *proclaim* the acceptable year of the Lord." Prophetic announcement dominates here. This is not to say that the Spirit endowment does not effect miracles; Luke also brings this out in the quotation of Isaiah: "to proclaim release to the captives" and "to set at liberty those who are oppressed."[24] However, note that in the context which immediately follows the Nazareth event, Luke first mentions that Jesus' teaching in Capernaum "was with authority" (vv. 31–32). Only after pointing out Jesus' inspired speaking does Luke begin recounting Jesus' deliverance and healing ministry.

Notes to Chapter 6

1. R. Bultmann, *The History of the Synoptic Tradition*, trans. J. Marsh (2d ed.; Oxford: Blackwell, 1972), 31–32, 361, 368. Bultmann identifies vv. 25–27 as traditional (see p. 32; Conzelmann, *Theology*, 29–30, 31 n. 1). According to Dibelius, "The whole narrative, however, is by no means new as a legend, but is only filled out by Luke or some older narrator. The traits of Mark's narrative still constitute the skeleton, viz. the amazement, the offence, and the saying about the despised prophet" (*From Tradition to Gospel*, trans. B. L. Woolf [New York: Scribner's, 1965], 110ff.; see also H. Anderson, "Broadening Horizons: The Rejection at Nazareth Pericope of Luke 4:16–30 in Light of Recent Critical Trends," *Int* 18 (3 July 1964): 259–75. Creed too states that there are non-Marcan sources but that the influence of the Marcan version can still be traced (*Luke*, 64; see also Leaney, *Luke*, 50ff.; Conzelmann, *Theology*, 31–33). For a survey of opinions see H. Anderson's "Rejection at Nazareth."

2. Leaney, *Luke*, 54.

3. "It seems reasonable to conclude that Luke wrote his version of the rejection at Nazareth as a substitute for Mark vi. 1–6, which he omitted" (ibid., 51).

4. Conzelmann assumes that since the place-name, Capernaum, appears to be out of chronological order, Luke must be using Mark as his source since in that Gospel, Capernaum comes after the introduction of Jesus' ministry and before the events in Nazareth (*Theology*, 33). The other source,

however, could reflect the same ordering of events as Mark (i.e., introduction, Capernaum, Nazareth) with the Nazareth event occurring sooner but still in proper succession, a succession which Luke does not observe in his haste to have Jesus affirm his own anointing with the Spirit. In a similar manner, Luke ignores the chronology involving John's arrest and John's baptizing Jesus (3:18–21).

5. Leaney observes, "It is not too much to say that Luke, in his desire to combine the narrative of a triumphant visit with a rejection, has given us an impossible story" (*Luke*, 52).

Some also have asserted that the Lucan version betrays its awkward composite nature in that it appears that the crowd at first speaks well of Jesus and then inexplicably turns against him. The short-lived approval of the crowd and then its animosity do not necessarily have to be viewed as awkward. In fact, Luke offers more by way of explanation than do either Matthew or Mark. Jesus deliberately antagonized the people with his refusal to perform miracles and his allusion to Gentiles as favored people. Furthermore, *thaumazō* and *martyreō* do not necessarily indicate crowd approval but indeed could mean the opposite, (cf. B. Violet, "Zum rechten Verständnis der Nazareth Perikope, Lc 4, 16–30," *ZNW*, 37 [1938]: 251–71; F. Gils, *Jésus Prophète d'Après les Evangiles Synoptiques* [Louvain: Université de Louvain Institut Orientaliste, 1957], 18ff.; Marshall, *Gospel of Luke*, 185ff.; J. Jeremias, *Jesus' Promise to the Nations*, trans. S. H. Hooke [London: SPCK, 1958], 44ff.).

Jeremias suggests that there is no essential change in the attitude of the audience. Following Violet's suggestion for a pejorative reading for *martyreō* and *thaumazō*, he proposes that the people were offended that Jesus left out the reference to "the day of vengeance" for the unrighteous in Isa 61:2 (J. Jeremias, *Jesus' Promise to the Nations*, 44ff.). This would explain their displeasure turning into blind rage when Jesus rebuked his hometown while at the same time admitting that he had performed miracles in Capernaum, probably for Gentiles. It does appear strange, however, for several reasons that omission of the reference to the "day of vengeance" would cause animosity in the general attitude of his audience. Jeremias is correct to maintain that there is no break at vv. 22–23 (see also Marshall, *Luke*, 180), but the more probable reason for the ambivalent attitude of the crowd is their hesitation to accept the "hometown boy" as a prophet. Luke reveals that this is the import of the question in v. 22, "Is this not Joseph's son?" by quoting the proverb, "Physician, heal yourself," in v. 23 (pace Anderson, "Rejection at Nazareth," 268). They could not quite accept him, though they acknowledged the truth of his words, and they wished to see more evidence to substantiate his claims. The absence of an explicit reference to the crowds taking offense at Jesus before he antagonized them in vv. 25–27 may be due to the influence of Mark's version on Luke or his source. It is assumed that offense was taken under the influence of the Marcan story. It must be pointed out, however, that this is not necessarily the case; many of the "problems" in our passage exist mainly when Mark is used as the measuring stick. The Lucan passage need not be supplemented by Mark for clarification; it makes sense on its own. Whether the Nazareth audience was initially pleased or confounded by Jesus' announcement, Luke makes it clear that Jesus himself deliberately provoked his hearers in the remainder of his speech.

6. H. Schürmann in " 'Bericht vom Anfang,' Ein Rekonstruktions-versuch auf Grund von Lk 4, 14–16" in *Traditionsgeschichtliche Untersuchungen zu der synoptischen Evangelien* (Düsseldorf: Patmos, 1968); and *Das Lukas-evangelium: Erster teil Kommentar zu Kap. 1.1–9, 50* (Freiburg: Herder, 1969), 227–28; Marshall, *Gospel of Luke*, 176–90; Chilton, *God in Strength*, 125–77. Also, especially see Jeremias, who identifies the bulk of 4:15–30 as traditional with even part of 4:14 as pre-Lucan (*Die Sprache*, 119–28). For a summary of major positions on the passage see Fitzmyer, *Luke*, 1.526–30.

7. Such as vv. 25–27 which could be added by Luke from another tradition. The reference to Capernaum in v. 23 probably does indicate a break in chronology, but this does not necessarily mean the break is due to appropriation of Marcan material. It may well mean that another tradition was reordered as Schürmann suggests for v. 14b (*Lukasevangelium*, 223).

8. Marshall, *Gospel of Luke*, 180.

9. Even Dibelius shies away from extensive Lucan creativity: "But in this case the author of Luke did not possess the author's freedom which, in Acts, helped him in the composition of the speeches. He dare not put such a 'speech' into the mouth of Jesus" (*Tradition*, 111). If Luke is dependent on a tradition for the Isa citation in vv. 18ff., then it is easier to explain the composite nature of the quotation which is uncharacteristic of Luke (Leaney, *Luke*, 53; Chilton, *God in Strength*, 143–47).

10. Jeremias, *Die Sprache*, 119–28.

11. In addition to Jeremias, *Die Sprache*, 117–27, see Schürmann, *Lukasevangelium*, 224–44; and Chilton, *God in Strength*, 127–77.

12. Schürmann, *Lukasevangelium*, 227; Jeremias, *Die Sprache*, 120–21; Chilton, *God in Strength*, 129.

13. Schürmann, *Lukasevangelium*, 227–28. Fitzmyer expresses caution here by noting that Matthew's inauguration of Jesus' ministry is to some extent dependent upon Mark 1:14 (*Luke*, 1.530). Nevertheless, Matthean conflation of his Marcan and non-Marcan source is plausible. Regarding the unique use of "Nazara" in Matt 4:13 and Luke 4:16, Streeter concludes, "It would look as if Q, which clearly had a word or two of narrative introduction to John's Preaching and the Temptation, had a brief notice of the change of scene in which the name Nazara occurred," (*Four Gospels*, 206).

14. In examining Luke's use of the eschatological discourse of Mark 13, F. C. Burkitt observes, "What concerns us here is not that Luke has changed so much but that he has invented so little" (*Christian Beginnings* [London: University of London Press, 1924], 115. F. F. Bruce follows up on the point: "If this is the verdict on Luke in places where his fidelity to his source can be controlled, we should not without good reason suppose that he was not equally faithful where his sources are no longer available for comparison" (*The Acts of the Apostles: The Greek Text with Introduction and Commentary* [Leicester: InterVarsity, 1952], 19). For a fuller discussion on historicity in Luke–Acts see Gasque, *Criticism of Acts* and Marshall, *Luke: Historian and Theologian*.

15. Such as the words that Luke often uses: *hypostrephō*, 32x in Luke–Acts out of 35x in NT; *atenizō*, 12x in Luke–Acts out of 14 in NT; Lucan preference for *hou* and *pros*. For a more detailed list see Jeremias, *Die Sprache*, 118–28.

16. The explanation that Luke has conflated two different Nazareth visits is not impressive; see H. K. Luce, *The Gospel According to St. Luke* CGTC (Cambridge: Cambridge University Press, 1933), 121; M.-J. Lagrange, *Evangile selon Saint Luc* (3d ed.; Paris: Victor Lecoffre, 1927), 146–48; J. P. Kealy, *Luke's Gospel Today* (Denville, N.J.: Dimension Books, 1979), 185. The presence of an apparent break between 4:22a and 4:22b "where acceptance and rejection of Jesus stand in uneasy juxtaposition" is cited as evidence of the two visits (Marshall, *Gospel of Luke*, 179). The possible pejorative meanings of *thaumazō* and *martyreō*, however, and the presence of both approval and rejection to some degree in all of the accounts, weaken the suggestion. Even if it is accepted, our observations will not be affected since Luke's creativity and/or his preference of one source over another would be responsible for the passage. Schürmann, Marshall, and Chilton consider Luke's source to be essentially non-Marcan and a parallel to the Marcan account, not a conflation.

17. Marshall, *Luke: Historian and Theologian*, 119. Conzelmann notes that if 4:16–30 is a "free adaptation by Luke of Mark's version," then "we should possess not only a striking illustration of his own theological outlook, but also of the degree to which he has modified his sources." Conversely, he notes, "Even if Luke has replaced Mark's account by a variant from another tradition, the fact remains that he was familiar with it. Why does he not adhere to Mark's course of events? . . . the question remains as to why he did so" (*Theology*, 32). We may not ascertain exactly how Luke modified his sources, but source reconstruction here does not obscure his pneumatological emphasis.

18. In Acts 10:37 note that Peter described John as "preaching a baptism." Obviously Luke uses baptism as a metonymy for repentance as is evident in Luke 3:3 and Acts 19:4.

19. Chilton, *God in Strength*, 156.

20. Ibid., 134.

21. To use P. S. Minear's title, *To Heal and to Reveal: Prophetic Vocation According to Luke* (New York: Seabury, 1976).

22. It is sometimes assumed that Jesus asked for the Isaiah scroll (Lagrange, *Evangile selon Saint Luc*, 138). Others make a case that this passage was scheduled in the Jewish lectionary to be read in the synagogues on that sabbath. For a summary of these positions see Chilton, *God in Strength*, 141–42, 160–61.

23. Given Luke's frequent emphasis on the Holy Spirit and salvation for the Gentiles, especially in Acts, one must admire his restraint here.

24. Note also the variant reading, "to heal the brokenhearted."

7

The Holy Spirit and Miracles

*F*ROM JESUS' CONCEPTION to the inauguration of his ministry at Nazareth, we have seen Luke's emphasis on the role of the Holy Spirit in the life of Jesus. This special interest of Luke's is one of his major motivations in writing his Gospel, for it supplements others that had already been written (Luke 1:1–4). He writes his Gospel because he wants to bring the synoptic tradition into conformity with the Christology of the early church's kerygma (preaching) as he understands it. Luke's main point is that Jesus is the Spirit-anointed Messiah and that he both spoke and performed wonders by the power of the Holy Spirit.

How Luke Links the Holy Spirit with Miracles

Although in much of his Gospel Luke portrays the Spirit as the author of inspired witness, he does not promote this special interest at the expense of the miracle ministries of Jesus and the early church.[1] Luke delays specific references to Jesus' performing miracles until after he presents the Nazareth ministry;[2] however, this does not mean that he is disassociating miracles from the activity of the Holy Spirit. The volume of references to miracles dispels any such notion.

Luke makes two major summaries which he considers paradigmatic of Jesus' ministry. One occurs in the Gospel and the other in Acts; both refer explicitly to healing miracles:

> How God anointed Jesus of Nazareth with the Holy Spirit and with power [*dynamei*]; how he went about doing good and *healing* all who were oppressed by the devil, for God was with him.
> —Acts 10:38, my ital.

> The Spirit of the Lord is upon me, because he has anointed me to preach good news to the poor. He has sent me to proclaim release to

the captives and *recovering of sight* to the blind, to set at liberty those who are oppressed, to proclaim the acceptable year of the Lord.
—Luke 4:18, my ital.[3]

In addition to these major references to the anointing of the Holy Spirit upon Jesus to perform miracles, Luke also specifically links the Holy Spirit to miracles in the following episodes:

—the conception of Jesus (Luke 1:35),

—Elizabeth's and John's prenatal discernment of Mary's pregnancy and divine visitation (Luke 1:41–44),

—Simeon's identification of Jesus as Messiah (Luke 2:22–35),

—the glossolalia at Pentecost (Acts 2:4),

—Stephen's wonder-working (Acts 6:3, 5, 8),

—Stephen's vision (Acts 7:55),

—the Samaritan reception of the Holy Spirit (Acts 8:14–19),

—the Gentile reception of the Spirit at the household of Cornelius (Acts 10:44–46),

—the Spirit's guidance of Peter (Acts 11:12),

—the Holy Spirit's choice of Barnabas and Saul (Acts 13:2, 4),

—Paul's cursing Elymas Bar-Jesus with blindness (Acts 13:8–11).

Furthermore Luke also uses the words, "power" (*dynamis*), "authority" (*exousia*), and "grace" (*charis*) to link the Holy Spirit with miracles, especially healings. Luke understands that these supernaturally effective qualities—power, authority, and grace—originate from the Holy Spirit in the ministries of both Jesus and believers.

The Spirit and Power

Luke usually maintains the traditional distinction between *dynamis* as kinetic effective power and *exousia* as official authority. Sometimes the two meanings overlap (see esp. Luke 4:36; 9:1; 10:19; and also 21:26; Acts 8:19). *Dynamis* usually refers to the miraculous in Luke, whereas the verbal form *dynamai* usually connotes ability in general. Luke apparently intends a specialized meaning for *dynamis:* ability to effect miracles. Of the twenty-five times Luke uses the word in Luke–Acts, eighteen specifically refer to miracles, especially healings.[4]

A virtually identical pattern arises in Luke's use of *dynatos,* which means "mighty, powerful, strong" (used 32 times in the NT). Of the ten times *dynatos* is found in Luke–Acts, six refer to miracles. Luke uses it only twice to describe conventional power and only once to describe powerful speech apart from miracles.[5] Sometimes *dynamis* appears with a definite article "to signify a mighty act" (e.g., Luke 10:13; 19:37)[6] and to refer to miracle-working power: "But Jesus said, 'Some one touched me; for I perceive that power [*dynamin*] has gone forth from me' " (8:46). This power could be given to Jesus' disciples (9:1).[7]

Luke links *dynamis* with the Spirit on several occasions and shows that the Holy Spirit is the source of both miracle-working power and inspired speaking:

—John calls people to repentance "in the spirit and power of Elijah" (Luke 1:17).

—Jesus is conceived in Mary because the Holy Spirit came upon her and "the power of the Most High" overshadowed her (Luke 1:35).

—"Jesus returned in the power of the Spirit" (teaching explicit, miracles implicit) (Luke 4:14–15).

—Jesus predicts that the disciples would witness because "the promise of the Father" would "clothe [them] with power from on high" (Luke 24:49). The Acts version makes it clear that this is the Holy Spirit (1:4–5).

—"But you shall receive power when the Holy Spirit has come upon you; and you shall be my witnesses" (Acts 1:8).

—Stephen, "full of faith and of the Spirit" and "full of grace and power," works wonders (Acts 6:3–8).

—God anoints Jesus "with the Holy Spirit and power" to heal (Acts 10:38). In the case of Luke 1:35 and Acts 10:38, the Holy Spirit and the power of God seem interchangeable. Luke identifies the Holy Spirit with miraculous power. Furthermore, Luke associates divine names such as "God," "Father," and "Lord" with miracle-effecting power.

—"The power of the Lord was with him to heal" (Luke 5:17).

—"The whole multitude of the disciples began to rejoice and praise God with a loud voice for all the mighty works [*dynameōn*] that they had seen" (Luke 19:37).

—Jesus will sit "at the right hand of the power of God" (Luke 22:69).

—"The promise of the Father" will clothe the disciples with power from on high (Luke 24:49).

—"Jesus of Nazareth, a man attested to you by God with mighty works and wonders and signs which God did through him in your midst" (Acts 2:22).

—God anoints Jesus with "the Holy Spirit and power" to heal (Acts 10:38).

—"God did extraordinary miracles [*dynameis*] by the hands of Paul" (Acts 19:11).

These references further demonstrate that Luke understands the *dynamis* of God to be the power of the Holy Spirit. Other references to miraculous power (*dynamis*) imply the active presence of the Holy Spirit. For example, C. K. Barrett observes, "Now it is comparatively clear that when Jesus exorcized an evil spirit, some inference is at hand about the Spirit of God; for there is a presumption that that which overcomes spirit is spirit."[8]

The Spirit and Authority

The word for "authority," *exousia*, functions similarly, although it is not used as extensively for miracles as *dynamis*. It explains the effecting of miracles or empowering of speech in the following: Luke 4:32, 36; 5:24; 7:8 by implication; 9:1; 10:19; and Acts 8:19. As noted before, the functions of *dynamis* and *exousia* appear closely related or even interchangeable in Luke 9:1 and 10:19. It follows that the Holy Spirit who is responsible for or attendant to the *exousia* is also responsible for the miracles.

The Spirit and Grace

We have already seen the interrelationship of *charis* (grace), the Spirit, and inspired speech when we looked at the relationship of Mary and the Holy Spirit in chapter 2. There we noted the Holy Spirit's gift of grace not only to Mary and Jesus but also to the martyr Stephen. Luke adorns his description of Jesus' conception with words from the *charis* word group (1:28, 30). God's favor or grace upon Mary (perfect participle) resulted in the conception and birth of Jesus. Luke tells us that the Holy Spirit was the agent of this grace (1:35). Similarly Stephen "full of grace *(charitos)* and power *(dynameōs)* did great wonders and signs" (Acts 6:8), and again Luke identifies the Holy Spirit as the source of Stephen's *charis* (Acts 6:3, 5, 10).[9]

In Luke–Acts *charizomai* ("to bestow grace or favor") "expresses the giving of something which is not due, but which reveals the favor of the giver toward the recipient."[10] This giving of grace can be miraculous in nature, for in Luke 7:21 Jesus "graces" (*echarisatō*) the blind with the power of sight. In the description of the boy Jesus in 2:40 and 52, Luke makes it clear that the wisdom of God is a grace bestowed. Grace in Acts describes the power of God to do miracles (6:8; 11:23; 14:26; 15:40; 18:27).[11]

A case can also be made for Jesus performing wonders by the grace of God through the Holy Spirit. In his address to the Nazareth synagogue, he announced that he was anointed by the Holy Spirit "to heal the brokenhearted" (4:18, KJV). If this refers to miraculous healing, then it can be seen as divine grace coming from the Spirit, for Luke said the people marveled at "the words of grace coming out of his mouth" (4:22, my trans.). In Luke's scheme of things *charis* here is not merely a way of saying that Jesus was a polished public speaker.[12] Rather, grace refers to the "matter of Jesus' preaching—its description of the works of divine grace—rather than the impression received by His hearers."[13] The use of the verb *charizomai* to describe Jesus' healings in 7:21 further supports this reading of 4:22. Thus in Luke's mind, the grace, power, and authority that perform the wonders of the kingdom originate in the Holy Spirit.[14]

The Interrelationship of Speaking and Miracles

The Spirit's endowment of grace, power, and authority enabled Jesus and believers to proclaim the inspired words of God (e.g., grace, Luke 4:22; Acts 4:33; 14:3; power, Luke 4:14–15, 36; Acts 1:8; authority, Luke 4:32, 36; 9:1 with 10:19). It is artificial in some respects for the working of miracles and inspired speech to be separated since they are both miraculous and since both are wrought by the same Holy Spirit. The two often overlap in Luke–Acts, and inspired words can result in healings and miracles (e.g., Luke 4:32, 36; 7:11–17; Acts 10:34–40; 13:9–12), and the miracles can attest to the truth of the words spoken (e.g., Luke 1:20; 1:36–37; 4:33–35; 5:20–26; Acts 2:22; 4:29–33; 6:7–8; 10:44; 13:9–12).

Inspired Speech Effecting Miracles

Luke often emphasizes an interrelationship between inspired speaking and miracles. He sometimes identifies speaking as the means of miracle-working even when the other Gospel writers mention another means, like touching, as the catalyst of the miracle. All of the Gospels contain accounts in which Jesus performed wonders by speaking a word, so this cannot be seen as an exclusively Lucan interest. Given the volume of miracles effected by word of mouth in all the Synoptics, Luke's attraction to such accounts does not appear obvious at first; however, the way he handles his Marcan source reveals his interest. After Jesus announced his divine anointing at the Nazareth synagogue, he entered the synagogue at Capernaum and exorcized a demoniac there (Luke 4:31–37). Like Mark (Mark 1:21–28), Luke records that Jesus performed the exorcism by rebuking the unclean spirit and demanding that it leave the victim. This is done verbally in both accounts. In Mark the witnesses ascribe the authority with which Jesus exorcized to the teaching that preceded the exorcism. In Luke the authority is associated with his word, *logos* (4:32, 36). Thus Mark's "What is this?" (*ti estin touto,* Mark 1:27) becomes literally, "What is this word?" (*tis ho logos houtos*) in Luke. While the Marcan crowd marveled at the event of the exorcism and its association with the previous reference to teaching, in Luke the crowd was amazed at the word which contained authority and power. Only Luke includes *dynamis* with *exousia* here. This associates the word of Jesus with the authority and power to perform miracles. While it could be suggested that the word, *ho logos,* does not refer to actual words but to the event itself in verse 36, it must be linked to "*his* words" (*ho logos autou*) in verse 32, which must be seen not as a mere reference to an event but as the words of Jesus. In Luke 4:32 the word is "in authority," and this authority is further explained by the exorcism account.[15] In Mark, however, it is Jesus who has the authority (1:22). Both accounts present a miracle wrought by the speaking of Jesus, but it is significant that Luke presents this first miracle of Jesus as one effected by inspired speaking and as the beginning of the fulfillment of the Spirit-filled program which Jesus announced at the Nazareth synagogue.

Following Mark's outline, Luke next includes the healing of Peter's mother-in-law. In this the second miracle Luke highlights the ability of Jesus' words to work wonders. He thereby consciously digresses from a synoptic tradition maintained by Matthew and Mark (Matt 8:14–15; Mark 1:29–31; Luke 4:38–39), who both note that Jesus healed the woman by touching her (Matt 8:15; Mark 1:31). Luke, apparently of his own volition or in deference to another tradition no longer available to us, records the healing in this manner, "And he stood over her and rebuked [*epetimēsen*] the fever, and it left her" (Luke 4:39a).

Similar instances soon follow in Gospel material unique to Luke. In the miracle of the catch of fish (5:1–11) Peter, after having made his protests known to Jesus, acceded to his request to let down the nets. The wording of Peter's response is interesting:

"But at your word [*rhēmati*] I will let down the nets." In this exclusively Lucan material the word of Jesus is specially accentuated as the means of the miracle. In the raising of the son of the widow of Nain (7:11–17)—again from one of Luke's non-Marcan sources—the word of Jesus appears to be the primary agent of the miracle.[16] The cleansing of the ten lepers (17:11–19), another miracle found only in Luke, is accomplished as the recipients of the healing act upon the words of Jesus. Luke does not record that Jesus used touch as the means of healing the ten lepers, whereas in the Marcan tradition a leper is cleansed by touching (Mark 1:41; see also Luke 5:13).

Speaking in the Name of Jesus to Heal

In the presentation of the arraignment of Peter and John before Annas, Caiaphas, and company in Acts 4:1–23, Luke indicates that there is a cause-and-effect relationship between authoritative speaking and miracles. The rulers and elders do not forbid the apostles to perform miracles, but they charge them "not to speak or teach at all in the name of Jesus" (4:18). Verses 16 and 17 show that the rulers believe that the healing of the lame man was caused by speaking in the name of Jesus. This is their presupposition when they address the question to the apostles, "By what power or by what name did you do this?" (4:7) and this is what Peter assumes when he responds in verses 8–12. Although the healing in question is wrought both by authoritative speaking (in the name of Jesus) and by touching (3:6ff.), the chief factor responsible for the miracle is the invocation of the name of Jesus (3:16; 4:10, 31) and the witness to Jesus by Peter and John under the direction of the Holy Spirit (4:8, 20). In Acts 3 and 4, miracles are associated with the name of Jesus, while in the same context Luke notes inspired speaking is associated with being filled with the Holy Spirit (2:4; 4:8, 31).

The activity of the Holy Spirit so often linked with inspired speaking is also responsible for healing. Invoking the name of Jesus causes healing, while being filled with the Holy Spirit results in inspired speaking. This division of roles overlaps at points, as is evident in Acts 4:29–31. Luke says the name of Jesus is responsible for healings in v. 30, and in the next breath he relates that "they were all filled with the Holy Spirit and spoke the word of God with boldness" (v. 31). After noting the believers speaking the word with boldness in verse 29, in verse 30 Luke observes that God's "hand" effects miracles through speaking. Here Holy Spirit-inspired speaking is associated with the working of miracles. Also present is the image of a hand extended to heal and to perform signs and wonders. Framed by the references to speaking in verses 29 and 31, the reference to miracles in verse 30 demonstrates that the inspired word is causatively related to the working of miracles.

Miracles Wrought by a Diversity of Means

It is also significant that Luke associates laying on of hands with healing as well (Luke 4:40; 13:13; Acts 9:12, 17; 14:3; 19:11ff.; 28:8; and perhaps 5:12). Of course, Luke is dependent upon Mark (5:23; 6:2;

7:32; 8:23; and perhaps 16:18) and upon the practice of the church at large for the concept of the laying on of hands for healing, but Luke also associates the laying on of hands with the Holy Spirit (Acts 8:17ff.; 13:3ff.; 19:6). Obviously, Luke is not trying to avoid accounts which record miraculous events wrought by means other than speaking. He is comfortable with the diversity within the synoptic tradition, as is seen in the miracle accounts exclusive to Luke where the means are varied (5:4–11, word; 7:11–17, word; 13:11–17, word and laying on of hands; 14:1–6, touching; 17:11–19, word, obedience, faith; 22:50ff., touching). Luke inserts associations of touching and healing into the Marcan material as well (e.g., 4:40), and he omits the words that cause the healing of the epileptic boy (Luke 9:42 contra Mark 9:25). Thus, Luke is not limited by his interest in the cause-and-effect relationship between speaking and miracles.

Nevertheless, it appears that this relationship between speaking with authority and power and performing miracles is an idea that Luke likes and which is common in his two-volume work. In Acts, the working of wonders is associated with the activity of the Holy Spirit, but usually the Holy Spirit is associated with inspired speaking, which may or may not effect miracles. In both the Gospel and Acts, Luke reveals a preference for describing the word of mouth as the means whereby a miracle is wrought. Just how much Luke is conscious of this apparent preference and how significant it is in relation to his overall program certainly are open to debate. Nevertheless, it must be noted that the relationship of inspired speaking and miracles as found in Luke–Acts parallels Luke's interest in the effectiveness of speech uttered under the direction of the Holy Spirit.

Witness Confirmed by Miracle-Working Power

Because of his Spirit-anointing, Jesus became "mighty in deed and word" (24:19; Acts 10:38). Both his works and words were evidence that he was God's prophet. Luke sees the "mighty works and wonders and signs which God did through him" (Acts 2:22) as paradigmatic for Jesus' ministry. For this reason, Luke characterizes Jesus' ministry as endowed with Spirit-words and Spirit-works in his two strategic summaries of salvation history: the beginning of Jesus' public ministry and the beginning of the mission to the Gentiles (4:18–19; Acts 10:38).

Knowing that the believers received from Jesus the same Holy Spirit that empowered him, Luke expects that the Spirit-words and Spirit-works will continue in the church. Even though he believes Jesus' anointing is unique, he consciously creates parallels between the activities of Jesus and his followers, as Charles Talbert carefully and convincingly demonstrates in his lists of similarities in *Literary Patterns, Theological Themes, and the Genre of Luke–Acts.*[17] The volume of such parallels cannot be due to chance. Empowered by the Spirit, the believers continue the works of Jesus and confront the authorities, and like Jesus they suffer for the kingdom.[18] The "architecture"[19] that Luke provides for the Gospel and Acts makes a strong statement: the common denominator between the acts of Jesus and the acts of the apostles is the power of the Holy Spirit.

Luke's message for his church is indeed a charismatic one. The Spirit-anointed Jesus performed miracles and poured out this same Spirit on the believers; therefore his church is endowed to perform God's wonders. Luke expects the church to be a people of the power of God. Nevertheless, he maintains a sovereign God who alone controls the gift of power (Acts 8:20). Lest the church become enamored with power for its own sake, as Simon the magician did (Acts 8:17–24), Luke directs his readers to witness boldly and not to worry about the power: "Do not be anxious how or what you are to answer or what you are to say; for the Holy Spirit will teach you in that very hour what you ought to say" (12:11b–12) and "I will give you a mouth and wisdom which none of your adversaries will be able to withstand or contradict" (21:15).

It is significant that when Luke describes the return of the apostles from the hostile Sanhedrin, he does not note that the believing community prayed for supernatural deliverance or for miracle-working power; rather, they prayed that they "speak thy word with all boldness, while thou stretchest out thy hand to heal, and signs and wonders are performed through the name of thy holy servant Jesus" (Acts 4:29–30). The community saw their primary task as being witnesses to their Lord. Granted they were a people of supernatural power, but only because they had a supernatural sovereign who was the Lord of the power. Miracles followed their prayers, but their prayers were primarily answered when "the place in which they were gathered together was shaken; and they were all filled with the Holy Spirit and spoke the word of God with boldness" (4:31). The power accompanied and affirmed their witness (4:33). Thus Luke, in his enthusiastic presentation of miracles, emphasizes the witness that the Holy Spirit gives.

Notes to Chapter 7

1. To minimize the miracles would violate Luke's all-inclusive view of salvation as expressed in Luke 4:18ff. and elsewhere (cf. Luke 1:71; 6:9–14;

7:36–50; 8:36, 48, 50; 9:56 [variant]; 17:11–19; 19:1–10; Acts 4:9; 13:26; 16:30).

2. In 4:23 Jesus mentions miracles in anticipating the thoughts of his audience, but only parenthetically and with no antecedent. As demonstrated in chapter 6, this reference to miracles is in Luke's sources which he uses to emphasize speaking by the authority of the Holy Spirit.

3. Note also the variant for 4:18: "to heal the brokenhearted."

4. Luke 1:35; 4:36; 5:17; 6:19; 8:46; 9:1; 10:13, 19; 19:37; Acts 2:22; 3:12; 4:7, 33; 6:8; 8:10, 13; 10:38; 19:11. Furthermore, *dynamis* is used in reference to inspired speech: 1:17; 4:14, 36; 24:49; Acts 1:18; 4:33; 6:3–10. Other references to *dynamis* are not specific enough, though even they have supernatural nuances (Luke 21:26, 27; 22:69).

5. The miraculous meaning occurs in Luke 1:49; 18:27; 24:19; Acts 2:24; 7:22; 11:17. The conventional meaning is used in Luke 14:31; Acts 20:16; 25:5. In Acts 18:24 Apollos is described as "mighty [*dynatos*] in the Scriptures" (NASB) referring to his teaching. Luke 24:19 and Acts 7:22 refer to Jesus and Moses as "mighty in word(s)" as well as "deed(s)." *Adynatos* occurs in Luke's writings only at Luke 18:27 to contrast human power with the power of God, and at Acts 14:8 for the Lystran's inability to walk.

6. C. K. Barrett, *Holy Spirit*, 71–72. Luke is indebted to the synoptic tradition for this usage (e.g., Mark 6:2, 14; 12:24; 13:25; 14:62).

7. Ibid., 75.

8. Ibid., 69.

9. The inadequacy of English translations to express the force of this perfect participle of *charitoō* is evident in the varied attempts: "favored one" (RSV), "thou that art highly favoured" (KJV), "you who are highly favored" (NIV). First, to accommodate the English readers the force of the perfect tense is not readily apparent. Second, the use of the word "favor" does not readily inform the reader that this is an exercise of grace which in Greek is repeated in verse 30 with the use of the noun, *charis*. The play on words between *kecharitōmenē*, *chaire*, and *charis* in 1:28, 30 is lost in English.

10. Navone, *Themes*, 56.

11. Ibid., 59–60; Esser, "Grace," 119; H. Conzelmann, "*charis*," *TDNT* 9:359–415.

12. This is similar to Plutarch's use of *charis* to describe Demosthenes' initial attempts at public speaking: "*Charin ouk echei pros ton dēmon*" (trans.: "He did not have grace with the people"). Zahn assumes that *charis* describes Jesus' ability to speak, *Lucas*, 239. Bengel describes it as "a sweetness or weighty impressiveness" or "becomingness," *Gnomen*, 54. Plummer calls Jesus' words "winning words."

13. Godet, *Luke*, 236. See also Marshall, *Gospel of Luke*, 186: "words filled with divine grace (Acts 14:3; 20:24, 32)." Double entendre may be intended here, H. Flender, *St. Luke: Theologian of Redemptive History*, trans. R. H. and I. Fuller (London: SPCK, 1967), 153ff. and Conzelmann, "*charis*," *TDNT* 9:392 n. 153.

14. Navone, *Themes*, 60.

15. Marshall, *Luke*, 191–92, Fitzmyer: 1.546–47.

16. In Luke 7:14 it is assumed that Jesus touched the coffin of the son of the widow of Nain not to transfer reviving power to the corpse but to

stop the bearers of the coffin (contra BAGD, 102§2b). The words of Jesus are what effect the miracle. Furthermore, it should also be noted that the act of seizing the bier and therefore stopping the funeral procession is temporally separated from the words which Jesus uttered thus causing the resuscitation of the young man. "And as he came up he grasped the coffin and the bearers stood still, and he said, 'Young man, I say to you, arise' " (7:14, my trans.). Thus, the effective agent is the word of Jesus, not the act of touching the coffin. Whether 7:14 is seen as a miracle effected by the touch or not, the interrelationship of inspired speaking and miracles is an association Luke likes and indeed cultivates.

Luke uses *haptō* elsewhere for touching in instances of healing and blessing in 5:13; 6:19; 8:44–47; 18:15; 22:51. In doing so he is utilizing the synoptic vocabulary four out of five times. In ten instances Mark uses the word, and every use is in relation to healing or blessing. Matthew follows suit using *haptō* in the same context in seven out of eight instances. Luke uses it in this context five times following Mark. Elsewhere he uses *haptō* differently or prefers another expression. In Luke 8:16 and 11:33 and in Acts 28:2 (the only use of *haptō* in Acts) it refers to lighting a lamp or fire. In Luke's version of the anointing of Jesus by the sinner woman at Bethany, he alone describes the woman's act as "touching" (*haptō*) the feet of Jesus. He does not use the term in the context of healing in his digression from Mark. In the non-Marcan material in 14:4, Luke describes a healing in which Jesus took hold of the man with dropsy and healed him. He did not use *haptō* to describe the action but *epilambanō*. Elsewhere, Luke describes healings which are effected by touching with the more Lucan phrase, *epitithēmi tas cheiras* (13:13; see also Acts 9:12, 17; 28:8; and probably Acts 5:12 as well: "Now many signs and wonders were done among the people by the hands of the apostles"). Thus it is not surprising that in this bit of non-Marcan material Luke does not use the term *haptō* to effect the miracle.

17. Charles Talbert, *Literary Patterns, Theological Themes, and the Genre of Luke–Acts*, SBLMS 20 (Missoula, Mont.: Scholars, 1974). Talbert builds especially on the work of R. B. Rackham as well as on that of F. B. Clogg, L. Cerfaux, and V. Wilkinson. See notes 4–5 on p. 30. For the parallel list see pages 16–18 in which Talbert gives 32 parallels.

18. R. B. Rackham notes the following parallels between Luke and Acts: (1) preface, (2) period of waiting and preparation, (3) a baptism with the Holy Spirit, (4) "followed by a period of active work and ministry," (5) a long passion or suffering section which includes (a) early predictions of the trials, (b) a journey to Jerusalem, (c) last words of the sufferer, and (d) the " 'passion' proper," (6) ending "with a period of victorious but quiet preparation for a further advance, or another volume" (*The Acts of the Apostles: An Exposition* [London: Methuen, 1930], xlvii).

19. To use Rackham's description (*Acts*, xlvii).

8 The Holy Spirit and Prayer and Praise

*T*HROUGHOUT LUKE-ACTS, Luke highlights prayer and praise. He tells his readers that the advent of Jesus and John was accompanied by the prayers of the righteous (Luke 1:6, 10, 13) and welcomed by praise (1:46, 64, 68; 2:14, 20, 28, 38). Only Luke's Gospel presents the eloquent prayers of praise found in the infancy narrative—the Magnificat (1:46–55), Benedictus (1:68–79), Gloria in Excelsis (2:14), and Nunc Dimittis (2:29–32). He, alone among the Gospel writers, presents certain teachings of Jesus on prayer (e.g., Luke 11:1–13; 18:1–14).

He often notes that praise occurs when the mention of praise is absent in the parallel accounts. For example in Nazareth, Jesus' hometown, the people's first response to him was praise (Luke 4:14–15, 22). After being healed from blindness, Bartimaeus glorified God as did all the people (18:43). At the triumphal entry, the multitude praised God in a loud voice because of the wondrous deeds of Jesus (19:37). The centurion praised God at the foot of the cross (23:47).

In addition to his infancy narrative, Luke presents events not in the other Gospels which also include praise and rejoicing: the healing of the crippled woman on the Sabbath (13:10–17), the parables of the lost coin and prodigal son (15:8–32), the cleansing of the ten lepers (17:11–19), the conversion of Zacchaeus (19:1–10), and the ascension (24:52).

Similarly, Luke alone relates Jesus at prayer in the following common synoptic events:

—The baptism of Jesus. Jesus is praying when the Holy Spirit descends (3:21).

—The cleansing of the leper. Luke concludes the event by saying that Jesus "withdrew to the wilderness and prayed" (5:16).

—The choosing of the Twelve. Jesus prays all night before he picks his followers (6:12).

—The Petrine confession. Jesus' questions are preceded by prayer (9:18).

—The transfiguration. Jesus "went up on the mountain to pray" (9:28).

—The Lord's Prayer. At the sight of Jesus in prayer the disciples ask him to teach them to pray (11:1).

—The prediction of Peter's denial. Luke specifically notes that Jesus prayed for Peter (22:31–32).

—Gethsemane. Luke records Jesus' words, "Pray that you may not enter into temptation" (22:40).

The point Luke is making is unmistakable: "one can say that Jesus' whole mission is accomplished in a spirit of prayer."[1] In Acts, Luke continues to stress prayer and praise. Several significant instances stand out. Luke tells us that on the day of Pentecost the disciples were praying when the Holy Spirit descended, and they began praising God (1:14; 2:11, 47). At the hour of prayer Peter and John healed a lame man who praised God (3:1–10). When the disciples prayed for boldness to witness, they were filled with the Holy Spirit, and "spoke the word of God with boldness" (4:29–31). Full of the Holy Spirit, Stephen prayed at his martyrdom (7:55–60). Paul (Saul) was praying when Ananias came and laid hands upon him for him to be healed and to receive the Holy Spirit (9:11, 17).

Both Peter and Cornelius prayed before Peter's vision and Cornelius' reception of the Holy Spirit (10:1–4, 9). Peter's release from prison was preceded by the prayers of the community (12:5, 12). The church at Antioch was fasting and praying when the Holy Spirit called Saul and Barnabas to a mission (13:2–3). Paul and his companions sought out the Philippian believers at "a place of prayer" (16:13–14). Paul and Silas prayed and sang hymns before they were miraculously released from prison (16:25). Other examples of Luke's emphasis on praise throughout Acts include 2:47; 3:8, 9; 4:21; 11:18; 13:48; 21:20.

Not surprisingly, Luke notes that the Holy Spirit enables people to pray and praise God. This is true for Mary (Luke 1:35, 46), Zechariah (1:64, 67ff.), Simeon (2:25–32), Jesus (10:21), the disciples at Pentecost (Acts 2:4, 11, 47), and later Cornelius (10:44–46). In Luke–Acts we also find that the activity of the Holy Spirit is often predicated upon prayer. At the expense of restatement we will isolate and list these instances. Jesus was praying when the Spirit descended at the Jordan (Luke 3:21). Jesus taught that the Holy Spirit is the answer to prayer (11:13 contra Matthew's "good gifts" in Matt 7:11). The disciples were at prayer before they were filled with the Holy Spirit (Acts 1:14; 2:4, 31).

Paul was praying before he was filled with the Holy Spirit (9:11, 17). Peter and Cornelius were praying before the Spirit was poured out on the Gentiles (10:1–4, 9, 44–46). Worship preceded the Holy Spirit's commissioning of Saul and Barnabas (13:2–3). Lampe calls this "one of the most characteristic features of St. Luke's teaching, namely, his insistence upon prayer as the means by which the dynamic energy is apprehended."[2] Spirit-empowerment is prefaced with and realized by prayer. In fact, Luke often relates that people were praying prior to momentous events in salvation history.[3] Praying became a means of human participation in and anticipation of divine intervention in history. Our major focus in this chapter, however, is the role of the Holy Spirit in enabling people to utter effective inspired prayer.

"Jesus Rejoiced in the Holy Spirit"

Both Matthew and Luke record this instance of Jesus' praise to the Father, but they differ in contexts. In addition, only Luke says that Jesus "rejoiced in the Holy Spirit." Matthew contrasts the "babes" who received the revelation with the unbelieving cities, Chorazin, Bethsaida, and Capernaum (Matt 11:20–30). Luke, like Matthew, includes the woes against the cities before this saying of Jesus (10:13–15), but Luke's immediate context is not disbelief and unrepentance as in Matthew (11:17–20).

Matt 11:25–27	Luke 10:21–24
At that time Jesus declared, "I thank thee, Father, Lord of heaven and earth, that thou hast hidden things from the wise and understanding and revealed them to babes; yea, Father, for such was thy gracious will. All things have been delivered to me by my Father; and no one knows the Son except the Father, and no one knows the Father except the Son and any one to whom the Son chooses to reveal him."	In that same hour he rejoiced in the Holy Spirit and said, "I thank thee, Father, Lord of heaven and earth, that thou hast hidden these things from the wise and understanding and revealed them to babes; yea, Father, for such was thy gracious will. All things have been delivered to me by my Father; and no one knows who the Son is except the Father, or who the Father is except the Son and any one to whom the Son chooses to reveal him."

Only Luke tells us that the occasion for the joy of Jesus and his followers is the successful mission of the Seventy. Matthew 11:25–26 suggests relates that Jesus gave thanks for belief over unbelief, but in Luke, Jesus and company also rejoice over a successful ministry complete with exorcisms and healings. "And the seventy returned with joy, saying, 'Lord, even the demons are subject to us in your name!' " (Luke 10:17). Jesus affirmed that Satan had indeed been shaken and that the disciples had exercised power over the enemy, but he also warned them against being enamored with power and suggested that they rejoice instead that their names were written in heaven (10:20). This mild rebuke, however, did not extinguish Jesus' joy; for "in that same hour" he praised the Father for revealing the fall of Satan and the coming of the kingdom in power to his disciples.

In Luke the belief of the "babes" produced results: preaching, healing, and exorcism. In contrast to Matthew, Luke emphasizes the powerful witness of the disciples as the occasion for the rejoicing of Jesus which, according to Luke, is inspired by the Holy Spirit.[4]

Original Context: Matthew or Luke?

As in the case of most of the Q material, scholars cannot say definitively which context—Matthew's or Luke's—is original. This is especially true here since no parallel for the mission of the Seventy exists. Neither can one easily choose between the Matthean or Lucan contexts for the benediction which follows Jesus' rejoicing.[5] "Blessed are the eyes which see what you see! For I tell you that many prophets and kings desired to see what you see, and did not see it, and to hear what you hear, and did not hear it" (Luke 10:23–24; Matt 13:16–17).

In Matthew the benediction alludes to the openness of Jesus' followers to the meaning of his parables in contrast to those referred to in the prophecy of Isaiah found in Matthew 13:14, "You shall indeed hear but never understand, and you shall indeed see but never perceive." In Luke the blessing is in response to the disciples who have seen and heard what the prophets and kings longed to see, i.e., the coming of the kingdom in power.[6] Luke's immediate context provides antecedents for both seeing and hearing; while in Matthew, the immediate context refers to parables. Therefore, Luke may better reflect the situation in which the saying occurred.[7]

Alternatively the saying could have circulated devoid of context. Both applications fit well and may reflect two genuine traditions. Regardless of the original form of Q, Luke's editorial motives are clear. If, on the one hand, Matthew more closely reflects the order and theological agenda of Q, then Luke has consciously restructured it to make a distinctive point. On the other hand, if Luke is a better preservation of Q, then one has to ask why he was attracted to it. In either event his motives are the same: he presents the disciples giving divine witness and working wonders and Jesus in turn giving an inspired response to their participation in the kingdom. In all probability Luke is responsible for the reference to the Holy Spirit, for he superimposes such references on the synoptic material and uses them freely in Acts.

"In the Holy Spirit"

The phrase referring to Jesus' having the Holy Spirit in Luke 10:21 stands only in Luke's version of Q and in several variant readings. Both "in the Holy Spirit" and "in the S/spirit" appear in the manuscripts.[8] The best evidence points to the variants with *tō hagiō* (the Holy),[9] thus "in the Holy Spirit" is the preferred reading. But even if the variant "in the S/spirit" is allowed to stand, Luke does not intend the phrase to be a reference to Jesus' spirit (i.e., his incorporeal members) or a generalized phrase for the spiritual realm. Had Luke intended this, he probably would have linked *pneuma* and a possessive pronoun to the verb *agalliaō* as he does in 1:47 ("my spirit rejoices in God my Savior"). Elsewhere Luke uses the expression to mean the Holy Spirit (1:17; 2:27; 4:1, 14), and there is nothing here in the text that demands a special reading.

Lucan Characteristics of the Phrase "Rejoiced in the Holy Spirit"

"Rejoiced in the Holy Spirit" is characteristically Lucan in contrast to the other synoptic Gospels. The phrase appears in the introduction to the praise-saying of Jesus, an introduction that Luke has apparently provided. Most of Luke's references to the Holy Spirit enabling someone to speak occur in his narration of the event rather than in the actual sayings. *Agalliaō* ("rejoice"), probably from Luke's own pen, contrasts with Matthew's simple *eipen*, "declared" or "said." Out of a total of eleven occurrences in the NT, *agalliaō* appears four times in Luke–Acts (one is a quote of a psalm, Acts 2:26), twice in John, and only once in the other Synoptics (Matt 5:12). Of the rest of the NT occurrences, three appear in 1 Peter and one in Revelation. [10]

Luke's more frequent use of *agalliaō* among the synoptic writers is in keeping with his frequent references to giving thanks, praising, and rejoicing. Often Luke relates that these activities occur during events paralleled in the other Gospels, but the parallels say nothing about praising or rejoicing. (For example, contrast with the synoptic parallels the following: Luke 4:14–15, 22; 18:43; 19:37; 23:47.) These themes are ever present in Acts as well (e.g., 2:26; 3:8–9; 4:21; 11:18; 21:20).

Luke's dominant use of the verb *agalliaō* is paralleled in his use of other words relating to this subject. In his Gospel are:

(1) Over twenty references to joy or rejoicing (*chara, chairō, synchairō*).

(2) Twenty-two references to glory or glorifying (*doxa, doxazō*).

(3) Four references to giving thanks (*eucharisteō*).

(4) The use of *aineō* for "praise." (Among the Gospel writers, only Luke uses this particular word. Of the eight times it appears in the NT, Luke–Acts uses it six times. *Aineō* is a distinctively Lucan word which serves his specialized interest in praise.)

(5) The use of *eulogeō* for "bless." Luke often uses this word in reference to God or Jesus. Of the forty-two times this word occurs in the NT, it appears fifteen times in Luke–Acts, and most frequently in Luke among the Gospels (Matt 5x; Mark 5x; Luke 13x; John 0x).

(6) Six references to *euphrainō* for "make merry" or "celebrate." (No other Gospel writer uses this word. Of the fourteen instances of the word in the NT, it occurs eight times in Luke–Acts.)

Luke frequently uses the phrase "in the Holy Spirit" and its parallels, such as "in the Spirit," "in the power of the Spirit," and "the Spirit," in the locative/instrumental case (Luke 1:17; 2:27; 3:16; 4:1, 14; 10:21; Acts 1:5; 6:10; 10:38; 16:18; 19:21; 20:22). The construction occurs elsewhere in the NT, but Luke's use of it is dominant among the Synoptic Gospels (Matt 3x; Mark 2x).[11]

The reference to the time for the rejoicing and benediction, *en autē tē hōra* ("in that same hour") is also distinctively Lucan.[12] Luke apparently uses this phrase to replace the phrase, *en ekeinō tō kairō* ("at that time"). By doing so he emphatically links the rejoicing of Jesus with the success of the mission of the Seventy. This contrasts Matthew whose temporal phrase links the rejoicing to the fact that the babes of the kingdom believed, while the cities who saw his miracles did not. Luke is responsible for this unique reason for Jesus' rejoicing. Thus we see that on the basis of his vocabulary preferences, his distinctive theological interests, and his preferred syntax, the entire phrase, "Jesus rejoiced in the Holy Spirit," is in all probability from Luke himself.[13]

The Significance for Luke's Agenda

Although Luke maintains much of the vocabulary and structure of his source in 10:21–22,[14] he also makes some adjustments to it.[15] This is especially true for the preface which he provides for the sayings: "In that same hour he rejoiced in the Holy Spirit and said . . ." (v. 21).

Here the reference to the Holy Spirit reveals several interesting points of Lucan pneumatology.

First, Luke points out that Jesus uttered this praise and experienced this joy by means of the Holy Spirit. The parallels between this act of inspired speaking, the events of Pentecost,[16] and the joy expressed by the witnesses in the infancy stories are clear.[17] They all joyfully witnessed concerning Jesus by the power and revelation of the Holy Spirit.

Second, the phrase, "rejoiced in the Holy Spirit," indicates that revelation has occurred; truth has been revealed. Leaney notes:

> The phrase is unique and well expresses the joy of those who, like Mary and Elizabeth, are permitted to share the knowledge of God's plan of salvation. In their case as in that of the Lord here, it is joy at an apocalyptic vision. Luke appears to be responsible for the phrase.[18]

Third, by rejoicing in the Holy Spirit, Jesus uttered an inspired statement.[19] The verbs *ēgalliasato* ("rejoiced") and *eipen* ("said") describe not separate events but the same sudden yet flowing action. This use of two verbs to express the act of speaking sounds semitic and may represent an introduction provided by Luke's source to which he appended the prepositional phrase, "in the Holy Spirit." Given Luke's use of *agalliaō* elsewhere, however, this may reflect Luke's semitizing style. Nothing in Luke's or Matthew's version suggests two separate actions described by the two verbs. Jesus' rejoicing is contained in the quotation that follows and does not indicate that Jesus rejoiced in the Spirit in another utterance before the clause, "Father, I thank thee." The utterance is directed to God and is in effect prayer. Luke probably recognizes this act of Jesus as a paradigm for the activity in the church identified as "praying in the Spirit" (1 Cor 14:15; Jude 20) and sees praise as being directed by the Holy Spirit.

Fourth, this means not only that Jesus was inspired to address his Father (vv. 21–22), but also that he was empowered by the experience to proclaim this truth to his disciples by telling them that they had seen the kingdom of God coming in power (vv. 23ff.). The reference to the disciples in verse 22 demonstrates that the praise-saying was not only for God's ear but also for the disciples' illumination.[20] The activity of the Holy Spirit is a prerequisite for revealing and proclaiming the salvation of God. In this passage Jesus witnesses, by the Holy Spirit, to the truth before God and those around him.

The context for the occasion of Jesus rejoicing in the Holy Spirit is firmly linked with the return of the Seventy, and it is this context which sheds much light on Luke's understanding of the phrase. In the mission passage (10:1–20), Luke preserves the twofold commission given by Jesus: to preach and perform wonders (10:9). The role of speaking in the mission is further heightened when the exorcisms occur by using the name of Jesus (10:17). Luke also describes Jesus' exorcism ministry in terms of speaking (4:18ff.) when Jesus, by the Holy Spirit's anointing, *proclaimed* release to the captives. (This is immediately followed by the exorcism in Capernaum, 4:31ff.) Jesus rejoiced that the disciples had experienced the kingdom of God through their own ministries. Luke sees authoritative speaking as the highlight of the Seventy's report (v. 17). Appropriately Luke observes that Jesus' response to the report was motivated by the Holy Spirit, the same Spirit who would soon empower the disciples (Luke 24:49; Acts 1:8).

Luke avoids making direct associations between the Holy Spirit and the disciples' pre-Pentecost activity, since they are not filled with the Holy Spirit until Pentecost. Instead, Luke preserves the saying in 10:19, "Behold, I have given you authority . . . over all the power of the enemy." This portrays Jesus as the source of their authority rather than the Spirit. This unique situation of having the disciples possess power before it was officially given to them by the Holy Spirit is created by Luke's observing the eras of the old and new covenants, a convention he ignores when he describes the ministries of many characters in the infancy narrative in post-ascension, Pentecostal terms. For the disciples he reserves references to the Holy Spirit until Pentecost, although in some sense they had the Spirit's power in their miracle mission in Luke 10:1–20.

Luke's explanation for the source of Jesus' praise of the Father (vv. 21–22) and his blessing of the disciples (vv. 23–24) is a model for the distinctly Lucan presentation of the work of the Holy Spirit. The main emphasis is inspired witness. By no accident the "rejoicing in the Holy Spirit" prefaces and amplifies Jesus' statement on his relationship as Son to God the Father, a revelation which shakes the kingdom of Satan and manifests the kingdom of God in power. Luke's special pneumatology affirms and reveals his ultimate christological statement: Jesus is the Spirit-anointed Son. Typically Luke expresses Christology via pneumatology (e.g., 1:35; 3:15–22; 10:21ff.; Acts 10:37ff.). Thus Luke tells us that the Holy Spirit reveals the nature of the relationship between the Father and the Son, but in so doing he also reveals the relationship between the Son and the Holy Spirit. The Holy Spirit anoints Jesus and gives rise to his words which reveal the relationship.

The Holy Spirit and the Lord's Prayer

"Let your Holy Spirit come upon us and cleanse us."

Close on the heels of the "rejoicing in the Holy Spirit" passage comes Luke's version of the Lord's Prayer. "Father, hallowed be thy name. Thy kingdom come" (Luke 11:2). In some ancient copies of Luke the prayer contains a reference to the Holy Spirit. In the writings of Gregory of Nyssa we read the following: "Father, hallowed be your name. Let your Spirit come upon us and cleanse [*katharisatō*] us." (Maximus and manuscripts 162 and 700 have similar readings.) Tertullian, perhaps quoting Marcion, mentions the request for the Holy Spirit before the request, "Let your kingdom come" (*Adversus Marcion* 4:26). While most of the textual evidence points to its absence, the reading that includes the reference to the Holy Spirit cannot be easily dismissed since the scribal tendency to adjust texts to Matthew's version seems early and widespread.[21] The manuscript Codex Bezae (D) appears to reflect knowledge of both traditions when it provides the conflation, "upon us let your kingdom come."[22]

The Validity of the Holy Spirit Variant

The concept of the descent of the Spirit is, of course, not alien to OT Judaism or the early church. Leaney notes similarities in Luke–Acts, John, and the epistles.[23] It fits well into Luke's pervasive interest in the Holy Spirit. Furthermore, "a reference to the Holy Spirit is fitting in a prayer that stands in contrast to a Johannine prayer (11:1),"[24] since John the Baptist predicted the coming of the Holy Spirit. It also corresponds to Luke's close association of the Holy Spirit with prayer and revelation.[25] An impressive parallel is in Luke 1:35 when the Holy Spirit came upon Mary, causing the child Jesus to be called holy (*hagion*). Especially important is the association of the Holy Spirit with the inspired speaking which consistently occurs in Luke's program. This prayer, like the Holy Spirit-empowered prayer in 10:21ff., elicits praise to God and revelation to a human audience.

Scholarship is divided over whether or not the variant stood in Luke.[26] The variant could be original (1) if Luke is editing Matthew or Q, (2) if Luke is citing an alternate to Q, (3) if he has a different version of Q, or (4) if the Lord's Prayer floated as an independent and varied tradition. The reading probably did not stand in Q as shared by the First and Third Gospels, for it is unlikely that Matthew would have jettisoned it had it been there.[27] Thus the originality of the reading in Luke must be based on a source other than Q or on Lucan redaction of either Matthew or Q.

It is not possible here to examine exhaustively these options concerning the variant reading or the question concerning the originality of the Matthean and Lucan versions of the whole Lord's Prayer. For our study it is irrelevant whether Luke is inserting the reference to the Spirit into his source or is favoring a tradition that contained it over a version that did not. Whatever the reason for the variant, if it stood in Luke, it was there because it served Luke's purpose, and it would modify the meaning of the prayer.

The Meaning of the Variant

The invocation of the Holy Spirit at the beginning of the prayer evokes several meanings in the context of Lucan theology. The immediate action of the Spirit is cleansing. If "hallowed be thy name" accompanies "let your Holy Spirit come upon us and cleanse us," then a word association between "hallowed" (*hagiasthētō*) and the Holy Spirit (*to pneuma sou to hagion*) is apparent. The implication is that the Holy Spirit of the holy (hallowed) Father creates a similar character in those upon whom he descends and whom he cleanses. Thus the suppliants expect to be of the same character and mind as of the One they address. Accordingly, the activity of the Spirit enables the suppliants to pray correctly. This enabling of believers to pray by means of the Holy Spirit's activity is further supported by the presence of "upon" (*epi*). This traditional concept of the Holy Spirit coming upon someone is similar to Luke's unique use of the phrase, "full of the Holy Spirit," and suggests a fresh endowment of the Spirit to pray in accordance with God's will. Furthermore, this activity fits well into early Christian teaching that only by the Holy Spirit can one call God "Abba, Father" (Rom 8:15; Gal 4:6).

This fits well into Luke's overall program. Several passages suggest that the activity of the Holy Spirit here (i.e., cleansing) enables inspired speaking on the part of the petitioner to take place. Luke records several instances where the activity of the Holy Spirit is noted prior to communication with God (Zechariah's blessing of God, 1:67ff.; Simeon's prayer, 2:29ff.; and in the previous context, Jesus' prayer of praise, 10:21ff.). Like all these prayers, the Lord's Prayer is not just for God's benefit, but it has a human audience as well. The "us" of 11:2 and the request of the disciples for instruction on how to pray (11:1) indicate that the Lord's Prayer has a wider audience. Thus a reference to the Holy Spirit in inspired prayer to God before witnesses has Lucan precedence (see also Stephen's prayer, Acts 7:55–60, and a similar situation in the prayer of the threatened disciples, Acts 4:24–31).

The references to the Holy Spirit here fit well with other Lucan tendencies. The close relationship between prayer and the work of the Holy Spirit is obvious.[28] As noted earlier, the Holy Spirit phrase follows, "Thy kingdom come." If Luke is responsible for its presence, then Luke sees the kingdom in terms of the activity of the Holy Spirit; to him the kingdom and the Spirit are inseparably linked. Both ideas have precedence in Luke. Dunn has pointed out that the connections between the Spirit and the kingdom are so close that the two blend together, and the distinctions between them are often blurred. This is seen in the commissioning of the disciples in Luke 24:36–53 and Acts 1:3–8. The two become interchangeable to such an extent that Dunn asserts, "Thus it is not so much a case where *Jesus* is there is the kingdom as where the *Spirit* is there is the kingdom."[29] S. Smalley goes a step further by observing that "Spirit, kingdom, and prayer are all closely related at important moments in the progress of salvation history."[30] He points out that these elements are present in many of the history-changing events recorded both in Luke's Gospel and in Acts.[31] He further notes that if the variant reading in Luke's Lord's Prayer is accepted, then all three elements are clustered together again. "It is even more significant that the alternative but probably inferior reading of some MSS at this point is 'thy Holy Spirit come upon us and cleanse us.' Once more Spirit and Kingdom are interchangeably associated in the context of petitionary prayers."[32]

The Value of the Variant to Luke's Program

The context Luke provides for the Lord's Prayer also fits well with the variant reading. Luke relates that at the sight of Jesus praying, the disciples asked him, "Lord, teach us to pray as John taught his disciples" (11:1). With the variant, the prayer of Jesus, which appropriately contains a reference to endowment with the Holy Spirit, contrasts well with John's probable teaching on prayer, which could contain only a promise of the Holy Spirit at best. Just as Jesus' Spirit baptism superseded John's water baptism, so too the prayer of Jesus, in contrast to John, becomes a "Spirit-prayer."[33]

The variant reading also fits in well with the greater context of the Lord's Prayer. In 10:21, Jesus is presented as an example of prayer, as he himself was inspired by the Holy Spirit to praise God. In 11:13, we see that the Holy Spirit who enabled the disciples (and Jesus) to pray in accordance with God's will and to affirm his truth was the same Spirit through whom all prayers are answered and all needs are met. Thus the theme of the Holy Spirit is intrinsic to Luke's larger context surrounding the Lord's Prayer. The Holy Spirit's pervasive influence over prayer provides a prelude and epilogue to Luke's Lord's Prayer. In 12:12, the believers are assured that the Holy Spirit will grant the appropriate words of witness. When its wider context is viewed, which also includes references to the Holy Spirit, the validity of the variant reading must be considered even though its textual attestation is weak. It fits well in Luke's program of Spirit and prayer and also parallels his minor theme of linking the Spirit and cleansing (see Acts 10:15 with 10:44; 11:9 with 11:16 and 15:8–9).

The Holy Spirit as the Answer to Prayer

Immediately after Luke presents the Lord's Prayer, he places more teaching on prayer: the parable of the persistent friend (11:5–8), the ask-seek-knock saying (11:9–10), and the incident of the son asking the father for a fish (11:11–13). In the last verse Luke concludes, "If you then, who are evil, know how to give good gifts to your children, how much more will the heavenly Father give the Holy Spirit to those who ask him!" (11:13). Luke's "Holy Spirit" stands in the place of Matthew's "good gifts" (Matt 7:11).

Scholarship is divided over which reading is original;[34] however, most believe that Matthew's "good gifts" is the original and that Luke interpreted the gifts of Matthew as the gift of the Holy Spirit (Acts 2:38).[35] It is also possible that Luke is preserving an alternate tradition. A case could also be made for Matthew's changing "Holy Spirit" to "good gifts."[36] But given Luke's redactional inclusion of "Holy Spirit" throughout Luke–Acts, it is clear that Luke is responsible for its insertion or preservation and that it serves a theological purpose. "Indeed, the evangelist would see this promise of Jesus in 11:13 as the basis for Pentecost."[37]

For Luke the Holy Spirit is the answer to prayer. The Spirit's power can remedy any situation. When 11:13 is linked with the Spirit and prayer context of 10:21 and possibly 11:2, the message of Luke is clear: the Holy Spirit is the means of asking for a gift, the sphere in which the request is made, and the essence of the good gift which is given. The Spirit superintends both the vertical and horizontal aspects of prayer: its praise to God and its witness to humans. For Luke the Spirit also superintends the answer to the prayer by becoming the answer. Spirit-prayer is in contrast to the blasphemous speech of Jesus' enemies, in the following verses of Luke 11, which we will discuss in chapter 9.

Notes to Chapter 8

1. Kealy, *Luke's Gospel*, 93.

2. G. W. H. Lampe, "The Holy Spirit in the Writings of St. Luke," in *Studies in the Gospels: Essays in Memory of R. H. Lightfoot*, ed. D. E. Nineham (Oxford: Blackwell, 1955), 159–200, esp. 169.

3. "I want to suggest that in both Luke and Acts, *Spirit, Kingdom and prayer* are all closely related to important moments in the progress of salvation history" (S. S. Smalley, "Spirit, Kingdom and Prayer in Luke–Acts," *NovT* 15 [1, 1973]: 59–71, esp. 64).

4. Marshall correctly notes that the event of Jesus' rejoicing is "the mighty works and preaching of Jesus as the signs of fulfillment" (*Gospel of Luke*, 431).

5. The following, however, hold that Matthew inserted the saying into his own context: Bultmann, *Synoptic Tradition*, 171; T. W. Manson, *The Sayings of Jesus* (London: SCM Press, 1949), 185ff.; U. Wilckens, "*sophia*," *TDNT*, 8:465–526, esp. 516ff. Dibelius and Norden, on the other hand, consider Matt 11:25–30 as an indissoluble unit by the time Matthew came across the three sections. Dibelius believes that Luke is responsible for the insertion of the prayer of praise into the context of the return of the Seventy, E. Norden, *Agnostos Theos: Untersuchungen zur Formengeschichte religiöser Rede* (Leipzig: Teubner, 1913), 277ff.; Dibelius, *Tradition*, 279ff. Marshall shows why Matthew is suspected of the insertion: "The blessing on the disciples has been inserted by Matthew into a Marcan context, and hence Luke may preserve the original setting in Q" (*Gospel of Luke*, 431). Marshall, however, thinks it may reflect "two originally separate sayings" (ibid., 431). Jeremias and Cadbury show evidence that a variant translation or tradition underlies Luke's version; see Jeremias, *The Prayers of Jesus* (London: SCM Press, 1967), 46; H. J. Cadbury, *The Style and Literary Method of Luke*, HTS 6 (Cambridge: Harvard, 1920), 142ff. Thus the possibility of a dual tradition with different contexts must be considered.

6. "It is hard to say which Evangelist reproduces the wording in Q, but the phrase is certainly based on Q and refers back to the occasion of whatever saying preceded it in Q (10:13–15 or 10:17–20). For Luke it refers back to the revelation of divine power seen in the exorcism of demons by the disciples, but in Mt. it gives a strong contrast between the rejection of Jesus' message by the Galilean cities and the acceptance of his message as divine revelation by the disciples," so Marshall, *Gospel of Luke*, 432.

7. "The contrast expressed in the saying between the wise and simple may perhaps favour Matthew's ordering of the sayings, but this is by no means conclusive" (ibid., 432).

8. Metzger reports that the UBS Translation Committee thought that the "strangeness" of the expression may have led to *tō hagiō* being omitted

from certain MSS (Metzger, *Textual Commentary*, 152); see also Plummer, *Luke*, 281. Marshall points out that although *en tō pneumati* "might appear to be supported by Lucan usage (2:27; 4:1; Acts 19:21)" in the references in the Gospel, "the adjective *hagios* is missing because the full phrase has just been used (2:25ff.; 4:1) which is not the case here." Since there is no antecedent for the simplified phrase in the context of 10:21, this reading is doubtful (Marshall, *Luke*, 433).

9. The presence or absence of *en* cannot be conclusively determined. The UBS Translation Committee opts for the reading with *en* since the LXX usually appends *en* to *agalliaō* (Metzger, *Textual Commentary*, 152).

10. Luke also dominates the use of the substantive form of *agalliaō* which is *agalliasis*. Of its five occurrences in the NT, three occur in Luke–Acts, one in Hebrews, and one in Jude.

11. Jeremias considers the use of *tō pneumati* as traditional and the bulk of Luke 10 as pre-Lucan, *Die Sprache*, 115, 189. Nevertheless, its frequency and related syntactical constructions show that if it is traditional, Luke took over the traditional expression and used it as his own. Marshall gives another opinion: "Since the following phrase is probably Lucan, the same may be true of the verb, which in any case is lacking in Mt. at this point" (*Gospel of Luke*, 433).

12. The phrase with its parallel expressions (*autos/auto/autē* with or without articles) + a substantive of time is found only in Luke–Acts (Jeremias, *Die Sprache*, 98, 189 [although he considers the temporal use of *en* as indicative of tradition]). See also Creed, *Luke*, 148; and Plummer, *Luke*, 281. Manson, however, suggests that Luke's phrase corresponds to a rabbinic phrase and that Matthew's expression, "at that season," is coined by him (*Sayings*, 79). Strack and Billerbeck see both Matthew's and Luke's references to times as having Jewish parallels; see Herman L. Strack and Paul Billerbeck, *Kommentar zum Neuen Testament aus Talmud und Midrash* (Munich: C. H. Beck, 1926), 1:606; 2:176. But Luke apparently has intensified the reference to time (if his source provided it), and he uses his own expression. Manson also considers Luke's phrase to be a reflection of rabbinic usage (*Sayings*, 79). Strack and Billerbeck's references to the convention that rabbis should be instantly ready to utter prayer is a peripheral point in that the phrase, "in that same hour," exists primarily to connect the words of Jesus with the return of the Seventy from a successful mission.

13. Creed notes the parallel between the phrase here and in 1:47 (*Luke*, 148). See also Zahn, *Lucas*, 424. A. H. McNeile sees much evidence for a Lucan contribution here. *Agalliaō* is Lucan, and so is the reference to the Holy Spirit (*The Gospel According to St. Matthew* [London: Macmillan, 1961], 161). Strack and Billerbeck note that the rejoicing in the Holy Spirit in the Spirit-inspired prophecy is similar to the case of Simeon in Luke 2:25. It is true that Luke and his community are indebted to Judaism for the concept, but the expression is Luke's own. M. Miyoshi considers Luke's use of *agalliaō* as a result of the influence of the LXX; see *Der Anfang des Reiseberichts, Lk. 9,51–10, 24: Eine redaktionsgeschichtliche Untersuchung*, AnBib 60 (Rome: Biblical Institute, 1974), 134. Bultmann recognizes that the verb's connection with the inspiration of the Holy Spirit is Lucan, "*agalliasis*," *TDNT*, 1:20.

14. The narrative providing an introduction to the logion undoubtedly is Lucan in theme and in wording; the sayings which follow, however, provide a semitic tone suggesting a pre-Lucan tradition. Since themes of sonship and Fatherhood resemble Johannine motifs, some scholars presuppose that such themes must reflect a later and more hellenistic origin for the logion or at least a later point in the evolution of the Q material; so Bultmann, *Synoptic Tradition*, 159; P. Hoffmann, *Studien zur Theologie der Logienquelle* (Munich: C. H. Beck, 1924), 210; E. Schultz, *Q-Die Spruchquelle der Evangelisten* (Zurich: Theologischer Verlag, 1972). This does not, however, take into account the semitic structure which cannot be accounted for by Lucan attempts to "semitize" his style since it is the common domain of the Q tradition. Manson describes the passage as full of semitic turns of phrase, and certainly Palestinian in origin (*Sayings*, 79). Jeremias sees *oudeis . . . ei mē* as semitic (citing K. Beyer in *Prayers*, 46). Oepke observes that the meaning, "to reveal," for *apokalyptō* is not typically Greek in "*kalyptō,*" *TDNT*, 3:556–92, 557. Creed notes that *exomologoumai soi* is frequently found in the LXX Psalms for *hwd l*, while *emprosthen sou* is "a Semitic periphrasis to avoid a too familiar manner in speaking of the Divine purpose" (*Luke*, 148; Strack and Billerbeck, 2:606). *Emprosthen* = Aramaic; G. Schrenk, "*eudokia,*" *TDNT*, 2:747; Jeremias, *New Testament Theology: The Proclamation of Jesus*, 1 (London: SCM Press, 1971), 190 n. 7. The address of God as Lord of heaven and earth is Jewish, and the saying about the babes has Jewish parallels as well (Strack and Billerbeck, 2:607). Jeremias identifies the Father-Son/Son-Father saying as a gnomic expression understood by the audience (*Prayers*, 50ff.) The asyndeton is not Lucan; neither is the parataxis found here typical of Luke. "The paratactic construction echoes Semitic idiom" (Creed, *Luke*, 148). This is semitic in character and probably is not due to Luke's style taking on a semitic flavor. Note that in the beginning of the third line of the praise-saying, the presence of the *kai* "cannot be attributed to Luke's editing as Luke cuts down on the frequent use of *kai* in his material and never alters an *oude* in the text of Mark to *kai*" (Jeremias, *Prayers*, 46, and *Die Sprache*, 189). Clearly, a semitic source lies behind the praise-saying and the benediction.

15. The passage does show signs of some Lucan emendation. The presence of *tis* in 10:22 is probably due to Luke's preference for hypotaxis and may be part of a Lucan attempt at abbreviation. The *oudeis/oude* is repeated in Matt 11:27, but Luke uses only one. Though he may never replace *oude* with *kai* in the Marcan material, Luke may be omitting the second one here since he omits the corresponding use of the verb (*epiginōskō*) for which *oude* serves as a subject in Matt 11:27. Luke avoids the repetition of the verb (which is part of the semitic parallel structure) "which Greek taste found ugly" (Jeremias, *Prayers*, 46). So, in jettisoning the verb and creating an ellipsis, he also decided to remove the corresponding subject. The *kai* in the phrase, *kai tis estin ho patēr ei mē ho hyios* (v. 22), may serve as a connective between the two relative clauses which are probably Lucan. Creed states, "The indirect question is prob. a stylistic alteration by Luke" (*Luke*, 149). In doing so, Luke has eliminated some of the parallel structures which Matthew retains and which Luke apparently continues to adjust in vv. 23–24. Luke does not maintain all the references to seeing and hearing which Matthew does in the blessing (10:23–24 contra Matt 13:16–17). Luke also seems responsible for

the Greek use of *hypo* after the passive *paredothē* (see v. 22); see G. Dalman, *The Words of Jesus*, 1 (Edinburgh: T. & T. Clark, 1902), p. 284 n. 1. Furthermore, Luke may be responsible for the participle *strapheis* in the transition he provides between the praise-saying and the blessing upon the disciples (v. 23; see also 7:9); see Marshall, *Gospel of Luke*, 438; Jeremias, *Die Sprache*, 155, 189.

16. At Pentecost the open praise of God's work and the bold, spontaneous public witness to God's truth which culminate on the lips of Peter closely parallel the intent of the utterance of Jesus.

17. Leaney, *Luke*, 279. See also Miyoshi, *Anfang des Reiseberichts*, 121.

18. Leaney, *Luke*, 279. See also Smalley, "Spirit, Kingdom and Prayer," 59–71; J. G. D. Dunn, "Spirit and Kingdom," *ExpT*, 82 (1970–71): 36–40; A. A. Trites, "The Prayer Motif in Luke–Acts," in *Perspectives in Luke–Acts*, ed. C. H. Talbert (Edinburgh: T. & T. Clark, 1978), 168–86.

19. "Jesus is filled with joy and the Spirit before uttering an inspired statement" (so E. Schweizer, *"pneuma," TDNT*, 6:332–455, 405. Miyoshi notes the emphasis on speaking here as well (*Anfang des Reiseberichts*, 134–36). Both Schweizer and Miyoshi identify this activity of Jesus as OT prophecy, but the characteristic description is Pentecostal. Clearly, the model for the speaking of Jesus and the infancy narrative witnesses is the all-inclusive view of prophecy in Acts and the early church and not just the OT. The parallels between the Spirit-filled Jesus in 4:18 who, by his speaking effects exorcisms (proclaims "release to the captives"), and his disciples who exorcise demons in his name (v. 17), demonstrate that the pneumatology of Luke does not fit the inadequate generalization that defines both OT prophecy and Lucan pneumatology as inspired speech *only*. It can be said, however, that the pneumatology in Luke *primarily* is concerned with inspired speaking.

20. While both of the Spirit-inspired statements of Zechariah and Simeon were at first addressed to God (Luke 1:67ff.; 2:29ff.), both address a human audience as well. See also Acts 4:24–31. See also Zahn, *Lucas*, 424, and Dibelius, who also cites John 11:41 as an example of prayer with more than one audience (*Tradition*, 281).

21. Leaney, *Luke*, 61, and G. D. Kilpatrick, *The Origins of the Gospel According to St. Matthew* (Oxford: Blackwell, 1946), 76ff. Manson, *Sayings*, 265.

22. E. Lohmeyer contests that this is the case in D. Lohmeyer, *The Lord's Prayer* (London: SCM Press, 1965), 258–61.

23. Leaney, *Luke*, 62.

24. Marshall lists several reasons why this variant cannot be lightly dismissed. He feels, however, that the weight of textual evidence is a telling argument for its exclusion from the Lucan text, and that the various manuscripts supporting its inclusion make it appear weak (*Luke*, 458). Metzger considers Tertullian's evidence weak since he mentions the variant during his "Montanist" period, while earlier he gives no reference to the variant in his references to the Lord's Prayer (*Textual Commentary*, 156–57).

25. Lampe, "The Holy Spirit in Luke," 169ff.

26. For: A. Harnack, *The Sayings of Jesus* (London: [n.p.], 1908), 63ff.; B. H. Streeter, *Four Gospels*, 277; Leaney, *Luke*, 59–68; E. Grässer, *Das Problem der Parusieverzögerung in den synoptischen Evangelium und in der Apostelgeschichte* (Berlin: A. Töpelmann, 1957), 109–41; W. Ott, *Gebet und*

Heil (Munich: n.p., 1965), 112ff.; Lampe, "The Holy Spirit in Luke," 170; R. Freudenberger, "Zum Text der zweiter Vaterunserbitte," *NTS* 15 (1968–69): 419–32.

Against: Metzger, *Textual Commentary,* 154ff.; Jeremias, *Prayers,* 83ff., who believes the association of the Lord's Prayer with the baptism of initiates led to the insertion of the invocation (p. 84); Marshall, *Gospel of Luke,* 458; Lohmeyer, *The Lord's Prayer,* 261–70; J. Carmignac, *Recherches sur le "Notre Père"* (Paris: n.p., 1969), 89–91. Barrett implies that the experience of the church is responsible for it (*Holy Spirit,* 46 n. 1).

27. Unless Matthew is substituting the version of the prayer with which he was familiar for the form preserved in Luke as suggested by Marshall, *Gospel of Luke,* 455.

28. So Lampe declares that "prayer is, in fact, complementary to the Spirit's activity since it is the point at which the communication of divine influence becomes effective for its recipients" ("The Holy Spirit in Luke," 169). See also Plummer, *Luke,* xlv. For an overview of scholarship on prayer in Luke–Acts see A. A. Trites, "Prayer Motif," 168–86.

29. Dunn, "Spirit and Kingdom," 38.

30. Smalley, "Spirit, Kingdom and Prayer," 64.

31. Ibid., 64ff. In some cases the presence of one of the elements is at best implicit, but nevertheless Smalley demonstrates a distinctive Lucan pattern.

32. Ibid., 68ff.

33. The reference to the activities of John the Baptist and to Jesus' activities superseding them may be due to the tendency of Luke and the church to absorb the Johannine elements into Christian preaching and worship.

34. Fitzmyer attributes "Holy Spirit" to Lucan redaction in keeping with his frequent interest in the Holy Spirit. He also sees the absence of the definite article before "Holy Spirit" as evidence of Luke's hand. *Luke* 2.915–16. See also E. Schweizer, *The Good News According to Luke* (Atlanta: John Knox Press, 1984), 192; R. Stronstad, *The Charismatic Theology of St. Luke* (Peabody, Mass.: Hendrickson, 1984), 46.

35. "The 'good gifts' in Mt. should certainly be understood in a spiritual sense (Rom. 3:8; 10:15; Heb. 9:11; 10:1; cf. Lk. 1:53)" (Marshall, *Gospel of Luke,* 470). "*Agatha* (Matt. 7:11) has the same eschatological significance as *pneuma hagion* since *ta agatha* frequently designates gifts of the Messianic Age" (Jeremias, *The Parables of Jesus,* 2d rev. ed. [New York: Charles Scribner's Sons, 1924], 145).

36. C. S. Rodd, "Spirit or Finger?" *ExpT* 72 (1960–61): 157–58.

37. C. H. Talbert, *Reading Luke: A Literary and Theological Commentary on the Third Gospel* (New York: Crossroad, 1986), 133. Stronstad suggests Luke has used a midrash pesher to interpret "good gifts" in terms of the "post-Pentecost reality of the gift of the Spirit" (*Charismatic Luke,* 46). See also R. Tannehill, *The Narrative Unity of Luke–Acts* (Philadelphia: Fortress, 1986), 239.

9 The Holy Spirit and Blasphemy and Witness

> And I tell you, every one who acknowledges me before men, the Son of man also will acknowledge before the angels of God; but he who denies me before men will be denied before the angels of God. And every one who speaks a word against the Son of man will be forgiven; but he who blasphemes against the Holy Spirit will not be forgiven. And when they bring you before the synagogues and the rulers and the authorities, do not be anxious how or what you are to answer or what you are to say; for the Holy Spirit will teach you in that very hour what you ought to say.
>
> —Luke 12:8–12

Luke's unique interest in the Holy Spirit is nowhere clearer than in his account of the blasphemy of the Holy Spirit saying. His context for the blasphemy saying concerns witness,[1] whereas Matthew and Mark do not mention witness in this context. Luke deliberately places the saying in a location quite different from Matthew and Mark.[2] Whereas in Matthew and Mark, Jesus addresses the saying to his enemies, in Luke he addresses it to his disciples. Furthermore, in Luke blasphemy against the Holy Spirit means something quite different than it does in Matthew and Mark. In Matthew and Mark, to blaspheme against the Holy Spirit is to call good evil and evil good; in Luke it is to fail to witness when called upon to do so.

The Context of the Blasphemy Saying in Matthew and Mark

Matthew and Mark relate that the occasion for the blasphemy saying was the curing of a mute demoniac. In response to this healing, Jesus' enemies—the Pharisees in Matthew and the scribes in Mark—

asserted that his power to perform wonders came from an evil source: "He is possessed by Beelzebul, and by the prince of demons he casts out the demons" (Mark 3:25; Matt 12:24). Jesus then warned them against blaspheming against the Holy Spirit. Jesus told them that they were in danger of eternal judgment: "Truly, I say to you, all sins will be forgiven the sons of men, and whatever blasphemies they utter; but whoever blasphemes against the Holy Spirit never has forgiveness, but is guilty of an eternal sin" (Mark 3:28–29; Matt 12:31–32). Immediately Mark adds, "For they had said, 'He has an unclean spirit' " (3:30). Mark is making it clear what this perilous sin is. He does not leave it to his readers to figure it out. In Matthew and Mark the sin of blaspheming against the Holy Spirit is calling good evil and evil good.

This saying of Jesus has caused much concern. But while Jesus was not precluding the possibility of pardon, he was predicting that persistence in such an erroneous belief and practice would result in irrevocable destruction.[3] What hope is there for one who persists in calling good evil and evil good? Such a presupposition would prevent one from recognizing salvation for what it is. Apparently the enemies of Jesus were about to make the same permanent error as Milton's Satan who said, "Evil be thou my good" (*Paradise Lost*, Book 4).

Luke's Relocation of Mark's Blasphemy Saying

In Luke's account of the healing of the mute demoniac (11:14ff.), he includes the exorcism and the Beelzebul accusation that follows without specifically identifying the accusers (*tines;* 11:15).[4] Furthermore, he omits Jesus' warning against blasphemy at this point, inserting instead, the return of the evil spirit pericope (11:24–26) and reserving the blasphemy saying until later. Apparently Luke feels that the saying, "He who is not with me is against me, and he who does not gather with me scatters" (11:23) adequately answers Jesus' accusers.

There is little doubt that in writing his Gospel, Luke is aware of the blasphemy saying, since he uses Mark as his source; and even if Matthew were his source, he would still be aware of it.[5] The parallel material in Matthew 12, Mark 3, and Luke 11 suggests that Luke has both Mark and Q before him. In this passage he sometimes reflects Mark's contents and order, while on other occasions he presents material common to both Matthew and himself which is not contained in Mark. Matthew's placement of the blasphemy saying may reflect Mark's order, and Luke's placement may reflect Q's.[6] Then again Luke may be following a source available only to him, or he himself may be responsible for the unique placement of the logion in his Gospel. Fortunately for our study, a definitive solution to questions of sources is not a prerequisite for the answer to our original question. The presence of the Beelzebub and blasphemy passages in Mark saves the detection of Luke's motives from becoming mired down in hypothetical reconstruction of Q. Whatever the case, Luke's motives and message are clear. He deliberately avoids Mark's version and presents another.

Witness: Luke's Context for the Blasphemy Saying

The context Luke prefers for the saying is found in Luke 12, and not in the chapter that contains the Beelzebul controversy (as Mark). This context presents Jesus exhorting his disciples to give bold witness:

> He began to say to his disciples first, "Beware of the leaven of the Pharisees, which is hypocrisy. Nothing is covered up that will not be revealed, or hidden that will not be known. Therefore whatever you have said in the dark shall be heard in the light, and what you have whispered in private rooms shall be proclaimed upon the housetops.

> I tell you, my friends, do not fear those who kill the body, and after that have no more that they can do. But I will warn you whom to fear: fear him who, after he has killed, has power to cast into hell; yes, I tell you, fear him! Are not five sparrows sold for two pennies? And not one of them is forgotten before God. Why, even the hairs of your head are all numbered. Fear not; you are of more value than many sparrows.

> And I tell you, every one who acknowledges me before men, the Son of man also will acknowledge before the angels of God; but he who denies me before men will be denied before the angels of God. And every one who speaks a word against the Son of man will be forgiven; but he who blasphemes against the Holy Spirit will not be forgiven."

> —Luke 12:1b–10 (Q parallel Matt 10:26–33;
> 16:5–6; 12:31–32; 10:19–20)

Jesus warned his followers to give a truthful witness in contrast to the Pharisees' hypocrisy. Then he warned that in the end, all things would be revealed anyway, so truth should be proclaimed. Jesus mentioned situations which would require witness though it might mean the forfeiture of the disciples' lives. God and his authority were to be respected over temporal rulers, and the believers' witness would have eternal ramifications. At this point Luke includes the blasphemy logion in an abbreviated form when contrasted with Matthew and Mark. Apparently Luke is familiar with both the Matthean and Marcan version of it, for it seems that his version is a conflation of both.

Luke's Version: Blasphemy versus Inspired Witness

Luke's presentation of the blasphemy against the Holy Spirit is both sobering and reassuring. In Luke's version the disciples, not the enemies, are warned of eternal apostasy. They are warned that God the eternal Judge is to be feared above any earthly rulers hostile to the faith; therefore their confession of allegiance to God on earth will procure eternal blessing before his angels. Failure to confess that allegiance, however, will have an equally eternal but negative effect. Thus for Luke, failure to give inspired witness is the blasphemy against the Holy Spirit. Luke gives a solemn commentary on this saying when he presents the betrayal and duplicity of Judas Iscariot as well as that of Ananias and his wife Sapphira. In both instances he tells his readers that they spoke under the influence of Satan (Luke 22:3, 4; Acts 5:3).[7]

Fortunately Luke tempers this sobering warning with hope and good news. Immediately following the quote about fearing God, who has the power to cast into hell (12:5), he points out the great value that God puts on the disciples. They are of greater value than sparrows, and God takes care of sparrows; therefore God will not forget them in their predicament (vv. 6–7). He also softens the force of the warning by appending verses 11–12 to it:

> And when they bring you before the synagogues and the rulers and the authorities, do not be anxious how or what you are to answer or what you are to say; for the Holy Spirit will teach you in that very hour what you ought to say.

Of the synoptists only Luke places this promise in the same context as the blasphemy against the Holy Spirit saying (contrast with Matt 10:19–20 and Mark 13:11). Thus, in the difficult situation where one's actions on earth determine one's eternal destiny, the disciple has great comfort and confidence. The same Holy Spirit whom the disciple must not blaspheme is the same Holy Spirit who will empower and instruct him/her to give a faithful witness for God. Luke spends much of the rest of Luke–Acts showing how this inspired witness was made before authorities in the trials of Jesus,

Peter, John, Stephen, James, Paul, and their colleagues. The disciples in Acts consistently "spoke the word of God with boldness" (4:31) as "they were filled with the Holy Spirit."

Luke sees denial as having the potential of being immediately threatening; however, this does not preclude grace and repentance. Luke relates Peter's denial in Luke 22 and his restoration and empowerment in Acts. As in the case of Judas and Ananias and Sapphira, Luke notes that Peter's denial of Jesus was the result of Satanic influence. Only Luke records the words of Jesus, "Simon, Simon, behold, Satan demanded to have you, that he might sift you like wheat . . ." (22:31). But in Peter's case he escapes the eternal woe of denial, for Jesus continues, " . . . but I have prayed for you that your faith may not fail; and when you have turned again, strengthen your brethren" (22:32).

The theme of inspired, fearless witness is so important to Luke that he preserves two versions of this teaching of Jesus, here at 12:11–12 and at 21:14–15:

> Settle it therefore in your minds, not to meditate beforehand how to answer; for I will give you a mouth and wisdom which none of your adversaries will be able to withstand or contradict.

One might wonder why Luke did not refer to the Holy Spirit in this second passage. Apparently Luke does not feel compelled to do so. By finding the "Spirit" version first, his readers would naturally interpret the second in terms of the first. In analyzing the Spirit of God/finger of God variation found in Matthew and Luke respectively (12:28; 11:20), C. S. Rodd observed that Luke does not always retain references to the Holy Spirit that he finds in his sources.[8]

Luke is not averse to using varied accounts and expressions in relation to the work of the Holy Spirit, in which he may or may not include a specific reference to the Holy Spirit. For example, Luke changes Mark's "David himself, inspired by the Holy Spirit, declared . . ." (Mark 12:36) to "David himself says in the Book of Psalms" (Luke 20:41). In Acts 1:16 Luke has "the Holy Spirit spoke beforehand by the mouth of David." This may be due to a stylistic variation to avoid excessive duplication. This seems to be the reason that Luke preserves two versions of believers' speaking in face of opposition. One refers to the Holy Spirit while the other refers to Jesus himself as the one who would aid the speaker (Luke 12:12; 21:15). This is in keeping with the blending of the work of the Holy Spirit and Jesus in Acts 4 and elsewhere. Luke believes that the two versions amplify the witnessing experiences of the church which center around both Jesus and the Holy Spirit. Not surprisingly, we also find two accounts of Jesus' promise of power to his followers

(Luke 24:44–49; Acts 1:4–8). Thus this duplication in reference to the Spirit's work appears to be a Lucan pattern.

Elsewhere Luke links wisdom, which is mentioned in 21:15, to the activity of the Holy Spirit. In the ministry of Stephen, the source of his wisdom was the Holy Spirit (Acts 6:3, 10; compare also with Luke 2:40). The second version (21:14–15), then, in which Jesus and not the Spirit is mentioned as the one who empowers inspired speech, fits well into Luke's overall program.

In conclusion, Luke deliberately prefers an alternative context for the blasphemy against the Holy Spirit directly, linking it with Spirit-inspired witness in the surrounding context. He jettisons the blasphemy statement in the pericope of the curing of the mute demoniac that he finds in Mark, which warns the enemies of the faith against blaspheming the Spirit by calling good evil. Instead, he wishes to simultaneously warn and encourage believers to avoid blasphemy against the Holy Spirit by confidently relying on the Holy Spirit to give bold inspired witness. Here Luke makes a deliberate choice to drop one synoptic version and replace it with a new application. His governing motive for such bold editing is his overriding interest in pneumatology and witness.

Notes to Chapter 9

1. P. Alexander, "Blasphemy Against the Holy Spirit," *Dictionary of Pentecostal and Charismatic Movements*, ed. S. Burgess, G. McGee (Grand Rapids: Zondervan, 1988), 88.

2. C. E. B. Cranfield lists several reasons for preferring Mark's context for the blasphemy saying over Luke's setting: (1) Matthew supports Mark's context making Q conform to it, (2) Luke 12:10 "does not seem particularly appropriate in its context," (3) Mark's version is more appropriate to the charge of the scribes, and (4) Mark links 3:28ff. with v. 22 by means of v. 30. Mark is restrained in giving links. "We are inclined therefore to regard vv. 28ff. as in its proper historical context." Given the appropriateness of the statement in Mark 3:28ff. which readily defines the sin against the Holy Spirit as ascribing the works of the Holy Spirit to Beelzebul, and the awkward problems created by Luke's context, one has to consider that Mark's context for the saying could have been Q's as well (Cranfield, *The Gospel According to Saint Mark: An Introduction and Commentary*, CGTC, ed. C. F. D. Moule [Cambridge: Cambridge University, 1959], 139). M. Black notes the Aramaic use of parataxis in Mark is reordered "with conspicuous hypotactic participles" in Luke's version of the Beelzebul controversy (*An Aramaic Approach to the Gospels and Acts*, 3d ed. [Oxford: Clarendon, 1967], 189). He suggests this is a "literary rewriting of a saying in the Lucan Q." With the use of *blasphēmēsanti* in Luke's blasphemy pericope (12:10), we have the same rewriting tendency which Black also observes in Luke 11:17ff. Black also identifies

Luke's deliberately soft-pedalling the harsh sentiment retained in Mark as "Luke's editorial work" consisting "of an accommodation of his Jewish material to the Gentile ways of thought and some of this editing consisted in the removal of some passages and the simplification of others" (*Aramaic Approach*, 189ff.). J. Jeremias describes *tō blasphēmēsanti* as redactional (*Die Sprache*, 214). After these non-semitic characteristics of the Lucan form of Q, Black leaves the possibility open that Q in Luke may not consistently reflect original Q (*Aramaic Approach*, 190).

3. The conversion of Saul, the vehement enemy of the church who was convinced that Jesus and his followers were evil, demonstrates that pardon is possible. Only those who persist in the fatal presupposition are doomed.

4. J. M. Creed (*Luke*, 51) has noted that Luke preferred a more generalized audience in contrast to a more specific identification in the synoptic parallels (e.g., Luke 11:15 comp. with Matt 12:24 and Mark 3:22; Luke 11:29 comp. with Matt 12:38, 39 and Mark 8:11; Luke 12:54 comp. with Matt 16:1 and Mark 8:11).

5. There are, of course, some scholars following Griesbach's suggestion that Mark as a source for Luke is not a safe assumption, e.g., W. R. Farmer, *The Synoptic Problem: A Critical Analysis* (Dillsboro, N.C.: Western North Carolina, 1976); B. Orchard and T. R. W. Longstaff, eds., *J. J. Griesbach: Synoptic and Text-Critical Studies 1776–1976*, SNTSMS 34 (Cambridge: Cambridge University, 1978); B. Orchard, *Matthew, Luke and Mark: The Griesbach Solution to the Synoptic Question* 1 (Manchester: Koinonia, 1976). Some who agree with Griesbach suggest that the two-source theory has been seriously challenged with Matthean priority gaining popularity. But much of present scholarship remains unconvinced, as Fitzmyer's article on the sources of Luke suggests: J. A. Fitzmyer, "The Priority of Mark and the 'Q' Source in Luke," in *To Advance the Gospel: New Testament Studies* (New York: Crossroad, 1981), 3–40. Some scholars have completely despaired of solutions to the source problems and suggest that redactional studies avoid making conclusions on the basis of Marcan priority or any particular source theory. Thus Talbert declared, "Employing Mark as a control today is about as compelling as using Colossians and Second Thessalonians to describe Paul's theology"; see "Shifting Sands: The Recent Study of the Gospel of Luke," *Int* 30 (1976): 381–95, esp. 393. A kindred view is expressed by J. B. Tyson. Observing that both the Griesbach and two-source hypotheses use the same data as evidence of proof, he concludes, "We, therefore, stand at a time at which it must be said that we have no dependable knowledge about the sources of Luke." Alternatively, he suggests a "holistic approach" as the basis for redaction studies (Tyson, "Source Criticism of the Gospel of Luke," in *Perspectives on Luke–Acts*, ed. C. H. Talbert [Edinburgh: T. & T. Clark, 1978], 24–39, 36, 39. Such an approach is employed by Talbert in *Literary Patterns*. Indeed no definitive solution to the synoptic source question appears in sight, and redactional observations should not be based on a particular source theory alone. The present author has observed redactional tendencies in the overall work of Luke–Acts, but this does not demand that the evidence that source criticism offers to a redactional analysis should be ignored, especially when the two-document solution still appears to be the best solution. Fortunately, our observations concerning Luke's use of the blasphemy of the Holy Spirit saying are

valid regardless whether the Farrar hypothesis, Griesbach hypothesis, or the two-source hypothesis is accepted. If these observations are true in the two-source system, then they are certainly true in the other two. The only theory that would preclude much of source criticism commenting on our passage is R. L. Lindsey's Lucan priority theory. In this case only general tendencies and more hypothetical sources could shed light on Lucan redactional questions. Lindsey's suggestions, though innovative, are not convincing and are generally not accepted; see his "A New Approach to the Synoptic Gospels: 'A Modified Two-Document Theory of the Synoptic Dependence and Inter-dependence,' " *NovT* 6 (1963): 239–69. For a critique of Lindsey's work see Tyson, "Source Criticism." Fortunately Luke's intense interest in pneumatology and inspired witness is demonstrable in any source theory. Nevertheless the evidence is strong that Luke has adjusted his sources to make the links between the Spirit and witness clear.

6. There are some overlaps between Mark and Q in this passage. See C. K. Barrett, *Holy Spirit*, 60ff. Although one cannot be certain, Q probably contained the blasphemy logion in the same context as Mark. I. H. Marshall suggests that Luke's context may reflect Q because of the repetition of "Son of man" in vv. 8, 10. Yet he also notes the disjointed themes that occur in vv. 8–10 and further suggests that the saying may have been independent and not fixed to any context in the Gospel tradition (*Gospel of Luke*, 510; see also Barrett, *Holy Spirit*, 131).

7. The *Sitz im Leben* for Luke's version is often discussed. Noting Luke's anticipation of the church era in his Gospel, it is suggested that the witness of the church in face of peril is the environment in which two sections of tradition in vv. 8–9, 10, and 11–12 coalesced. This could have occurred in the compilation of Q or by Luke's hand. Others suggest that the saying resulted as a prescience of Jesus himself: M.-J. Lagrange, *Evangile Selon Saint Luc*, 355ff.; Barrett, *Holy Spirit*, 131; H. E. Tödt, *The Son of Man in the Synoptic Tradition*, trans. D. M. Barton (Philadelphia: Westminster, 1965), 119. It is significant that Luke is fond of presenting such situations both in the Gospel and in Acts. Confession and witness are themes close to Luke's heart.

8. C. S. Rodd, "Spirit or Finger?" 157ff. Rodd observes that Luke not only adds references to the Holy Spirit but also deletes them; therefore, the possibility must be considered that Luke deleted the "Spirit of God" reading in favor of the "finger of God." He suggests that Spirit of God may have been inserted in Q to remove an anthropomorphism. Luke may be reintroducing this rare anthropomorphism (which occurs only here in the NT and rarely in OT) because "it may be that the variant form of the saying which Luke knew comes nearer to the originality of the mind of Jesus" (ibid., 58).

10 | The Holy Spirit and Jesus' Farewell Address and Ascension

Then he said to them, "These are my words which I spoke to you, while I was still with you, that everything written about me in the law of Moses and the prophets and the psalms must be fulfilled." Then he opened their minds to understand the scriptures, and said to them, "Thus it is written, that the Christ should suffer and on the third day rise from the dead, and that repentance and forgiveness of sins should be preached in his name to all nations, beginning from Jerusalem. You are witnesses of these things. And behold, I send the promise of my Father upon you; but stay in the city, until you are clothed with power from on high."

Then he led them out as far as Bethany, and lifting up his hands he blessed them. While he blessed them, he parted from them, and was carried up into heaven. And they returned to Jerusalem with great joy, and were continually in the temple blessing God.

—Luke 24:44–53

Jesus' farewell speech and ascension are other important passages for Luke's theme of inspired speaking. In Luke's Gospel, Jesus, in anticipation of the ministry of the early church, gives his farewell address, which is a synopsis of teachings about himself and his ministry in a form frequently paralleled in the sermons in Acts. Jesus commissioned the disciples to be witnesses of this message and told them to wait until they had received the power to do so. Here the stress is on witness, although wonder-working is implicit in the reference to *dynamis* and in the allusion to Elisha's succession to the office of Elijah ("clothed with power from on high"). Although the Holy Spirit is not named specifically in reference to witness (the "promise of my Father" is mentioned, v. 49), Luke's presentation of the lives of Jesus and others in the Gospel demonstrates that the Holy Spirit is indeed the source of the powers being dispensed. More importantly, in Acts Luke explicitly defines the descent of the Holy Spirit as the means by which the disciples spoke authoritatively (2:4). Furthermore, Luke quotes Jesus as specifically identifying the promise received from the Father as the Holy Spirit in his second account of Jesus' ascension (Acts 1:4, 5, 8).

The Ascension as the Catalyst for the Release of the Spirit

Luke's Emphasis on the Ascension

The ascension of Jesus plays a prominent role in the theology of Luke. As early as Luke 9:51 he anticipates it, "When the days drew near for him [Jesus] to be received up [*analēmpseōs*], he set his face to go to Jerusalem."[1] Also, a few verses earlier in the transfiguration account, there is a possible reference to the ascension. Moses and Elijah "spoke of [Jesus'] departure [*exodon*], which he was to accomplish at Jerusalem" (9:31).[2] Luke spends more time discussing the ascension in his Gospel than any other Gospel writer. In Matthew, the ascension is not described, and in Mark no mention is made except in the longer ending, and it is brief: "So then the Lord Jesus, after he had spoken to them, was taken up into heaven, and sat down at the right hand of God" (16:18). Luke not only gives a fuller description in his Gospel, but he also repeats the account of the ascension in Acts, where it immediately follows Jesus' promise of power to witness through the Holy Spirit (1:8ff.). Luke refers to the ascension no less than three times in the first chapter of Acts (vv. 2, 9–11, 22). By carrying over the theme of "the promise of the Father," Luke makes the transition from his Gospel to Acts.

The ascension account in Luke–Acts emphasizes the exalted Christ in his heavenly role. Yet with this christological statement, Luke makes a strong pneumatological statement. The Holy Spirit descends as a result of the Jesus' ascension to the Father: "Being therefore exalted at the right hand of God, and having received from the Father the promise of the Holy Spirit, he has poured forth this which you see and hear" (Acts 2:33). For Luke the ascension triggers the release of the power of the Holy Spirit upon Jesus' followers.

Luke's Hand or Tradition?

Although Jesus' farewell address and the ascension narratives reveal some traditional elements,[3] much of the passages is redactional.

The language and themes bear Luke's stamp.[4] This is especially evident in the vocabulary and syntax. For example, *eipen de* ("then he said") with *pros* ("to") and the use of the preposition *syn* for "to" in 24:44,[5] and the articular infinitive with the genitive to indicate purpose in the phrase, *tou synienai tas graphas* ("to understand the scriptures," v. 45), are typical of Luke.[6] In verse 46 the use of *pathein* for "suffer" is Lucan; of the six times it occurs in the NT it appears five times in Luke–Acts in reference to Christ's death.[7] The prepositional phrase, "from the dead," occurs in the kerygma in Acts, where it modifies "raise" (*egeirein*) and "rise" (*anastēnai;* Acts 3:15; 4:10; 10:41; 13:30; 17:3, 31). R. Dillon considers this part of "the gradual crystallization of the Lucan kerygma."[8]

The idea of witness and the word "witness" itself (vv. 47–48) play a dominant role in Luke–Acts. Of the fifteen occurrences of *martyres* (witness) in the NT, it is used eleven times in Luke–Acts and in the Gospels only at Luke 24:48.[9] Jesus' name and witness are closely related in Acts and may indicate Lucan redaction when found together.[10] The phrase, "repentance for the forgiveness of sins," which occurs in Luke 3:3 and is referred to in Acts 2:38; 3:19; 5:31; 8:22; 26:18, has a specialized meaning and function in Luke–Acts.[11] Yet he may appropriate it from Mark (Mark 1:4; Luke 3:3).

In Luke's mind, Jerusalem dominates as the locus for the church's mission and reception of the Spirit (24:47). It is, as Conzelmann observes, a geographical-theological symbol for Luke.[12] We have already noted Luke's interest in *dynamis* and his deliberate associations of Jesus with Elijah; thus "clothed with power from on high" (v. 49) has a Lucan flavor. Luke concludes the passage with a characteristic reference to joy and praise. Although we do not wish to exhaustively analyze the origins of the passage, we present these distinctively Lucan characteristics to make a point: *If Luke's hand is so heavy in this passage he no doubt has personal theological motives for saying it this way.*

The Message of the Farewell Address

Curiously, with so much Lucan activity present in the farewell speech Luke has Jesus refer to the descent of the Holy Spirit only as "the promise of my Father" (which he identifies as the Holy Spirit in Acts 1:4ff. and 2:33). The question of why Luke does not mention the Holy Spirit by name at this point will be investigated as the elements of the farewell speech are analyzed. This analysis will not only attempt to answer this question, but it will also demonstrate that Luke used elements of the early church kerygma, i.e., preaching, to construct the farewell address and provide a summary of the historical and theological significance of Jesus' ministry.[13] We will see that this is part of Luke's greater program of using the preaching of the early church to provide structure for his Gospel. We will also see that this farewell speech mirrors Luke's understanding of the role of the Holy Spirit.

Fulfillment of Scripture and Inspired Exegesis

Then he said to them, "These are my words which I spoke to you, while I was still with you, that everything written about me in the law of Moses and the prophets and the psalms must be fulfilled." Then he opened their minds to understand the scriptures.

—Luke 24:44–45

The last sermon of Jesus in the Gospel of Luke began like his first public speech: Jesus spoke with authority and interpreted scripture concerning himself (4:18ff.). At Nazareth the Holy Spirit is the guarantor of Jesus' words and exegesis; in the case of the last sermon, an added divine affirmation of his words and his understanding of scripture is his resurrection from the dead. The resurrection provides a divine and irresistible mandate both to speak and to listen. The supernatural affirmations of Jesus' baptism and transfiguration afforded similar opportunities, "This is my Son, my Chosen; listen to him!" (Luke 9:35; see also 3:22). In the farewell address, Jesus summarized his ministry in a divinely appointed speech emphasizing the fulfillment of scripture in his death, resurrection, and preaching, as well as in the Holy Spirit-directed witness of the church. The working of miracles, though an interest in Luke, momentarily fades in the dazzling brilliance of the primacy of the inspired spoken word.

Luke later lets his readers know that the Holy Spirit is responsible for Jesus' interpretation of scripture here. In Acts 1:1–2, Luke says that he has already presented the things which Jesus did and taught "until the day when he was taken up, after he had given commandment through the Holy Spirit to the apostles whom he had chosen" (v. 2). Thus the Holy Spirit directed the first public words of Jesus at Nazareth and his final words to the apostles in Jerusalem.

The Early Church Preaching Summarized

In Luke 24 and Acts 1, Luke relates that Jesus' last words, inspired by the Holy Spirit, correctly interpreted OT scripture. In doing so he authenticates the message of the preaching of the earliest community as he perceives it; for essentially what Jesus says in Luke 24 is a distillation of the early kerygma found in Acts which emphasizes the passion, death, and resurrection of Christ and the call for repentance unto forgiveness of sins. Thus for Luke, the church's preaching carries the highest authority—the authority of none other than Jesus the Christ, the Holy Spirit, and holy writ. It is from this tripartite authority that the church receives its commission, justification, and power to witness to all nations.

The Death and Resurrection of Jesus

> Thus it is written, that the Christ should suffer and on the third day rise from the dead.
>
> —Luke 24:46

The death of Jesus is central in the preaching of the church in Acts, and it is a basic tenet of Christian proclamation throughout the NT.[14] Luke does not speak of the death of Jesus with the theological precision of Paul. He presents Jesus' suffering, death, and resurrection as a process through which salvation is imparted. The meaning of Jesus' death in Luke has been open to debate,[15] but it is not in the purview of this work to resolve the issue.

The resurrection of Jesus, like the death of Jesus, is an important part of the kerygma of the early church, and for that reason Luke spends much time speaking of it. It is important to him and his program because it helps identify Jesus as the Messiah[16] and provides assurance that a similar salvation is available to Jesus' believers.[17] Luke stresses the reality of the resurrection; he goes to great lengths to show that it was a bodily resurrection.[18] Jesus' dying and rising as a man are crucial to Luke. According to J. Neyrey, in Luke's presentation of the resurrection, we see "several major themes which pervade Luke–Acts: (a) he saved others, (b) the Christ cannot save himself, (c) faith saves, and (d) Jesus exhibits faith in God." Neyrey goes on to say:

> In this context Luke portrays Jesus in his crucifixion and death as the Saved Savior. The one who had faith in God-who-raises-the-dead was ultimately saved because of his faith and obedience. And in being saved and exalted, the Saved One became the Savior of others, just as the Lukan Gospel has always proclaimed.[19]

Even though Luke presents Jesus to some extent as otherworldly, he nevertheless considers him human. Failure to recognize the human side of Jesus calls into question the nature of the passion and resurrection, for if he had not been human then his passion would have been a mere sham. Luke links suffering and resurrection together (Luke 24:26 and Acts 17:3). His presentation of Jesus as the Spirit-led man who is led forth to suffer (Luke 4:1–13) challenges any later docetic claims that Jesus was not human.[20] It is not surprising then that the resurrection became an indispensable part of the preaching of the early church as reconstructed in Acts.

Repentance and Forgiveness

And that repentance and forgiveness of sins should be preached in his name to all nations, beginning from Jerusalem.

—Luke 24:47

Although repentance and forgiveness of sins correspond to the work of Jesus, here they are probably in the farewell speech because they characterize the preaching in Acts and in Paul.[21] In verses 47–49 Jesus commissioned his followers to be witnesses of these truths. It is not then surprising that Jesus' recapitulation of that preaching follows the outline of the preaching in Acts. Dillon observes that repentance and forgiveness are "no less effective in qualifying this appointed ministry [that of the apostles] as a continuation of his [Jesus'] own."[22] These two points, especially repentance, are a reflection of the early kerygma which provides a structure for the ordering of Luke's Gospel.[23]

We have seen in previous chapters that in John the Baptist's ministry Luke emphasized repentance, while he emphasized other aspects in Jesus' ministry. This too is a result of Luke's superimposing upon the ministries of John and Jesus the structure of the basic formula for conversion and initiation into the kingdom contained in the kerygma of Acts.

The structure of the salvation message proclaimed in Jesus' farewell address in Luke's Gospel is the same as the order proclaimed in the speeches in Acts. They generally lead to a call to repentance.[24] Conzelmann correctly observes that for Luke, repentance is a specific point in the conversion process and not a general description of conversion as in Mark.[25] The basic steps for conversion in the early church sermons are also reflected here: repentance, often represented by baptism;[26] the name of Jesus as the effective agent in providing forgiveness; and the reception of the Holy Spirit.[27]

Luke often uses the name of Jesus to explain how the ascended Christ can be at work in the post-ascension church.[28] The reference to preaching to all nations, though a prediction and command from Jesus common to the synoptics (Matt 28:19ff.; Mark 13:10; 16:15), is characteristic of Luke's presentation of the work of the church in Acts. The geographical reference, "beginning at Jerusalem," has programmatic implications both in the Gospel[29] and in Acts. In the case of the former,

Lucan redaction seems an inescapable conclusion.[30] The use of "his name" here in verse 47, in contrast to "my name" in verse 49, creates a less personal tone which reflects more the post-ascension preaching of the church than the instructions of the pre-ascension Jesus. The concepts of repentance and forgiveness of sin are indeed a continuation of the ministry of Jesus as Luke's sources presented it, and even the name of Jesus is employed by the Seventy (10:18): The "name" and references to the mission beginning at Jerusalem in chapter 24, however, seem characteristic of the preaching mission of the church which Luke presents in Acts.

Witnesses and the Promise of Power

> You are witnesses of these things. And behold, I send the promise of my Father upon you; but stay in the city until you are clothed with power from on high.
>
> —Luke 24:48–49

The reference to witness in verse 48 is taken by some to be primarily a witness to the resurrection (Acts 1:22; 4:33),[31] but witness must take on a wider significance in the immediate context of Luke 24 and in the overall program of Luke–Acts. The witnesses attest not only to Jesus' resurrection but also to his inspired exegesis and his order for the salvation message and its components. Here the ministry of Jesus is intended as a model for the disciple. This greater function of witness is clearly a Lucan contribution to and expansion of the resurrection account. Witness of the resurrection here is seen by Luke as an attestation of the preaching of Jesus and the church, and the call to witness is also presented as an integral part of that preaching. Fuller observes, "The Evangelist himself integrated the resurrection narrative into his scheme of salvation-history."[32] Dillon likewise notes concerning verse 48: "In *hymeis martyres toutōn* (v. 48) the risen Christ's self-disclosure *through interpretation of the scripture* becomes a mandated 'ministry of the word' for his disciples and his Easter instruction of them therefore seems to become the crucial fundamental of their *martyria*."[33] Furthermore, the concepts of Jesus' name and witness are closely related in Luke–Acts and may indicate Lucan redaction when found together.[34] As a witness to the fact that the scriptures reveal the necessity of preaching to all the nations, the disciples of Jesus in effect are called to fulfill it.[35]

Witness must, then, be seen as having a wider significance elsewhere. The theme of "seeing and hearing," especially in the context of miracles (7:18ff.), shows witness has a larger meaning which continues in Acts. Furthermore, failure to witness in Luke is associated with the blasphemy of the Holy Spirit, while fearless confession is evidence of the Spirit's activity (12:8–12). This shows the concept of witness is an integral part of the greater plan of Luke–Acts, and for that matter, the plan of salvation history. In 24:44–49 witness is clearly part of the proclamation of the good news and not just affirmation of Jesus' resurrection.

In verse 49 Jesus promised to send the promise of his Father before the disciples' ministry began at Jerusalem. This promise is further described as "power from on high." Luke places this reference to the descent of the Holy Spirit (Acts 1:8; 2:33) here to demonstrate how the witness of the disciples will effectively fulfill scripture as predicted by Jesus (Luke 24:49). Luke repeats this in the parallel in Acts 1:8, where Jesus said that as a result of the Holy Spirit's coming upon them, his followers would be witnesses throughout the world. This association of witnessing with the promise of the Father (i.e., the Holy Spirit) makes a redactional statement of paramount importance in Luke–Acts. This entire speech of Jesus summarizes the pre-ascension ministry of Jesus and his pre-Pentecost witnesses, and gives a preview of the witness of the post-ascension church.

When Luke notes that the followers would be clothed with power, he consciously compares the transfer of power from Jesus to his followers with the succession of Elisha to Elijah's office by receiving the prophet's mantle.[36] Like Elijah and Jesus, the church witnessed by the power of the Spirit.[37] This passage, like the rest of Luke–Acts, emphasizes the speaking ministry of the church and the Holy Spirit; it does not, however, deny the secondary yet complementary work of the Spirit in miracles and healings. Luke's use of *dynamis* for "power" here supports this, for elsewhere he often uses it for working wonders.[38]

Why the Absence of the "Holy Spirit" Title?

Given Luke's frequent references to the Holy Spirit, and especially those in the ascension passage in Acts 1:4–8, it is surprising that he does not explicitly say in Luke 24:49 that the Holy Spirit will enable the disciples to witness effectively. Rather he uses the phrase, "the promise of my Father." Since the parallels in Acts 1:4–8 and 2:33 make it clear that the Holy Spirit is synonymous with the promise of the Father, why does he use this variation here? Is it stylistic, or is there another reason? Although Luke is not beyond stylistic variation, the absence of a reference to the title, "Holy Spirit," is uncharacteristic of this Lucan situation. It could be that a source behind the Lucan ascension account contained the reference to the promise of the Father, but since the existence of such a source is uncertain we cannot be sure that this is the case. Apparently Luke wishes to reserve any full explanation of the nature of the empowering of the followers of Jesus until later, when the event actually occurs—in Acts. Thus using the phrase, "promise of my Father," for the Holy Spirit may be here to generate anticipation:

> It is clear that a certain pathos of expectation is meant to be aroused here at the end of the first volume. The disciples are to await the divine "promise" meant for them, a "power" to equip them for their missionary endeavour. It is this momentum of anticipation, artfully built into the junction of his two books, that must account for Luke's choice of words to begin the momentous Pentecost story, Acts 2,1: *en tō symplērousthai tēn hēmeran tēs pentēkostēs* . . . On hearing those words, one will know that the period of waiting is over, and he will be ready to hear the astonishing account of the birth of a new people.[39]

However, more than anticipation is at work here. Luke is conscious that Pentecost was the pneumatic catalyst for the disciples' ministry. Before Pentecost their ministry was only indirectly associated with the Holy Spirit through the spiritual authority invested in Jesus. In making this distinction, Luke is preserving an epochal division which not he but tradition had maintained. The divisions between the era of the OT and John, the era of Jesus, and the era of the universal outpouring of the Spirit are not always maintained by Luke, but in the case of the disciples and the Spirit, he follows the traditional division of time.

Luke describes the work of the witnesses in the infancy narratives as well as the ministry of John and *even* that of Jesus in post-Pentecost terms. Even the reference to the work of the Seventy in "Jesus' name" anticipates the Spirit-empowered work of the post-ascension church (Matt 28:19; Acts 2:38; 3:6, 16; 4:7, 10, 30; and passim). Luke has to restrain himself in order to maintain some semblance of a distinction in the epochs, for he wishes to see all of them, even the era of Jesus, in terms of the post-ascension church's experience with the Holy Spirit.

Luke exercises this restraint in his Gospel, however, in the case of the apostles. When offered opportune situations to describe the apostles' activities in terms of the Holy Spirit, he declines; however, he often describes the work of Jesus in terms of the Holy Spirit. This restraint is especially noticeable in the commissioning of the Twelve (Luke 9:1ff.), the commissioning of the Seventy (Luke 10:1–21), the Petrine confession (Luke 9:18ff. contrasted with Matt 16:13–20, esp. v. 17),[40] and here in the ascension speech (Luke 24:44–49). To the end of the Gospel, Luke avoids describing the pre-Pentecost apostles and disciples of Jesus in the same pneumatological terms as they are presented in Acts, or as the ministries of John, Jesus, and the heralds of the infancy narrative are presented earlier in Luke. Refraining from describing the disciples in these same terms is part of Luke's overall plan for Luke–Acts as well as the general pattern presented in the traditions (John 1:31–33; Q [Luke 3:16]; Acts 1:5; 2:33; 13:24ff.). Luke reveals that the Spirit baptism prophecy uttered by John is not to be fulfilled until after Jesus has ascended to heaven. Only after he records that event in the Gospel, and as the time approaches for the fulfillment of the prophecy in Acts, does Luke explicitly define the witness of the disciples in terms of the Holy Spirit. Luke avoids the explicit association of the ministry of the disciples and the Holy Spirit in Luke for this very reason. Rather, Luke reserves it until he presents the Acts of the Apostles as a fulfillment of John's pneumatological prophecy. Just as he presents the inauguration of Jesus' ministry (4:14, 18) and the beginning of his journey to Jerusalem in terms of fulfillment (9:51), so too, he notes the time had been *fulfilled* for the empowering of the disciples (Acts 2:1). At the right time the disciples too began their mission with power. Thus Dillon notes:

> But, in a typically Lucan mixture of perspectives, those words will also direct the reader's attention *back* to Lk. 9,51 *en tō symplērousthai* that is being inaugurated on the Pentecost: the ascended Lord's "witnesses" will be embarking on the "journey" that is to repeat his own![41]

The Ministry of Jesus as a Paradigm for the Church

Luke sees the ministry of Jesus as analogous to the ministry of the disciples. Pneumatological succession is clearly indicated in the allusion to Elijah and Elisha. In regard to Jesus' ministry as an earthly man the prophetic ministries of both Jesus and his disciples are qualitatively, if not quantitatively, the same.[42] Thus the disciples cannot fully start their ministries until they, like Jesus at his baptism, are empowered with the Holy Spirit, and therefore they wait until the time is fulfilled.[43]

The ascension provides the primary transition between the Gospel and the Acts of the Apostles; it appropriately appears both in the end of Luke and in the beginning of Acts. When the ascension material from both is compiled, major Lucan interests emerge. Jesus gave final instructions to his apostles by the Holy Spirit (Acts 1:2). This pneumatological endowment enabled him to correctly interpret the scriptures, to present the essentials of the gospel, and to predict the empowerment of his spiritual successors. The Acts account supplies further information on the disciples' empowerment: the same Holy Spirit who empowered Jesus would soon clothe them with power (1:5, 8). As a result of this power, the disciples, like Jesus, would give inspired witness. In both of his books, Luke specifically states that the Spirit's power is for witnessing (24:48; Acts 1:8; 2:4ff.; 4:8, 29–31). This transfer of power takes place when Jesus ascends to the Father and pours forth the Holy Spirit upon believers (Acts 2:3, 33). The dominant theme of the Holy Spirit directing inspired speaking is the connection between Luke and Acts. The witness theme provides the important transition between Luke's Gospel and Acts.

Notes to Chapter 10

1. *Analēmpsis* could refer to death as in Pss Sol 4:18; however, in light of the use of the verb *analambanō* in Acts 1:2, 11, 22, "the Lucan references in Acts almost certainly give it a larger connotation," Fitzmyer, *Luke* 1.828. Marshall thinks the primary reference here is death, "but it is hard to resist the impression that there is also an allusion to Jesus being 'taken up' or 'taken back' to God in the ascension especially in view of the presence of Elijah typology in the context (9:54)" (*Gospel of Luke*, 405). See also Plummer, *Luke*, 262.

2. *Exodon* here could be a euphemism for death as in 2 Peter 1:15 (Schürmann, *Lukasevangelium*, 1:588); however, more likely it refers to the death, resurrection, and ascension (Zahn, *Lucas*, 383); J. Maneck, "The New Exodus in the Books of Luke," *NovT* 2 (1955): 8–23; Ellis, *Luke*, 142; Marshall, *Gospel of Luke*, 384; Fitzmyer thinks the broader meaning "seems to fit better with the geographical perspective of Lucan theology," in which Jerusalem symbolizes all three (*Luke*, 1.800).

3. Jeremias sees several phrases as traditional or Aramaic in character in Luke 24:44ff. (*Die Sprache*, 321ff.). Black, *Aramaic Approach*, 59, 115, notes that several items in the Acts passage reflect Aramaic as does Bruce, *The Acts of the Apostles: The Greek Text with Introduction and Commentary* (Leicester: InterVarsity, 1952), 68–71. E. Haenchen detects asyndeton in Acts 1:7, but thinks it is there for effect (*The Acts of the Apostles: A Commentary*, trans. B. Noble, G. Shinn, H. Anderson, R. Wilson [Oxford: Blackwell, 1971], 143). R. H. Fuller, *The Formation of the Resurrection Narratives* (New York: Macmillan, 1971), 116ff., thinks sources underlie our passage. The Aramaic-like structure may or may not reflect the presence of sources at any given point; but given the increased frequency of semitisms in the first part of Acts, it seems unlikely that a Lucan semitizing style would account for them all.

4. E.g., Bultmann, *Synoptic Tradition*, 286; Conzelmann, *Theology*, 157ff.; U. Wilckens, *Die Missionsreden der Apostelgeschichte*, WMANT 5.2 (Neukirchen: Neukirchener Verlag, 1962), 98 n. 1. R. H. Fuller calls the address a "compendium of kerygmatic-christological instruction" (*The Forma-*

tion of the Resurrection Narratives [New York: Macmillan, 1971], 116ff.); see also I. H. Marshall, "The Resurrection of Jesus in Luke," *TynB* 24 (1973): 55–98, esp. 91, and idem, *Gospel of Luke*, 907ff. Marshall agrees that Lucan editing and rewriting occurred but thinks it likely that Luke had some traditional basis for his work. C. H. Talbert (*Literary Patterns*, 58ff.) contends that two distinct traditions could stand behind the ascension accounts of Luke 24 and Acts 1, but the farewell speech in the Gospel "is in its entirety a literary production of Luke, a speech like the speeches in Acts" (p. 60). See also C. H. Dodd, "The Appearances of the Risen Christ: A Study in Form-Criticism of the Gospels," in *More New Testament Studies* (Grand Rapids: Eerdmans, 1968), 117ff.; R. J. Dillon, *From Eye-Witnesses to Ministers of the Word*, AnBib 82 (Rome: Biblical Institute, 1987), 167.

5. Plummer, *Luke*, 561. Use of *syn*: Matt 4x, Mark 6x, John 3x, Luke 23x, Acts 52x, Luke–Acts 75x. See also Fitzmyer, *Luke*, 2.1582; Jeremias, *Die Sprache*, 33, 321.

6. Plummer, *Luke*, lxii; Jeremias, *Die Sprache*, 28, 321.

7. Jeremias, *Die Sprache*, 286; Marshall, *Gospel of Luke*, 905. Fitzmyer, *Luke*, 2.1565–66, esp.1583; B. Gärtner, "Suffer," *NIDNTT* 3:719–26, esp. 723. (Luke 24:26, 46; Acts 1:3; 3:18 with 3:15; 17:3.)

8. Dillon, *From Eye-Witnesses*, 207.

9. Jeremias accepts the word as Lucan but thinks the phrase in which it stands, "You are witnesses of these things" is traditional (*Die Sprache*, 322). Other members of the *martys* word-group occur in the Gospels often in a legal sense. Luke is probably getting his specialized meaning for witness from the tradition of witnessing for the faith before authorities (*martyrion*, Mark 13:9).

10. Dillon, *From Eye-Witnesses*, 212, citing J. Zmijewski.

11. Jeremias, *Die Sprache*, 322; Conzelmann, *Theology*, 99ff.

12. Conzelmann, *Theology*, 189, 213.

13. The traditional sources behind Luke 24 may be responsible for the basic elements of the speech in vv. 44–49, but the terminology parallels the language of the preaching as presented in Acts. This passage indicates that certainly the concepts and perhaps the terms and mission charge come from earlier tradition; but the summary character of this speech resembles the sermons in Acts, and one must consider it likely that Luke had a big hand in expressing the farewell address in these terms. See Fuller, *Formation*, 117ff., where he not only notes synoptic precedents for the elements in the address but also identifies Luke's own hand as well.

14. See C. H. Dodd, *The Apostolic Preaching and Its Developments* (New York: Harper, 1952), who traces the proclamation of the death of Jesus in the Gospels, in Acts, and in the Epistles.

15. See Fitzmyer's discussion of Lucan soteriology, *Luke*, 1.219–27; J. Neyrey, *The Passion According to Luke: A Redactional Study of Luke's Soteriology* (New York: Paulist, 1985), 154–92.

16. "The messianic nature of Jesus" is "proven not necessarily by the resurrection so much as the passion (vv. 7, 26, 46), yet not fully understood except through the resurrection" (G. Osborne, *The Resurrection Narratives: A Redactional Study* [Grand Rapids: Baker, 1984], 145).

17. Ibid., 145–46; Neyrey, *The Passion*, 154–55.

18. Osborne, *Resurrection Narratives*, 145.

19. Neyrey, *The Passion*, 154–55.

20. Gärtner, "Suffer," 3:724.

21. Kerygmatic outlines as reconstructed by Dodd in *Apostolic Preaching*.

22. Dillon, *From Eye-Witnesses*, 213.

23. Jeremias sees "repentance unto forgiveness of sins" as a "fundamental idea in Lucan theology" (*Die Sprache*, 322). This is true, but it is, of course, not his invention but a theme which he readily appropriates. Note that it has parallels in Mark 1:4 (Luke 3:3) and in the remaining references which occur in the preaching in Acts. It is probably a part of the kerygmatic tradition.

24. Wilckens, *Missionreden*, 54, 179; Conzelmann, *Theology*, 213; J. Dupont, *Etudes sur les Acts des Apôtres*, Lectio Divina 45 (Paris: Editions du Cerf, 1967), 433, 440, 460ff.; Dillon, *From Eye-Witnesses*, 213.

25. Conzelmann, *Theology*, 99, 228ff.

26. As noted earlier, baptism has become a metonymy for the proclamation of repentance (Luke 3:3).

27. Dillon also recognizes this correspondence between our passage in Luke 24 and conversion-initiation formulae in Acts (or as he calls it, "ordo salutis"; *From Eye-Witnesses*, 213).

28. Wilckens, *Missionreden*, 179; Dillon, *From Eye-Witnesses*, 210.

29. In Luke 23:5 the work of Jesus is described as beginning in Galilee and proceeding to Judea (i.e., in Jerusalem where the comment was made). See also Acts 10:37–39. Here *arxamenos + apo* ("beginning from") is used as it is in Luke 24:47.

30. Furthermore, Luke uses *arxamenos + apo* in Luke 23:5; 24:27, 47; Acts 1:22; 8:35; 10:37. Clearly it is a Lucan expression. See Jeremias, *Die Sprache*, 301, 322. See Fuller, *Formation*, 118, for discussion of the Lucan character of the reference to Jerusalem. See Conzelmann, *Theology*, 93ff.

31. Flender, *St. Luke*, 120; C. H. Talbert, *Luke and the Gnostics: An Examination of the Lucan Purpose* (Nashville: Abingdon, 1966), 17–32; Marshall, *Luke: Historian and Theologian*, 42ff.; E. Franklin, *Christ the Lord: A Study in the Purpose and Theology of Luke–Acts* (London: SPCK, 1975), 166 (although Franklin notes 24:45–48 "makes the witness wider than to the resurrection alone").

32. Fuller, *Formation*, 119.

33. "You are witnesses of these things," Dillon, *From Eye-Witnesses*, 169. Out of fifteen times in NT, *martyres* occurs eleven times in Luke–Acts and never in the Gospels apart from Luke 24:48. The term appears to have a Lucan flavor. Jeremias accepts the word as Lucan but thinks the structure in which it stands, *hymeis martyres toutōn*, is traditional (*Die Sprache*, 322). Other forms of *martys* occur elsewhere in the Gospels, but it often has a legal meaning there. Other members of the word group occur in the Gospels, and it is probably the synoptic tradition concerning witness before authorities from which Luke inherits this specialized application (Mark 13:9).

34. Dillon, *From Eye-Witnesses*, 212, citing J. Zmijewski.

35. The preaching to the nations is to be taken as part of Jesus' opening their minds to understand the scriptures. Note the parallel structure between the three infinitives, all of which are connected by the coordinate

conjunction *kai.* The last infinitive cannot be separated from *gegraptai* (contra J. Wellhausen, *Das Evangelium Lucae* [Berlin: Georg Reimer, 1904], 141). Thus "to suffer," "to be raised from the dead," and "to preach to all nations" are all fulfillment of the scripture and part of the program of the resurrected Jesus and his church. See Creed, *Luke,* 301; E. Klostermann, *Das Lukas-evangelium,* Handkommentar zum Neuen Testament 5 (Tübingen: Mohr [Paul Siebeck], 1929), 242. Dupont, *Etudes,* 404; Fuller, *Formation,* 117; J. Jervell, *Luke and the People of God: A New Look at Luke–Acts* (Minneapolis: Augsburg, 1972), 56; Dillon, *From Eye-Witnesses,* 207ff.

36. The terminology is common in the NT and LXX (Plummer, *Luke,* 564), but given the common context of prophetic succession, the allusion to Elijah/Elisha seems inescapable. Furthermore, we have already noted that Luke abounds in allusions to Elijah and Elisha. Miracles are intimated here, for after Elijah departed, Elisha—like his mentor—performed the miracle of parting the waters of the Jordan with his mantle. P. Hinnebusch acknowledges the analogy between endowment of the disciples of Jesus with power and the empowering of Elisha by Elijah. He further considers the reference to the cloud in the ascension account in Acts 1:8–9 as another parallel to the ascension of Elijah and the empowering of Elisha (*Jesus the New Elijah* [Ann Arbor, Mich.: Servant Books, 1978], 9ff. See also W. Wink, *John the Baptist in the Gospel Tradition* [Cambridge: Cambridge University, 1968], 44ff.).

37. Should anything else be expected from a passage serving as a summary of the ministry portrayed in the Gospels and Acts where divine speaking is attested by signs and wonders, especially in Acts? The Lucan hand is present here.

38. As forceful as this statement on the Holy Spirit and inspired speaking is, one must merely say that in Luke the Holy Spirit is the "spirit of prophecy" (Schweizer, "*pneuma,*" *TDNT* 6:409). If the spirit of prophecy is taken to mean inspired speaking alone, then it is not an adequate description of the pneumatology of Luke. While it is true that Luke more explicitly identifies speaking with the Holy Spirit, he also associates wonder-working to some extent with the Holy Spirit (e.g., Luke 4:14) as well as with inspired speaking. If Barrett's observation is correct that *dynamis* is the means of working wonders in Luke (*Holy Spirit,* 75ff.), then its presence here in v. 49 would make one think of miracles. Certainly in this passage *dynamis* effects inspired speech as it is apparent that in our context, the promise of the Father, the endowment of power, and witness are inseparably fused together into one event. It is also apparent that the *dynamis* effects the geographical expansion of the witness since the disciples are not to leave Jerusalem until they are clothed in power. It would appear that Luke does not have in mind only one result of the power, i.e., just speaking or just wonder-working.

39. Greek phrase being, "When the day of Pentecost had come" or "had been fulfilled" (Dillon, *From Eye-Witnesses,* 218–19, following J. Kremer).

40. Barrett notes, "There is no occasion then to find in the missionary charge any indication that the Spirit had been given, or was then given, to the apostles" (*Holy Spirit,* 129). In Luke's Petrine confession, he is content to allow Peter to describe the Messiah's ministry in pneumatological terms, the Christ (the Anointed One) of God (subjective genitive). This is unlike Matthew's expanded saying, "You are the Christ, the Son of the living God"

(16:16), and Mark's terse title, "the Christ" (8:29). Unlike Matthew's, Luke's version does not describe the response of Peter in terms of revelation, "Blessed are you . . . for flesh and blood has not revealed this to you but my Father who is in heaven" (16:17). In Acts, Peter again speaks forth revelations, and then it is in the state of being filled with the Holy Spirit. No such reference is made in Luke's Petrine confession.

41. The Greek phrase refers to the "fulfillment" of the time for Jesus' ascension in Luke 9:51 (Dillon, *From Eye-Witnesses*, 219).

42. Conzelmann, *Theology*, 180. As "full of the Spirit" Jesus is not set apart from believers. See also Barrett for similarities (*Holy Spirit*, 101).

43. Dillon, *From Eye-Witnesses*, 219.

11 | *The Holy Spirit and Believers in Acts*

L UKE'S INTEREST IN THE Holy Spirit continues and even increases in the Acts of the Apostles. In Acts, as in his Gospel, Luke predominantly presents the Holy Spirit as the originator of inspired witness. Other issues also revolve around the activity of the Holy Spirit in Acts: the Holy Spirit as judge (e.g., Acts 5:3, 9; 7:51; 13:8), as the giver of joy (Acts 11:23, 24; 13:52; cf. Luke 10:21), and as the inspiration behind OT scripture (Acts 1:16; 4:25; 28:25). However, mission and conversion comprise the crucial issue when examining his pneumatology.

The Holy Spirit as Director of Missions

Throughout Luke's account of Jesus' ministry, we see the Holy Spirit at work in his teachings and miracles, in his prayer and praise, and in every area of his life. Luke even begins the book of Acts with a reference to the Holy Spirit superintending the work of Jesus: "he [Jesus] had given commandment *through the Holy Spirit* to the apostles whom he had chosen" (1:2). Acts 10:38 summarizes the ministry of Jesus as "anointed . . . with the Holy Spirit." Thus Luke sees Jesus' entire mission as directed by the Holy Spirit. Following this same pattern established for the ministry of Jesus, Luke portrays the Holy Spirit as the director and enabler of the activities of the church.

In Acts the Holy Spirit instructs the followers of Jesus to move from one place to another, to refrain from moving, to endure hardship, to foresee future events, and to give inspired witness. Very early in Acts, Jesus himself informs the disciples that they will "receive power" (Acts 1:8). Although this power would enable them to perform wonders, its primary purpose was to enable them to witness (see 1:8; 4:29–31).

In addition to the frequent references to the Holy Spirit's tactically directing the mission of the church, Luke also presents the Holy Spirit as the strategist and director of the larger mission. That is to say, the Holy Spirit not only enabled the believers to witness, but he also directed when and where the witness was to take place. In the case of the ministry of Philip the deacon, "an angel of the Lord" (8:26) and the Spirit (8:29) directed him to go and preach to the Ethiopian official on the road to Gaza. This action took Philip away from the successful Samaritan campaign to minister to one man. What the long-range result of this strategic diversion was is left to the readers' imagination.

Equally surprising is the manner in which Philip left the new convert: "the Spirit of the Lord caught up Philip; and the eunuch saw him no more" (8:39). Here the Holy Spirit not only determined the direction of the mission but also transported Philip to another mission starting at Azotus. Here he preached the gospel along the coast "till he came to Caesarea" (8:40).

In the case of Cornelius and Peter, Luke presents one of the most strategic orders of the Holy Spirit. After both men had received supernatural visitations from God (a vision of an angel for Cornelius and a vision of clean and unclean animals for Peter), the Spirit said to Peter, "Behold, three men are looking for you. Rise and go down, and accompany them without hesitation; for I have sent them" (10:19–20; see also 11:12). Both the angelic visitation and Peter's vision are works of the Holy Spirit. In keeping with the Spirit's strategy, Cornelius' devout soldier and two servants advanced to the south to Joppa, and two days later Peter was accompanying the party north to Caesarea. Peter's ministry in Caesarea was a strategic event in the advancement of the gospel; it provided divine precedent for Gentile participation in the kingdom of God. The Holy Spirit confirmed that indeed a vital shift had taken place in the mission when the Holy Spirit descended upon the household of Cornelius even as the Spirit had fallen on the Jewish church at Pentecost (10:47). Peter told it this way, "The Holy Spirit fell on them just as on us at the beginning" (11:15).

In Paul's ministry the same thing occurred. The Holy Spirit originates the mission of Barnabas and Saul: "the Holy Spirit said, 'Set apart for me Barnabas and Saul for the work to which I have called them' " (13:2; see also v. 4). In Paul's second missionary journey the Holy Spirit forbade him "to speak the word in Asia" (Acts 16:6), and the "Spirit of Jesus" did not permit the evangelization of Bithynia (16:7); rather, the Spirit gave direction for a western Aegean ministry. Paul's journey to Jerusalem and subsequent arrest were also directed by the Holy Spirit: "I am going to Jerusalem, bound in the Spirit" (20:22; see also 19:21). This change in direction was also confirmed by the Holy Spirit through the prophetic activity of Agabus and other church members (20:23; 21:4, 11).[1] Clearly, in Acts the followers of Jesus received direction and empowerment from the Holy Spirit much the same way that Jesus did.

The Holy Spirit and Conversion in Acts

The role of the Holy Spirit in conversion in Luke–Acts has become a point of contention in church circles. Until recent emphasis on redactional distinctives in the NT, it was often assumed that Paul's view of the role of the Holy Spirit in conversion-initiation explained the phenomenon in Luke–Acts. Although Luke is not averse to associating the Holy Spirit with conversion, this is not his major pneumatological thrust. Some misunderstanding has arisen when the role of the Holy Spirit in empowering for witness is confused with conversion.

Pentecost and Conversion (Acts 2)

The issue of the Holy Spirit's role in conversion immediately arises in the first two chapters in Acts. Many assume that the Pentecost experience is a conversion to Christ and an initiation into the church,[2] when in reality, Luke primarily considers it an experience of empowerment for mission.[3] The assumption that it is a conversion-initiation experience is often made because Luke's pneumatological motives are assumed to be the same as Paul's. For example, in Romans 8:9 Paul declares, "Any one who does not have the Spirit of Christ does not belong to him." Paul is talking about the necessity of the presence of the Holy Spirit in a person's life in order for that person to *be* a Christian. Paul is addressing the ontological question: How is one a Christian? It is often assumed that Luke is addressing that same question.[4] In reality, however, this is not the issue that Luke is addressing here. Luke relates the events of Pentecost to answer the question, How do we witness? While the answer to both Paul's and Luke's question is the same— through the Holy Spirit—their questions are different. Each writer's unique view here is like a specialized optical lens. Luke's lens brings the issue of witness up close and in doing so narrows the field of vision, while Paul's view is broad and includes many issues of the Holy Spirit at the expense of the fine detail. To assume that they view the Spirit the same way only creates confusion and misunderstanding. From everything we have seen so far, Luke's emphasis is on empowerment to witness through the Holy Spirit; he continues this at Pentecost. Luke makes this clear in several ways.

First, as we have seen in chapter 10, Luke stresses empowerment in the ascension in Luke 24 and Acts 1–2. The disciples were witnesses who were "clothed with power from on high" (24:49). In Acts 1:8, Jesus indicated that the descent of the Holy Spirit was to empower the witness of the disciples. Clearly, in the fulfillment of the promise Luke emphasizes *not* repentance, initial confession of Jesus as Lord, or baptism of the disciples, but *witness* inspired by the Holy Spirit: "And they were all filled with the Holy Spirit and began to speak in other tongues as the Spirit gave them utterance" (2:4, 11).

The language of Luke demonstrates that witness and not conversion is paramount in his mind here. He describes the recipients of the Holy Spirit in the same terms in which he presented the witnesses in the infancy narrative in the Gospel: they gave inspired witness when "filled with the Holy Spirit" or when the Holy Spirit "was upon them" (see chapter 2). Luke does not intend Jesus' experience with the fullness of the Spirit to connote conversion (Luke 4:1). Rather, it refers to inspired witness (see chapter 4). Nor does Luke intend the phrases, "filled with . . ." or "full of the Holy Spirit," in the early part of his Gospel to describe conversion. On the contrary, the Holy Spirit inspired witnesses are described in terms of holiness and devotion to God prior to their empowerment (1:6, 28, 30, 35; 2:25, 37).[5] It seems incredible that Luke would present the disciples as witnesses of Jesus' death, resurrection, and ascension; as recipients of his commission (24:47–49) and blessing (24:51); as joyful (v. 52; Paul defines joy as a fruit of the Spirit in Gal 5:22), united (Acts 1:14, Paul refers to "unity of the Spirit" in Eph 4:3); and devoted to prayer (1:14); and yet not see them as converted. Apparently Luke considers the pre-Pentecost believers as just that—believers in Jesus, converts to his message, who were about to be empowered for a special mission.

Clearly, Luke ignores the so-called Lucan epochs when he speaks of the Holy Spirit and participation in the kingdom. For Luke, the infancy narrative, John the Baptist, Jesus, and his faithful followers are part of the same kingdom movement; they all function with the same Spirit of the kingdom. It seems, therefore, rather arbitrary to assume that Romans 8 provides adequate commentary on the descent of the Spirit at Pentecost. If one must include Paul in the discussion, then why not apply Romans 10:9: "If you confess with your lips that Jesus is Lord and believe in your heart that God raised him from the dead, you will be saved"? Surely the pre-Pentecost disciples fulfill these criteria for conversion.[6] Caution must be used in calling on other NT writers to clarify Luke since other canonical writers sometimes address different questions in their pneumatologies.

The Spirit and Conversion in Peter's Pentecost Sermon (Acts 2:38)

Like Paul, Luke is probably not averse to associating the Holy Spirit with conversion. One can infer from the conclusion of Peter's sermon that this is so: "Repent, and be baptized every one of you in the name of Jesus Christ for the forgiveness of your sins; and you shall receive the gift of the Holy Spirit" (2:38). Yet this interpretation is not the only option. Presumably those present at Pentecost experienced a temporal gap between their repentance and the empowerment of the Holy Spirit. So too in the conversion of the Samaritans, there was a hiatus between repentance-baptism and reception of the Holy Spirit (8:6, 14–17). This somewhat parallels the experience of Jesus in which there appears to be a delay between his baptism and the descent of the dove: "After Jesus had been baptized [*baptisthentos*, aorist participle] and while praying [*proseuchomenou*, present participle], the heaven was opened, and the Holy Spirit descended upon him in bodily form, as a dove" (Luke 3:21–22a, my trans.). Here Luke is responsible for the shift in tense from aorist to present. He superimposes it and other distinctive syntax upon the synoptic tradition (see chapter 4).

One could argue that Luke's conversion formula is intended to be one process on the basis of the experience of Paul in Acts 9, of Cornelius in 10, and of the twelve disciples at Ephesus in 19.[7] Haenchen notes that Luke "says nothing in v. 41 of the newly baptized speaking in tongues, although in v. 38 they have received the Holy Spirit."[8] Yet this omission does not preclude Luke's intent of empowerment for the reference to the Holy Spirit. Stronstad observes:

> Peter restricts the eschatological gift of the Spirit to the penitent, the saved. As he addressed the crowd Peter announced that the last days had arrived—both the Christ and the Spirit were operative in Israel. Undoubtedly, this announcement aroused a false expectation among the pilgrims, namely, that they would also freely participate in the promised eschatological gift of the Spirit which they had just witnessed. Having first denied their automatic participation in salvation, Peter now denies their automatic reception of the Spirit. While Joel announced the eschatological gift of prophecy "for all mankind," Peter informs his audience that the term means "all penitent, not all Israel." . . . Peter announced that the prophetic gift of the Spirit is potentially universal.[9]

In the following context, witness by the new Christian community resulted; they "spoke the word with boldness" (4:31). While it is apparent that the new converts of 2:38 were empowered for ministry, it cannot be said that either the reference to "filled with the Holy Spirit" in 4:31a or Peter's reference to the "gift of the Holy Spirit" in 2:38 resulted in the recipients of the Spirit speaking in tongues. On the contrary, neither context refers to glossolalia.[10] Furthermore, the reference to the gift of the Holy Spirit does not have to have an explicit fulfillment for Luke to intend it to have an empowerment meaning. It could have salvific import here, but Luke's pattern usually is empowerment for witness, and he apparently has the same in mind here with conversion, at best, a peripheral intent. Luke himself is responsible for the ambiguity here. In the events that follow as well, it is not always clear whether Luke is referring to the Holy Spirit in relation to conversion or to inspired witness. Elsewhere, when Luke refers to the gift of the Holy Spirit, an endowment for witness is intended (e.g., Acts 8:20; 10:45–46; 11:17).

The Samaritan Pentecost (Acts 8:4–17)

Without question, in the conversion of the Samaritans there is a period of time between the baptism of the converted and their Spirit-empowerment. As a result of Philip's proclamation of the gospel, which was accompanied by miracles, they were baptized (8:12). Then the apostles from Jerusalem sent Peter and John who laid their hands on the Samaritans, "and they received the Holy Spirit" (8:17). This delay of Spirit-reception is not without precedent, as we have seen earlier. The delay in the reception of the Holy Spirit causes a problem only if it is assumed that Luke sees the Holy Spirit primarily as an agent of conversion in this passage.[11] However, some have seen the reception of the Holy Spirit subsequent to salvation as necessary so that the Samaritan believers would be recognized as full members of the church receiving the Holy Spirit from the hands and with the blessing of the Jerusalem apostles.[12]

While the delay of Spirit-reception may well have served to confirm another race as *bona fide* Christians, it would have also afforded an equally important opportunity for an *apostolic* condemnation of Simon's avaricious and misguided assumption that the Spirit of God was a spirit of magic. It is safe to assume that here among the Samaritans, as elsewhere in Luke–Acts, the activity of the Holy Spirit reflects inspired witness of the power of God, even to a magician (or later to a false prophet and seven counterfeit exorcists; see 13:4–12; 16:16–18; 19:11–20).

The Spirit and the Conversion of Saul of Tarsus (Acts 9:22)

After Saul/Paul was blinded by a vision of Jesus on the road to Damascus, the disciple Ananias was sent to lay hands on him that he might regain his sight and "be filled with the Holy Spirit" (9:17). Paul experienced an immediate healing and then was baptized. A case could be made here that Paul was filled with the Holy Spirit when he was baptized.[13] Elsewhere in Luke–Acts the phrase, "filled with the Holy Spirit," effects inspired witness. Is this an exceptional use of the phrase to note conversion? Probably not,[14] for in 9:20, as a result of being filled with the Holy Spirit, "in the synagogues *immediately* he [Paul] proclaimed Jesus, saying 'He is the Son of God' " (my ital.). Bruce suggests that the filling "was necessary for the prophetic service indicated in ver. 15."[15] Ananias did not proclaim Jesus as Lord to Paul; the risen Jesus himself did—before Paul arrived at Damascus (9:3–8). Paul was already in a state of prayer *before* Ananias arrived (v. 11). A case could be made for Paul's conversion on the road to Damascus instead of in the city of Damascus. Ervin argues that Ananias addressed Paul as brother (*adelphe*) because he was already a Christian at their meeting.[16] Double entendre could be on Luke's mind: the Holy Spirit in conversion and witness. We will discuss this passage more when we examine fullness in the Spirit below.

The Spirit, Conversion, and Cornelius (Acts 10)

The incident of Cornelius' reception of the Holy Spirit also raises the issue of the relationship between the Holy Spirit and conversion. Again we find that Luke does not address the issue with clarity. He describes Cornelius in terms that one would expect to be used of one already converted. Luke calls him devout (*eusebēs*) and a God-fearer, i.e., an adherent of the Jewish faith yet not a proselyte who has accepted circumcision.[17] Cornelius was engaged in liberal almsgiving among the Jews[18] and was in constant prayer (v. 2). These latter two activities particularly met with divine approval, for the angel in the vision said, "Your prayers and your alms have ascended as a memorial before God" (v. 4). Even his household and some of his military unit apparently were God-fearers, for he dispatched two servants and a "devout soldier" [*stratiōtēn eusebē*] to Joppa to summon Peter. "We may say, indeed, that he [Cornelius] had every qualification short of circumcision which could satisfy Jewish requirements."[19]

Furthermore, Cornelius and his household apparently had some previous knowledge of the ministries of John, Jesus, and the repentance-kingdom movement; for in his sermon Peter said to them, "The word which He sent to the sons of Israel, preaching peace through Jesus Christ (He is Lord of all)—you yourselves know the thing which took place throughout all Judea, starting from Galilee, after the baptism which John proclaimed" (Acts 10:36–37, NASB). Cornelius' lifestyle displayed the fruits of repentance which Luke alone carefully defines in the preaching of John the Baptist (Luke 3:10–14). It would be difficult not to see Cornelius as converted prior to Peter's arrival in the same sense that the believers in Luke's infancy narrative, whose experiences Luke describes in post-Pentecost terms (see ch. 2), were converted (Acts 11:9).

Yet at the same time, Luke vaguely associates the events at Caesarea with repentance. Baptism in the name of Jesus Christ is belatedly administered (10:48). The descent of the Spirit is seen as proof that belief in Jesus has occurred: "If God therefore gave to them the same gift as He gave to us also after believing in the Lord Jesus Christ, who was I that I could stand in God's way?" (11:17, NASB; see also v. 16).[20] In Peter's justification of the Gentile outreach to the Jerusalem brethren, Luke recounts that the Gentiles received the Holy Spirit as did the Jerusalem church at the beginning. On the basis of this manifestation of pneumatic activity, the Jewish-Christians "glorified God, saying, 'Then to the Gentiles also God has granted repentance unto life' " (11:18). This reference to repentance could indicate that repentance and conversion on the part of Cornelius' household occurred either during Peter's sermon, or at the moment they interrupted the sermon with speaking in tongues and praising God as a result of the Holy Spirit's falling upon them (10:44–46).[21] This interpretation seems to be supported by Peter's report to the church at Jerusalem. He related that Cornelius told him that the angel said, "[Peter] will declare to you a message by which you will be saved" (11:14). On the other hand, the reference to repentance in 11:18 could mean that the Holy Spirit's descent upon the Gentiles was evidence that a lifestyle of repentance had already been established and that repentance did not initially occur in the middle of Peter's sermon. The household of Cornelius was empowered by the Holy Spirit to give witness explicitly concerning God's greatness and implicitly concerning their own repentant and therefore acceptable state before God.[22] Luke does not say exactly when the conversion occurred or what the Holy Spirit's role was in the conversion. On one hand, it appears as though Cornelius' conversion was close to, if not simultaneous with, his reception of the Holy Spirit. But on the other hand, Cornelius' fruits of repentance preceded Peter's ministry. Luke's primary point is that Cornelius' reception of the Holy Spirit with the resulting Spirit-inspired witness was evidence that conversion had occurred at some time. Here the speaking in tongues and praise to God served both as a witness to God and as a sign to the people that the Gentiles too could be participants in salvation history. Although the precise moment of conversion is not clear, the Spirit-witness of Cornelius and his household confirmed that at some point they had repented and believed in Jesus. The empowerment presupposed conversion.

Luke's reference to the Gentiles' reception of the Spirit in terms of witness clouds the issue. Apparently Luke is not addressing the same question that some of his modern readers ask of him, such as: What is the role of the Holy Spirit in conversion? Luke does not say receiving the Spirit effected the conversion as Paul might, but only that the Spirit confirmed through Spirit-witness that it had occurred. For Luke, the precise definition and description of conversion is not necessary for his purpose; rather, Spirit-inspired witness dominates his thoughts and vocabulary. In the experience of Cornelius and that of the Samaritans in Acts 8, we see that Luke's understanding of the relationship between conversion, baptism, and Spirit-reception is fluid. Luke's pneumatology refuses to fit into neat little boxes.

The Spirit, Conversion, and the Ephesian Disciples (Acts 19:1–7)

Luke perpetuates this ambiguity between conversion, Spirit reception, and inspired witness in Acts 19. When Paul arrived at Ephesus, Luke notes that Paul found some disciples who had neither received the Holy Spirit when they believed nor "even heard that there is a Holy Spirit" (19:2). They had received only the baptism of John the Baptist. Paul acknowledged that while John's baptism was related to repentance, his ministry also called for people to anticipate the greater ministry of the Messiah. These disciples then accepted rebaptism in the name of the Lord Jesus and the laying on of hands. As a result, "the Holy Spirit came on them; and they spoke with tongues and prophesied" (v. 6). Several questions arise in this event: Whose disciples were they, John's or Jesus'? Was Paul rejecting John's baptism? Why were these disciples rebaptized? Was the coming of the Holy Spirit indicative of their conversion or their empowerment?

The Disciples. Is Luke intimating that these men were followers of the Baptist only? Probably not. When Luke refers to followers of John in his Gospel they are specifically called "disciples of John" or "his disciples" (Luke 5:33; 7:18, 19; 11:1). Usually in Luke's Gospel "disciples" without further description refer to Jesus' disciples. In Acts, disciple (*mathētēs* or *mathētria*) consistently refers to followers of Jesus[23] (29 times; see especially 11:26 where the disciples are specifically called "Christians"). Apparently, Paul at first assumed these "certain disciples" were full-fledged followers of Jesus.[24] Having submitted to repentance baptism certainly would not preclude them from being considered part of the Christian community. One would expect Luke to specifically refer to these people as "John's disciples" as he does elsewhere if that were his intent.[25]

Also this incident immediately follows another case of a believer in Jesus who was acquainted only with the baptism of John. Apollos "had been instructed in the way of the Lord; and being fervent in spirit, he spoke and taught accurately the things concerning Jesus, though he knew only the baptism of John" (18:25). He subsequently received from Priscilla and Aquila instruction concerning "the way of God more accurately" (v. 26). Luke does not describe this instruction as a conversion, nor is Apollos rebaptized. Paul initially raised the question about the Holy Spirit because he was primarily interested in empowerment. If he were assuming that reception of the Spirit automatically occurred at the point of belief as sometimes is assumed,[26] then why would he ask, "Did you receive the Holy Spirit when you believed?" Furthermore, how would Paul have expected to receive affirmation of an internal work of the Holy Spirit? Assuming that an empowerment is the intent of the reference to the Holy Spirit here is less problematic.

The disciples' response that they "have never even heard that there is a Holy Spirit" (v. 2) is obviously hyperbolic. It should not be assumed that lack of information about the Holy Spirit is an indication that they are not Christians. One also could argue that not knowing anything about the Holy Spirit would be indicative that they knew *little* about Jesus and John. In the synoptic and Johannine presentation of John the Baptist's preaching, the Holy Spirit has a prominent role, and Christian writers would have us believe that prophecy about the Holy Spirit was an integral part of John's message.[27] Furthermore, it does not seem possible that any initiates of John's baptism could be ignorant of the role of the Holy Spirit in the Hebrew scriptures.

Why Rebaptism? Paul (and Luke as well) was not rejecting the efficaciousness of John's baptism; for he expressly said that it was effective for repentance (19:4). In his Gospel Luke describes John's baptism as "a baptism of repentance for the forgiveness of sins" (Luke 3:3; see also Acts 10:37 where John's baptism is a metonymy for the call to repentance). Since the Christian rite of baptism also involved repentance and forgiveness of sins (Luke 24:47; Acts 2:38), John's baptism was accepted and perpetuated by the church. Because it also pointed his initiates to Jesus the Messiah, it had a link with the name associated with salvation, i.e., Jesus (Acts 4:12). (In Luke–Acts the ministries of John and Jesus are not as separate as first appears.)

Why then did Paul rebaptize these disciples? Was it that Paul considered John's baptism ineffective? For repentance and subsequent forgiveness it was not ineffective, but for empowerment it was. The baptism of Jesus is effective for both, but apparently the disciples did not need to repent at that point. In Luke–Acts Jesus is presented as the Baptizer in the Holy Spirit in keeping with the synoptic tradition (Matt 3:11; Mark 1:8); however, in Luke–Acts the empowering aspect of Jesus' baptism is emphasized (see chapter 3; Luke 3:16, 21–22; Acts 1:5; 2:33). So in Paul's ministry to the Ephesians, he first further explained the faith; second, he baptized them in the name of Jesus; and, third, he laid hands on them resulting in the Holy Spirit coming upon them. This visitation of the Spirit empowered them to witness by speaking in tongues and prophesying (19:6). In like manner Apollos, being fervent in spirit/Spirit, was able to witness more effectively concerning the Lord Jesus (18:25, 28). Here, as elsewhere, Spirit-reception effects a powerful witness, a witness which may indirectly cast light on the question of conversion.[28]

Conversion or Empowerment?

In these instances the question, "What is the role of the Holy Spirit in conversion?" keeps recurring. One cannot too readily assume that the dominant role of the Holy Spirit is in conversion; inspired witness is also present. Some too quickly read Luke's pneumatology with Pauline-colored spectacles. Yet blatant harmonization is not the only reason for confusion; Luke himself is partly responsible for the ambiguity.[29] Luke does not clearly delineate between the Spirit's role in conversion and empowerment for mission. This is especially true in Acts 5:29–32 where the preaching of repentance, witness of believers, and witness of the Holy Spirit are mentioned in close proximity. Why is Luke not clearer? It is primarily because the role of the Holy Spirit in conversion is not his major interest. His fundamental concern is to show how the witness concerning Jesus spread. Luke is not averse to associating the Holy Spirit with conversion but, unlike Paul, he does not ardently press ontological issues onto his pneumatology. Luke's major emphasis concerning the role of the Holy Spirit is much simpler: inspiring and empowering witness.

As we saw elsewhere, Luke does not always honor the bound-
aries of the so-called Lucan epochs of the salvation history; the old,
middle, and new often flow together. The differences between John's and
Jesus' roles are not stringently maintained. Luke does not make clear
what the status of the infancy narrative witnesses, John the Baptist, and
pre-Pentecost disciples is in the kingdom of God as compared with that
of the post-Pentecost disciples. It is especially true that Luke ignores
epochal distinctions when he presents the Holy Spirit's empowering
inspired witness. Therefore, it is not surprising that Luke leaves his
readers with unanswered questions about the role of the Holy Spirit and
conversion. We must not go beyond his questions concerning the Holy
Spirit and superimpose Paul's pneumatology or our own onto Luke's
pneumatology. The results inevitably will be confusing, disappointing,
and divisive. Luke's redactional interests must be respected, and we must
not read too much into the text concerning the converted state of the
recipients of the Holy Spirit since Luke himself does not clarify the
point. As will be apparent in the remaining material in Acts, inspired
witness dominates Luke's pneumatology.

"Filled with the Holy Spirit," "Full of the Holy Spirit," and Inspired Speech

Luke employs phrases that appear both traditional and Lucan
in character to indicate the presence of the Holy Spirit in instances of
inspired speaking. "Baptism in the Holy Spirit," "receiving the Holy
Spirit," "the gift of the Holy Spirit," and "the Holy Spirit coming upon"
an individual or group are apparently traditional phrases that Luke
employs to express his specialized pneumatological interest. The phrases
"filled with the Holy Spirit" and "full of the Holy Spirit," however, have
an unmistakably Lucan stamp, although these expressions themselves
may antedate Luke. The concept of fullness in relation to the Holy Spirit
has a specialized meaning in Luke's work regardless of its ultimate origin.

Luke uses this expression to provide crucial theological transition throughout his two-volume work. The phrase, "filled with" or "full
of the Holy Spirit," indicates primarily that inspired witness about Jesus
or against the devil is occurring. Any other significance of the expression
is probably peripheral to Luke's intentions. Its use in the infancy narratives, in the post-Pentecost church, and in the life of Jesus himself serves
to blend the so-called three epochs of Luke[30] into an indivisible pneumatological unit. Luke's overall program is one of witness to the Spirit-
anointed Christ and his impending kingdom from Jerusalem to Rome.

By using the same phraseology for the witnesses provided by the precursors to Jesus, Jesus himself, and his followers, Luke is declaring that the same provision of the Holy Spirit authenticates the message of salvation. In this, Luke demonstrates that the kingdom movement—of which Zechariah, Elizabeth, Mary, John, as well as Jesus and his followers, are a part—is in the mainstream of Jewish salvation history. This is the main task to which Luke addresses his pneumatology.

Specialized Meanings for "Filled" and "Full"?

Luke's presentation of the Holy Spirit is indeed varied. The concept of "filled with the Holy Spirit" (*pimplēmi* + genitive of Holy Spirit) is used perhaps to describe the initial reception of the Holy Spirit (Acts 2:4) and to indicate that a special dispensation of the Spirit was responsible for the authoritative speaking of believers (2:4; 4:8, 31; 9:17; 13:9). Even when the phrase occurs where initial reception of the Spirit is mentioned, inspired speaking is also present in the context. The phrase, "full of the Holy Spirit" (*plērēs* + genitive of the Holy Spirit), also has more than one use in Acts. It can refer to the quality of a personality (6:3, 5; 11:24)[31] or to the presence of divine power in a person enabling him/her to speak or act authoritatively (e.g., 7:55; Luke 4:1, 14). It may be generally true that Luke uses "full of the Holy Spirit" to express the character of a disciple and "filled with the Holy Spirit" to indicate the empowering of an individual on a specific occasion to speak authoritatively.[32] Yet the contexts for both expressions reveal Luke's interest in inspired speaking. Thus the uses of *plērēs* and *pimplēmi* do not always fit into a simplified pattern. Both expressions, however, do occur in contexts in which inspired speaking is the major theme. Marshall notes the use of both "filled" and "full" to designate that believers spoke "effectively as witnesses to Christ."[33]

Analysis of Passages with the Phrase, "Full of the Holy Spirit"

Stephen: Acts 6:3, 5, 8, 10; 7:55. It is significant that Stephen, who along with the other deacons is described as "full of the Spirit and wisdom" (6:3),[34] is later singled out and described with references to fullness of the Holy Spirit (6:5 with v. 8)[35] immediately prior to the narration of his disputing with the men of the synagogue of the Freedmen (6:9–12) and before his defense speech at his trial (7:2–53). It is stated that all of the deacons are full of the Spirit of wisdom or full of the Holy Spirit and wisdom (6:3), but in the actual lists of names (6:5) only Stephen is described as "full of the Spirit and faith." It is true that the expressions of fullness denote quality and that this quality may effect various manifestations (6:8).[36] The instances of "full of the Spirit" may be traditional descriptions of Jesus and his followers,[37] but *plērēs* is a Lucan preference word (in Luke–Acts 10 times; rest of NT 6) and especially so in association with the Holy Spirit. It would appear that Luke has his usual meaning in mind when he includes the phrase here, i.e., enabling to speak authoritatively. The observation is inescapable when one notices that after references to Stephen's spiritual fullness (6:3, 5, 8), the main task in which that influence is employed is in speaking: "But they could not withstand the wisdom and the Spirit with which he spoke" (6:10). The capstone to this specialized use of "fullness" in relation to speaking occurs in 7:55 when Stephen, again described as "full of the Holy Spirit," saw a vision of Jesus with God and related it to his audience. Both the perception of the vision and Stephen's description of it are results of being "full of the Spirit."[38]

Barnabas: Acts 11:24. The last use of "full of the Holy Spirit" in Acts occurs in 11:24. The context is insightful: "And he exhorted them all to remain faithful to the Lord with steadfast purpose; for [*hoti*] he was a good man, full of the Holy Spirit and faith" (11:23b–24). This reference to Barnabas is a description of his character, but Luke includes this description because of the activity of Barnabas in verse 23. Barnabas exhorted (*parekalei*) the new church in Antioch. The *hoti* ("that") in verse 24 functions as a causal conjunction and should be translated "for,"[39] which is characteristic of Luke's usage elsewhere (Luke 9:12; 13:31; 16:24). (Note that in 9:12 Luke inserts this use of *hoti* into the Marcan material.) The question arises: Why does Luke call Barnabas "full of the Holy Spirit and faith"? Luke provides the answer: because of his exhortation.[40]

The Gospel Parallel: Luke 4:1, 14, 18. These uses of "full of the Holy Spirit" parallel Jesus' experience expressed in Luke's Gospel. Jesus is described as "full of the Holy Spirit" (4:1) after his baptism and prior to his temptation. Nowhere is evidence of Luke's redactional contribution clearer, for only Luke among the Synoptic Gospels inserts "full of the Holy Spirit" here (Matt 4:1; Mark 1:12; Luke 4:1). As we noted earlier, this is not just a superlative compliment to Jesus' nature and character nor just a summary of the results of his baptism; rather, it explains how Jesus successfully combatted Satan in the temptation. Jesus accomplished this not by means of miraculous self-attestation or through public wonder-working, but through inspired speaking while being "full of the Holy Spirit." In 4:14, Jesus is described as "returning in the power of the Spirit" to Galilee prior to his inaugural speech at Nazareth where he announced that he was anointed of the Holy Spirit (4:18). Here too he refused to perform wonders; the ministry at his hometown was inspired speech. (See chapter 6.) Thus Luke's primary use of "full (*plērēs*) of the Holy Spirit" is to demonstrate that the speaker is divinely inspired.

"Filled with the Holy Spirit" and the Reception of the Holy Spirit

Pentecost: Acts 2. "Filled with the Holy Spirit" (*pimplēmi* + genitive of Holy Spirit) also occurs in Acts in contexts where inspired speaking is the dominant theme. The classical passage around which much commentary and controversy revolve is Acts 2, Luke's Pentecost account. Interpretation of this event is crucial for the classical Pentecostal and charismatic movements. Only here, and perhaps in Acts 9:17 and Luke 1:15, is the reception of the Holy Spirit described in terms of the fullness of the Holy Spirit. Elsewhere the experience is described as baptized in the Holy Spirit (Luke 3:16; Acts 1:5; 11:16); the Holy Spirit coming upon someone (Luke 24:49; Acts 1:8; 2:17; 19:6); receiving the Spirit or the power of the Spirit (Acts 1:8; 2:38; 8:15, 17, 19; 10:47; 19:2); the gift of the Holy Spirit (Acts 2:38; 10:45; 11:17); the promise of the Spirit (Luke 24:49; Acts 1:4; 2:33, 39); and the Holy Spirit falling upon a group (Acts 8:16; 10:44; 11:15). In each of these instances inspired witness dominates the context. Initial reception and/or conversion probably are not the main thought in these passages. Considering Luke's frequent use of *plērēs* and *pimplēmi* in connection with the Holy Spirit in his Gospel, it is indeed surprising that a term so suited to the description of the believers' reception of the Holy Spirit would be used so little in such contexts. It is true that Luke feels free to interchange the various phrases expressing the coming of the Holy Spirit, for we have seen this in his use of the Holy Spirit filling or coming upon someone in relation to inspired speaking. This substitution of one phrase for another, though somewhat stylistic in places, cannot be viewed as a merely random variation. In each case where "filled with the Spirit" might indicate initial reception of the Holy Spirit, it occurs in the context of inspired speaking, in proclaiming the gospel, and/or in witnessing to the messiahship of Jesus.

The context in Acts 2 makes it clear that the experience of being filled with the Holy Spirit is responsible for inspired speaking that attracts the attention of the pilgrims in Jerusalem. The result is not ecstatic speech in the sense that the speaking is unintelligible or a catalyst for unintelligible confusion,[41] but the speaking in tongues provides a multilingual testimony to the mighty works of God (2:6, 8, 11). Here the result of being filled with the Holy Spirit is a proper, well-ordered evangelization complete with accommodation for those who were from foreign lands. Only those who do not recognize the foreign languages and consider them unintelligible to anyone else accuse the disciples of being drunk. In fact, unintelligible speech is the only evidence the text gives for such an accusation. To assume that the audience condemned them for emotionalism or an altered state of consciousness requires a considerable amount of presupposition being read into the text.[42]

The reaction in the text is to the language and may reflect the Judean prejudice that we meet elsewhere, "Can anything good come out of Nazareth?" (2:7; John 1:46). Here the main result of being filled with the Holy Spirit is inspired speaking, as is proven by the Galilean Peter who addressed the onlooking gainsayers by speaking to them in their own language: "Men of Judea and all who dwell in Jerusalem" (v. 14). The context and vocabulary Luke provides here make it clear that Peter was "filled with the Holy Spirit" when he spoke.[43] By expressing the reception of the Holy Spirit in terms of "filled with the Holy Spirit," Luke is commenting not only on the inspired nature of the message in tongues, but also on the inspiration behind Peter's Spirit-directed interpretation of the scripture, the Christian presentation of the salvation history, the confrontation of sinners with a call for repentance, and the promise of Holy Spirit.

It appears that Luke has explained this event in terms of filling because of the dominant role of inspired speaking and witness which abounds both in the predictions of Pentecost (Luke 3:16; 24:49; Acts 1:4, 5, 8) and in the recounting of the event itself. Luke has superimposed the phrase, "filled with the Holy Spirit," upon the event here. Like the Holy Spirit coming upon (*epi*) someone, "filled with the Holy Spirit" can indicate both inspired speaking and reception of the Holy Spirit. Perhaps Luke feels justified in doing this because he has an OT precedent: when the Holy Spirit came upon Saul at his anointing, divine speaking accompanied the endowment of the Spirit (1 Sam 10:6, 10).

Paul: Acts 9:17–20. As discussed earlier in this chapter, by all appearances the use of the phrase, "filled with the Holy Spirit," in connection with Ananias' laying hands on Paul is a reference to the reception of the Spirit (9:17,18). The question is: Reception of the Spirit to what end: conversion, healing, or empowerment for mission? We have already discussed the passage as it relates to conversion and concluded that conversion is probably not Luke's intent here. Apparently Paul's filling occurred after his conversion on the road to Damascus (vv. 3–8) when Ananias laid hands on him not only for filling with the Holy Spirit but also for restoration of his sight.[44] The result of Ananias' obedience is curiously expressed, for only the restoration of Paul's sight is mentioned. No reference to the reception of the Holy Spirit accompanies the confirmation of the healing (v. 18) unless the result is implicit in that he then was baptized (v. 19). Probably the phrase, "filled with the Holy Spirit," is mentioned mainly for a reason other than to indicate initial conversion. The subjunctive phrase, *plēsthēs pneumatos hagiou* ("might be filled with the Holy Spirit"), is left dangling with no explicit fulfillment in the indicative. It is, of course, not mandatory for Luke to give us an explicit indicative fulfillment paralleling each promised subjunctive action. Paul's baptism could be seen as affirmation that the promise had been fulfilled and that therefore reception did indeed occur, not unlike Cornelius' experience.

The verses which follow, however, offer a better explanation of how Ananias' prayer for "filling with the Holy Spirit" was answered. After noting that Paul (Saul) did not immediately leave the disciples at Damascus, Luke relates that "immediately [*eutheōs*] he proclaimed [*ekēryssen*]" that Jesus was the Son of God (v. 20). *Eutheōs* places Paul's preaching into temporal proximity to the reference to "filled with the Holy Spirit," and it could well be taken that the expression of fullness describes the power behind his preaching.[45]

Even if "filled with the Holy Spirit" refers to Paul's conversion (which is doubtful), double entendre must be considered because of the force of *eutheōs* in verse 20 and because of the dominant use of the fullness of the Spirit in relation to speaking in Luke's writings. Peter's Pentecost sermon provides a parallel to this situation. After having received the Holy Spirit in terms of being filled (2:4), Peter was empowered (Luke 24:47–49; Acts 1:8) to explain the significance of the Pentecost event, to proclaim Jesus as Christ and Lord, and to offer salvation.

John the Baptist as a parallel: Luke 1:15. In his Gospel, Luke presents a similar situation with the infant John who is "filled with the Holy Spirit, even from his mother's womb" (Luke 1:15). Surely Luke does not intend the phrase to refer to the infant John's conversion. Luke is saying that John as an unborn infant or as an adult (or both) gave witness to Jesus. Of course the infant John did not "speak" as such, but one could make a case that he did witness to the Lordship of Jesus while still in the womb when he leaped for joy (Luke 1:44). His mother Elizabeth, also filled with the Holy Spirit, relates that John's movement was out of joy[46] which he experienced when the "mother of the Lord" entered the house (1:41–45). If this interpretation is to be rejected then the fullness of the Spirit which the prenatal John experienced was to prepare him to give witness to Jesus in his adult ministry (1:16; 3:2).[47] Zechariah his father, filled with the Holy Spirit, described John's ministry in terms of prophetic exhortation in anticipation of the coming Messiah (1:67, 76–79). This is fulfilled in John's preaching in Luke 3. John, who was previously identified as filled with the Holy Spirit, began his ministry when the word of the Lord came upon (*epi*) him (3:2), a circumstance with striking parallels in Luke 2:25–27, Acts 1:8, and 4:31. (See chapter 3.) Luke's description of both the infant John and Paul as "filled with the Holy Spirit" causes fewer problems if the phrase is primarily understood in terms of witness. Conversion was not paramount in his mind.

Paul's preaching as "comfort of the Holy Spirit": Acts 9:28–31. Luke concludes the section on Paul in chapter 9 with another connection between Paul's preaching and the Holy Spirit. After he preached in Damascus he witnessed about Jesus in Jerusalem "preaching boldly in the name of the Lord" (v. 29). Therefore (*oun*), as a result of his preaching the church was edified "in the comfort of the Holy Spirit" (v. 31). It is true that Luke does not imply that Paul's ministry was the sole cause of the church's peace, edification, and growth. He does, however, introduce this description of the church with Paul's bold preaching as an example of the comfort received from the Holy Spirit. And what comfort it was! The dread enemy of the church returned to Jerusalem as its champion. The dominant interest Luke has in presenting Paul and the Holy Spirit in Acts 9 is Paul's witness. Luke presents a similar link between the word of the Lord spreading as a result of Paul's and Barnabas' first mission and the disciples being "filled with joy and the Holy Spirit" (13:49, 52).

The Function of Fullness of the Spirit Contrasted with Other Pneumatological Expressions in Luke–Acts

Luke's distinctive use of the phrase, "filled with/full of the Holy Spirit," can be demonstrated statistically in the chart on page 143:

If Acts 6:3 and 6:5 are included as uses of fullness of the Spirit in relation to inspired speaking, and if fullness in Luke 1:15 and 4:1 is taken to refer to reception of the Holy Spirit, then in Luke–Acts there are eleven instances of fullness of the Spirit in relation to inspired speaking outside of contexts where initial reception of the Holy Spirit is mentioned.[48] As well, there are four instances where it appears in a

	A Used for speaking with no reference to reception	B Used to indicate reception of the Holy Spirit (speaking role may be present as well)
1. Baptism in the Holy Spirit	0	3
2. Holy Spirit was upon or came upon, or rejoiced in the Holy Spirit in col. A and Luke 3:22 in col. B	2	4
3. Received the Spirit or the power of the Spirit	0	9
4. Gift of the Holy Spirit including Acts 11:17 in col. B	0	3
5. Promise of the Spirit	0	4
6. Holy Spirit fell on believers	0	3
Subtotals	2	26
7. Filled with the Holy Spirit or full of the Holy Spirit including Luke 4:1 and excluding Acts 6:3,5 in col. A	9	3
8. Filled with the Holy Spirit or full of the Holy Spirit including Luke 4:1 in col. B and excluding Acts 6:3,5 in col. A	8	4
9. Filled with the Holy Spirit or full of the Holy Spirit including Luke 4:1 and Acts 6:3,5 in col. A	11	3

passage noting initial reception (73% and 27% respectively). This pattern is significant. When "filled" or "full" is contrasted with other references to the activity of the Holy Spirit, the differences are striking: "filled with the Holy Spirit" or "full of the Holy Spirit" are often phrases associated with inspired speaking. The ratios *reverse* when the data for rows 1–6 of the chart are contrasted with rows 7, 8, or 9. When a x^2 contingency statistical test is applied we find that all three configurations are less than 0.1 percent due to chance.[49] This test can tell us only the odds of this grouping happening by chance. It tells us merely that it is very remote that this is a random grouping. The evidence does *not* reflect a random change of phrases for mere stylistic variation. Only by observing the contextual use that Luke gives for the phrases can the reason for the configuration be answered. He usually reserves *one* meaning for fullness of the Spirit.

Inspired Speaking and the Fullness of the Holy Spirit in the Program of Luke–Acts

Luke does not isolate his use of the phrases, "full of the Holy Spirit" and "filled with the Holy Spirit," to contexts specifically addressing the reception of the Holy Spirit. Rather, he also uses the latter phrase in situations where no reference is made to reception of the Spirit as a part of a conversion-initiation process but where inspired speaking occurs. It is primarily in these situations of inspired speaking that Luke uses the expressions of fullness of the Holy Spirit to contribute to the witness motif that dominates the structure of Luke–Acts. It becomes Luke's preferred expression for the motif.

Peter's Inspired Speaking and Fullness of the Spirit (Acts 4:8). Like his sermon on the day of Pentecost, Peter's response to the rulers and elders in 4:8 is a result of his being "filled with the Holy Spirit." Since this phrase is in the narration, it is Luke's own observation and is characteristic of his use of the expression and similar phrases in Luke–Acts. In keeping with the synoptic tradition that the Holy Spirit would aid in the disciples' defense before rulers, Luke notes the activity of the Spirit.[50] The expression of fullness describing Peter's defense is Luke's own, one which replaces the more traditional structure, i.e., "the Holy Spirit" or "the Spirit of your Father speaking through you," "the Holy Spirit will teach you," or Jesus giving to the witness "a mouth and wisdom" (Mark 13:11; Matt 10:20; Luke 12:12; 21:15). Characteristically, Luke seldom presents actual accounts of legal self-defense in these frequent instances of believers before authorities (e.g., Acts 4:1–14; 5:17–32; 6:12–7:53; 23:1–9; 24:10–21; 26:1–23). Rather, witness for Jesus occurs. The notable exception in these instances is Paul, whose genuine self-defense statements also provide an opportunity to present the gospel. Luke's double reference to the disciples witnessing before authorities in his Gospel makes this synoptic emphasis all the stronger (Luke 12:8–12; 21:12–15). For example, in Acts 4 Peter presents to the Sanhedrin elements parallel to his Pentecost sermon. Here Luke notes that Peter, under the direction of the Holy Spirit, preached Jesus (v. 10), correctly interpreted scripture (v. 11), and proclaimed salvation (v. 12) as he did at Pentecost (2:14–40). Luke describes Peter as "filled with the Holy Spirit" (v. 8) because at that moment (*plēstheis*, aorist participle) Peter was empowered to speak, not because the reader needs a reminder that he had already been filled at Pentecost.[51] In Peter's next confrontation with the authorities, Luke reminds us that witness in the face of opposition is a divine-human operation: "We are witnesses of these things, and so is the Holy Spirit whom God has given to those who obey him" (5:32).

Disciples and Inspired Speaking (Acts 4:31). Luke presents another example of Holy Spirit-inspired speaking after Peter's and John's release from custody: the believers' response to Peter's bold testimony before the rulers (4:24–31). After noting that the hostile action of the authorities was predicted in scripture (vv. 24–28), the disciples prayed that in spite of this threat they would speak God's word "with all boldness" (v. 29) while the Lord attested the validity of their speaking through signs and wonders (v. 30). As a result of this prayer, "They were all filled with the Holy Spirit and spoke the word of God with boldness." Here again fullness with the Holy Spirit emphasizes speaking, while signs and wonders validate the words spoken by Jesus' followers.

"Filled with the Holy Spirit" here is not a reference to initial reception of the Holy Spirit.[52] Although this passage has parallels to Pentecost in Acts 2, it is not an alternative version of Pentecost as Harnack suggests.[53] The strength of the witness theme in the immediate context dispels such a notion. Likewise, attempts to identify 4:31ff. as the initial reception of the Spirit for the converts who joined the church as a result of Peter's first sermon come to ruin under the weight of the immediate context.[54] First, the apostles who had already received the Holy Spirit (2:4) apparently "took part in the prayer of 4:24–30" and were filled with the Holy Spirit along with the other Christians.[55] This is supported in the reference to the apostles' witness in the summary in verse 33 as well. Second, the immediate context demands that the filling with the Holy Spirit is indicating the means whereby the disciples "spoke the word of God with boldness."[56]

Peter, Paul, Stephen, and Spirit-Filled Speech. There is a similar example in Paul's ministry as Luke records it in Acts. Like so many other characteristics of Paul's ministry, the references to "filled with the Holy Spirit" parallel the ones in Peter's ministry. Both Peter and Paul began their work after an initial reference to being filled with the Holy Spirit. This filling can be seen to some extent as corresponding to the initial reception of the Holy Spirit, and in both cases it resulted in preaching (Acts 2:4, 14–40; 9:17, 20–22). Peter addressed Jerusalem while Paul preached to Damascus. Elsewhere Luke says that both Peter and Paul were filled with the Holy Spirit to speak. Peter, filled with the Holy Spirit, addressed the rulers of the Jews (4:8–20), while Paul, filled with the Holy Spirit, spoke a word of rebuke and condemnation to Elymas the magician and called down temporary blindness upon the enemy of the gospel (13:9–11). Peter's filling with the Holy Spirit in order to answer authorities had been foretold by Jesus himself (Luke 12:12). Paul's filling with the Holy Spirit in order to confront verbally the powers of evil corresponds to Jesus' being "full of the Holy Spirit" in order to confront the temptations of the devil in the wilderness (Luke 4:1ff.). Like Jesus, both men preached the good news aided by the presence of the Holy Spirit (Luke 4:14, 18, 19).

It cannot be said that Paul was filled with the Holy Spirit only to "look intently at" Elymas (Acts 13:9). He was filled primarily for the purpose of speaking as well as for participating in the Lord's act which caused the blindness. The syntax makes this clear. *Athenisas*, the aorist participle, has its meaning completed by *eipen*.[57]

This structure in 13:9 parallels how Luke expresses the experience of Stephen prior to his martyrdom: "But he, full of the Holy Spirit, gazed into heaven and saw the glory of God, and Jesus standing at the right hand of God, and he said . . ." (Acts 7:55–56a). In the Stephen account, "being full of the Holy Spirit" and having "gazed into heaven" explain the two consequent actions, "said" and "saw." The translation should be as follows if the tense of the two participles is observed: "but while (or since) he was full of the Holy Spirit, after he looked into heaven he saw . . . and said," or "but being full of the Holy Spirit after having looked into heaven he saw . . . and said" (my trans.). Here the tense of the present participle ("being full") appears to correspond more to the verb of speaking than to seeing, although technically it could modify both.[58]

Other Expressions of Spirit-Inspired Speech

Luke does not limit his associations of the Holy Spirit and inspired speaking to the concept of fullness. In other passages where authoritative speaking occurs, but the Holy Spirit is not explicitly named as the agent behind the speaking, the work of the Spirit is often implied by the presence of particular items in the context. Luke does not feel compelled to preface every statement of the faithful with a reference to the Holy Spirit. He is content to let the reader understand this implicitly. Furthermore, he is content to let the summaries of several preaching accounts indicate that the power of the Holy Spirit is behind the speakers by mentioning the activity of the Holy Spirit (Acts 4:31, 33; 9:27–29, 31; 13:49, 52) or by referring to the signs and wonders that confirm the words (e.g., Acts 2:43 as related to the Pentecost sermon and the apostles' teaching; Acts 4:8–20 as an explanation of the healing and sermon of Acts 3).

Once he mentions the presence of the Holy Spirit in a speaker, Luke does not repeat this each time he introduces one of that individual's speeches. He considers the first reference as adequate unless he wishes to emphasize the Holy Spirit's activity in a special circumstance. The frequency of references to the Holy Spirit's activity in the speaking ministry of the church demonstrates that Luke considers it the norm in the progress of the early church. In the first chapter of Acts, Luke establishes this precedent, "You shall receive power when the Holy Spirit has come upon you; and you shall be my witnesses" (v. 8). Reception of the Spirit also effects inspired witness at Pentecost (2:33). Luke makes reception equivalent to "poured out" and "prophesy" in 2:17, 18. Reception is implied in Peter's promise that his hearers would "receive the gift of the Holy Spirit" (2:38).[59] The examples provided before and after Peter's sermon emphasize the Spirit and witness. The same is apparently true in the Samaritans' reception of the Holy Spirit since it produced manifestations which witnessed to Simon the sorcerer of the power of God (8:14–19). When the household of Cornelius received the gift of the Holy Spirit ("fell" 10:44; "gift" and "poured out" 10:45; "received" 10:47; "fell" 11:15; "baptized" 11:16; "giving" 15:8), they too gave inspired witness (10:46; 11:15, 17). The same is true in the Ephesian Pentecost. "Receiving the Holy Spirit" (19:2) and "the Holy Spirit coming upon them" (19:6) resulted in prophetic utterance. The context for "baptized with the Holy Spirit" is also dominated by references to Spirit-witness (1:5, 8; 11:15–16). Thus the dominant theme of Luke's pneumatology in his presentation of the early church is: "We are witnesses to these things, and so is the Holy Spirit" (5:32).

Since we have already discussed the relationship between Jesus and the Holy Spirit in previous chapters, it remains for us in this chapter on Acts to define the relationship between believers and the Spirit as well as the interrelationship between Jesus, believers, and the Spirit. As in his Gospel, Luke views Jesus' experience with the Spirit as paradigmatic though not directly equivalent to that of his followers' experience with the Spirit. Luke presents a Spirit-anointed Messiah who, as a result of that anointing, was empowered to perform miracles and to utter the words of God (Acts 10:38; Luke 4:18). Luke also tells us that the resurrected Jesus gave instructions to his followers by the Holy Spirit (Acts 1:2).[60] Jesus' experience with the Holy Spirit is unique in the Gospel in that he was conceived of the Spirit (1:35), and the Spirit as a dove descended upon him (3:21); while in Acts he is uniquely the dispenser of the Holy Spirit after his ascension (2:33). Yet in pouring out the Holy Spirit upon his followers, Jesus enabled them to function in ministry in a manner similar to his own.

In Acts the Holy Spirit performed miracles, directed the mission of the church, judged the enemies of Jesus, and infused the believers with joy. Luke also identifies the Spirit as the divine source of OT scripture. Luke associates the Holy Spirit with conversion to some degree, but he does not clearly describe that role since his attention is centered on another major role of the Spirit: inspired witness. This witness is attended by signs and wonders provided by the Spirit (e.g., 2:4; 4:31; 5:9–10; 6:5, 8; 8:17–19; 9:17–18; 10:38, 44–46; 13:9–11). Even the witness itself coming through human beings can be classed as miracle (see chapter 7).

Notes to Chapter 11

1. Luke obviously understood the witness of the Holy Spirit "in every city" (Acts 20:23) as a confirmation that he indeed was on the right path and not as a divine warning not to go to Jerusalem. It is incorrect to assume the latter on the basis of Acts 21:4: "Through the Spirit they told Paul not to go on to Jerusalem." Apparently the disciples "in every city" received a message from the Holy Spirit that if Paul went to Jerusalem he would be arrested. Some presumed that this could not possibly be the will of the Spirit. Notice that the renowned prophet Agabus did not deliver a value judgment on Paul's intended journey but simply said, "Thus says the Holy Spirit, 'So shall the Jews at Jerusalem bind the man [Paul] who owns this girdle and deliver him into the hands of the Gentiles' " (21:11). Paul understood these messages from the Holy Spirit as confirmation to go anyway, for he said in response to their dissuasions, "What are you doing weeping and breaking my heart? For I am ready not only to be imprisoned but even to die at Jerusalem for the name of the Lord Jesus" (21:13). The disciples responded in resignation, "The will of the Lord be done" (21:14). Presumably in the events that followed it was.

2. For example, Dunn says, "There were no Christians (properly speaking) prior to Pentecost" (*Baptism*, 51), and "For Luke Pentecost was the beginning of the new covenant in the experience of the disciples." It is a new era (ibid., 47). Although Dunn sees empowerment for mission here, he still argues, "The Baptism in the Spirit, as always, is primarily initiatory, and only secondarily an empowering" (ibid., 54). Bruce sees Spirit baptism as distinct from filling with the Holy Spirit. *Commentary on the Book of Acts*, NICNT (Grand Rapids: Eerdmans, 1954), 56. See also M. Green, *I Believe in the Holy*

Spirit (Grand Rapids: Eerdmans, 1975), 141–42; and Marshall, *Acts: An Introduction and Commentary*, TNTC, gen. ed. L. Morris (Leicester: Inter-Varsity Press, 1980), 305.

3. Marshall recognizes empowerment here in Acts 2 (*Acts*, 69). H. Ervin sees no reference to conversion at Pentecost but only empowerment, *These Are Not Drunken as Ye Suppose* (Plainfield, N.J.: Logos, 1968), 89; and *Spirit Baptism* (Peabody, Mass.: Hendrickson, 1987), 69. See also R. Stronstad, *Charismatic Theology*, 52.

4. Dunn, *Baptism*, 46ff., 55, 86.

5. If "filled with the Holy Spirit" refers to conversion at Pentecost, then to be consistent, John the Baptist "filled with the Holy Spirit, even from his mother's womb" (Luke 1:15) would mean a prenatal conversion of John! Obviously Luke does not intend that meaning for John, nor does he intend that at Pentecost.

6. This is especially true if one is allowed to allude to the Johannine testimony of the disciples' faith in the risen Christ prior to Jesus' ascension (John 20:25, 28).

7. See Marshall, *Acts*, 81, who says that the two gifts of forgiveness and the Holy Spirit "are closely linked, since it is the Spirit who accomplishes the inner cleansing of which baptism is the outward symbol." Haenchen argues that when the candidate is baptized in the name of Jesus Christ, "he comes under the power of Jesus, his sins are in consequence, remitted and he 'receives the Holy Spirit.' The few cases in Acts when reception of the Spirit is separated from baptism are justified exceptions." Haenchen goes on to assert that "by the time of Luke, it was not every Christian (if it ever had been) who received the *ecstatic* Spirit at baptism. Rather was the Spirit now regarded as a gift no longer bound to any outward sign" (*The Acts of the Apostles*, trans. B. Noble, et al. [Oxford: Basil Blackwell, 1971], 184).

8. Ibid., n. 4.

9. Stronstad, *Charismatic Theology*, 57.

10. Ervin, *Spirit-Baptism*, 69–71.

11. Here Dunn argues that the Samaritans' conversion must have somehow been defective. He specifically cites Rom 8:9 to argue that they were not Christians until they received the Holy Spirit after the apostles had arrived (*Baptism*, 55, 63–68). This does not respect the redactional motives of Luke and Paul which are *not* completely interchangeable. Stronstad is correct in calling this a "methodological error" (*Charismatic Theology*, 9–12, 64). This does not respect Luke's independent views which sometimes differ from Paul. See Marshall, *Luke: Historian and Theologian*, 75.

12. G. W. H. Lampe, *The Seal of the Spirit: A Study in the Doctrine of Baptism and Confirmation* (London: SPCK, 1967), 70–72.

13. Characteristically Dunn asserts that only when Paul is filled with the Holy Spirit is he a Christian (*Baptism*, 78).

14. "In describing Saul's encounter with the risen Lord, Luke emphasizes his calling, not his conversion. The stress falls upon what Saul must do, to bear the name of Jesus before the Gentiles." The Holy Spirit for Paul effects vocation and empowering (Stronstad, *Charismatic Theology*, 66).

15. Bruce, *Acts: Greek*, 202. See also Marshall, *Acts*, 172; K. Lake and H. J. Cadbury, *The Beginnings of Christianity*, Part I: The Acts of the

Apostles vol. 4, gen. ed. F. J. Foakes-Jackson and K. Lake (London: Macmillan, 1933), 104. W. Neil assumes that "Paul experienced the Pentecostal ecstasy" (*The Acts of the Apostles*, [London: Morgan, Marshall, and Scott, 1973], 131).

16. Ervin, *Spirit-Baptism*, 76. See also W. Neil, *Acts*, 131, and A. Robertson, *Word Pictures in the New Testament: The Acts of the Apostles*, vol. 3 (Grand Rapids: Baker, 1930), 121.

17. See Rackham, *Acts*, 147; Neil, *Acts*, 137; Bruce, *Acts*, 216; Haenchen, *Acts*, 346. Haenchen notes that this is the intent of the phrase, "God-fearer," yet it is not clear if it was a proper title.

18. The word for people (*laos*) refers to the Jews as opposed to Gentiles (*ethnē*) similar to Luke's use in Luke 7:4ff.; Lake and Cadbury, *Beginnings of Christianity: Acts*, 4:113; Haenchen, *Acts*, 347.

19. Bruce, *Acts*, 216.

20. In 11:17 *pisteusasin* ("having believed") does not necessarily note that Spirit reception occurred immediately at the moment of belief. The aorist participle could mean "after having believed" as easily as "when having believed." Both translations accommodate the idea that the action of the participle preceded the action of the main verb although sometimes it could indicate action coincident to the verb. This is not Luke's intent; in light of the events at Pentecost to which Peter referred in his explanation of the Gentiles' reception of the Spirit, this did not immediately take place. In Luke 24 belief apparently had occurred before the ascension, and the believers "tarried" for the empowerment of the Holy Spirit (Acts 1) for several days before Pentecost. Contra Dunn, *Baptism*, 86ff.

21. Marshall, *Acts*, 193. Dunn says that before hearing Peter's sermon, Cornelius' "repentance and faith had not yet reached that level or had been turned to that object, which would enable Luke to call them *metanoia eis zōn* and *pistis eis Christon Iēsoun*; and so he was without the forgiveness and salvation they bring. He only entered into this Christian experience when he received the Spirit" (*Baptism*, 82). This does not, however, reflect Luke's understanding of repentance as effective for forgiveness of sins (Luke 3:3). In the exclusively Lucan parable of the praying Pharisee and publican, Luke relates that the penitent attitude of the publican resulted in justification (*dedikaiōmenos*, Luke 18:9–14).

22. Stronstad, *Charismatic Theology*, 67. Ervin is correct to note that "the Pentecostal baptism in the Spirit for power in mission" is Luke's intent here. But it is too much to say that this event makes it clear "[t]hat tongues are the normative evidence of the baptism in the Holy Spirit" (*Spirit-Baptism*, 78). Luke's motives for his presentation of the Holy Spirit only indirectly involve investigating and thoroughly identifying the role of the Holy Spirit in conversion or the "normative" signs of Spirit reception.

23. "*mathētēs* for Luke always signifies 'Christian' " and "These men must—as *mathētai*—be Christians" (Haenchen, *Acts*, 553, 556). See also Bruce, *Acts*, 385; Stronstad, *Charismatic Theology*, 68. Nor is it enough to say that Paul mistakenly assumed that these men were disciples of Jesus (Marshall citing K. Haacker in *Acts*, 305ff.). Why would Luke allow the misunderstanding to remain even for his readers? If this were Luke's intent, he could have said they were *supposed* disciples.

24. The use of the adjective pronoun "certain" does not distinguish between the Christian disciples and these twelve men. Ananias and Timothy are both described as "a certain disciple" (*tis* in Acts 9:10; 16:1). See Stronstad, *Charismatic Theology*, 68 n. 4.

25. "Disciples . . . is a term which he [Luke] commonly uses for Christians, and had he meant to indicate that they were disciples not of Christ but of John the Baptist (as has sometimes been deduced from v. 3), he would have said so explicitly" (Bruce, *Acts*, 385).

26. Marshall, *Acts*, 305–306; Dunn, *Baptism*, 83–89.

27. Bruce, *Acts*, 385ff.; pace Haenchen, *Acts*, 553 n. 3.

28. Stronstad correctly notes, "There is no tension between the fact of the indwelling of the Holy Spirit in the life of every believer and an additional experience of receiving the prophetic or charismatic gift of the Spirit" (*Charismatic Theology*, 68).

29. Lampe has also noted "an inconsistency in Luke's picture of the Church as the eschatological Spirit-inspired community." Luke does not meticulously address the role of the Holy Spirit in the community life. Furthermore, he presents "a distinct class of prophets . . . [who] are singled out as being specially inspired, such as Stephen and Barnabas, described as 'full of faith and the Holy Spirit' and the group of the Seven, who are 'full of the Spirit and of wisdom' " (*God as Spirit: The Bampton Lectures, 1976* [Oxford: Clarendon, 1977], 67).

30. The unity of Luke's pneumatology weakens H. Conzelmann's suggestion that Luke has created three distinct epochs, cf. *Theology*. The pneumatology of the infancy narrative is the Achilles' heel of Conzelmann's epochs, cf. Minear, "Luke's Use of the Birth Stories," 111–30.

31. Haenchen suggests that Luke is maintaining two different theologies of the church in using "filled" as a special endowment for a special function and "full of the Holy Spirit" as the durative presence in a person (*Acts*, 187, 216). If this is the case, then Luke utilized traditional phraseology to express his special interest: the Holy Spirit and authoritative speaking.

32. As held by M. Turner in "Spirit Endowment in Luke–Acts: Some Linguistic Considerations," *VoxEv* 12 (1981): 45–63. He is correct in noting that "full of the Holy Spirit" indicates that the church felt the impact of the Spirit "through that person's life" (pp. 53–55), but the specialized use of this fullness (i.e., speaking) is not recognized. Bruce is close to our observation here: "After the initial receiving or filling with the Spirit, individuals may be described in a distinctive sense as being 'full' of the Spirit, like the seven almoners of Acts 6, especially Stephen (6:3, 5; 7:55), or like Barnabas (11:24); or they may be 'filled' with the Spirit for a particular purpose, especially for authoritative or oracular utterance"; as in "The Holy Spirit in the Acts of the Apostles," *Int* 27 (1973): 130–204, 180. Earlier Bruce maintained the iterative nature of "filled" and the durative nature of "full" (*Acts*, 99; *Acts: Greek*, 120; cf. also Neil, *Acts*, 89).

33. Marshall, *Luke: Historian and Theologian*, 199.

34. The double expression in 6:3, *plēreis pneumatos kai sophias*, may have a twofold meaning, but it seems likely that this is not an overt reference to the Holy Spirit but a reference to wisdom, the Spirit of wisdom, or "wisdom

inspired by the Spirit." See Haenchen for the former meanings (*Acts*, 262), and Marshall for the latter one (*Acts*, 126–27). Haenchen notes that wisdom is emphasized in the following context (vv. 8, 10). He also correctly notes Luke's penchant for such double phrases but also points out that the LXX uses *sophia* in such pairs and uses the expression *pneuma sophias* in Exod 31:3; 35:31 and Wis 1:4; cf. *Acts*, 262, n. 4.

J. Kilgallen, *The Stephen Speech: A Literary and Redactional Study of Acts 7, 2–53*, AnBib 67 (Rome: Pontifical Biblical Institute Press, 1976), 49, identifies wisdom as a Lucan interest here so that Luke is probably responsible for the expression. *Sophia* is often used by Luke, and it occurs in similar situations in Luke 2:40, 52; 21:15. In Stephen's speech, wisdom is used to describe Joseph (Acts 7:10) and Moses (7:22). Cf. also Wilckens, *Missionsreden*, 210 n. 2. Several MSS add *hagiou* after *pneumatos*, while the shorter form occurs in others. Metzger suggests that Christian scribes would naturally provide the reading, "Holy Spirit" (*Textual Commentary*, 337). It would not be beyond Luke to have inserted the adjective into a traditional description of the major requirement of wisdom for admission into the early diaconate.

35. Technically only Stephen, the preacher whose speeches occupy the following context from 6:10–7:60, is described as full of the *Holy* Spirit. The adjective "holy" does not occur in 6:3 which describes the apostolic guidelines for selection of deacons of which wisdom is paramount (see preceding note). Luke may be responsible for the elaboration of *pneuma* in v. 3 into the work of the Holy Spirit in the following context.

36. Leadership, counseling, and teaching could be intended in the meaning of the phrases as well; cf. J. D. G. Dunn, *Jesus and the Spirit* (London: SCM Press, 1975), 176. Luke may intend the wonders to be attestations of the inspired speaking. Stephen is described in terms similar to Barnabas, "full of the Holy Spirit and of faith" (11:24). These descriptions accompany the speaking ministries of both men.

37. The traditional background of the Stephen material has often been noted in scholarship. For a summary of criticism see Haenchen, *Acts*, 264–69; see also G. Stanton, "Stephen in Lucan Perspective," *Studia Biblica 1978: Papers on Paul and Other New Testament Authors*, JSNTS 3, ed. E. Livingstone, (Sheffield: JSOT, 1980), 345–60. Harnack saw 6:1–7:50 as a "single connected narrative" (*The Acts of the Apostles: A Commentary*, Crown Theological Library 27, trans. J. R. Wilkinson [London: William & Norgate, 1909], 169–70), while more recent scholarship has acknowledged a source for 6:1 but identifies redactional elements as well, e.g., M. Dibelius, *Studies in the Acts of the Apostles*, trans. M. Ling (London: SCM Press, 1956), 11 n. 20.

Conzelmann also notes the presence of tradition. "Behind this account lies a piece of tradition which Luke must have had in written form; note the manner in which the 'Hellenists' and 'Hebrews' are introduced." These two categories suggest that it is tradition because "up to this point there have been no indications of the coexistence of two groups. Observe also the list in vs 5, which no longer fits with the material as Luke has revised it." Furthermore, the fact that "Luke does not know of any concrete miracles performed by Stephen" seems to betray an earlier source (*A Commentary on the Acts of the Apostles*, trans. J. Limburg, A. T. Kraabel, D. H. Juel [Philadelphia: Fortress,

1987], 44, 47). See also idem, *History of Primitive Christianity*, trans. J. E. Steely (Nashville: Abingdon, 1973), 35.

Kilgallen thinks signs and wonders (v. 8) should be linked to the miracles of Moses mentioned in Stephen's speech (7:36; *Stephen Speech*, 81). Nevertheless the main event is the speech. Signs and wonders accompany the word as in 4:31–33. It is also surprising that the apostles assigned the deacons the daily administrative tasks so that they would have time to minister the word of God, only to have the deacon Stephen to be described as a preacher. Luke has apparently provided a panorama of the ministry of Stephen, presenting its beginning, middle, and end as one section. The tradition concerning the deacons gives Luke another opportunity to present another significant step in the church's expanding mission. J. Lienhard suggests that Luke learned from his source the names of the deacons and that they were appointed to wait tables. He also questions whether the source would have especially noted that they were filled with the Holy Spirit for this purpose; see "Acts 6:1–6: A Redactional View," *CBQ* 37 (April, 1975): 228–36, esp. 230. This observation is more in keeping with the ability to preach and do missions than to wait on tables. Lienhard notes Luke's motive for his restructuring of the "Stephen Cycle" in 6:1–6, "The final redactor of Acts (i.e., Luke) intended to associate 6:1–6 with the narrative about Stephen which follows it."

M. Scharlemann also considers the deacon's "gift of the Spirit" (6:3) as an indicator that Stephen (in anticipation of his speech) was "obedient to the Spirit of God and had a Messianic understanding of the Old Testament"; see his *Stephen: A Singular Saint*, AnBib 34 (Rome: Pontifical Biblical Institute, 1968), 12. Kilgallen also notes that Stephen was enabled to present a proper exegesis of the OT (*Stephen Speech*, 5). If Dunn's suggestion is correct that "the description of various individuals as 'full' (*plērēs*) of the Holy Spirit" was acquired by Luke "from a special and primitive source (6.3, 5, 8; 7.55; 11.24)," then we may be face to face with an early church concept of the enduring quality of the Holy Spirit as the means of "sureness of insight and conviction of speech" (*Jesus and the Spirit*, 171). Cf. also Haenchen who identifies this as a "Hellenistic Christian view" (*Acts*, 187). It is of interest that the dominant context of the passages with "full of the Spirit" is inspired speech. It is equally valid to view the associations of "fullness" with inspired speaking as Luke's own contribution. He uses traditional descriptions of persons (e.g., full of wisdom or "spirit of wisdom" for deacons) as an opportunity to emphasize the role of the Spirit in the preaching mission of the early church. Luke may indeed be indebted (at least in part) to a source for the designation of deacons as "full of the Spirit." It seems unlikely that Luke would describe deacons as continually full of the Spirit to speak while the apostles were filled to speak only on occasion. Certainly in his use of "filled with/full of the Spirit" to designate authoritative speaking, the differences in iterative and durative meanings are minimized.

38. Both *eiden* (saw) and *eipen* (said) are parallel and connected by the coordinate conjunction *kai*. For more on the grammatical structure of this phrase see J. Shelton, " 'Filled with the Holy Spirit' and 'Full of the Holy Spirit': Lucan Redactional Phrases" in *Faces of Renewal*, ed. P. Elbert (Peabody, Mass.: Hendrickson, 1988), 83–84.

39. BDF, §456.1.

40. Note also that rejoicing is mentioned here (v. 23) in relation to the Holy Spirit. This is similar to Luke's presentation of Jesus rejoicing in the Holy Spirit in Luke 10:21.

41. The word "ecstatic" has often been used to describe the events at Pentecost. It often carries a pejorative nuance. What happened at Pentecost, although supernatural, was a well-ordered evangelization complete with interpretation.

42. These assumptions seem to suppose that the abuse and excesses that Paul tries to correct in 1 Cor 12–14 were the norm in such phenomena in the early church.

43. The context and general practice of Luke make it clear that Peter addressed the onlookers (Acts 2:14) as a result of being filled with the Holy Spirit with the other believers in 2:4. The term Luke uses to describe Peter's speaking also reinforces this observation. *Apophthengomai* can refer to oracular or prophetic speech in classical and hellenistic Greek, and in the LXX. It occurs three times in the NT, all in Acts: in 26:25, here, and in 2:4 (cf. BAGD, 102). Wilckens considers the connection between the "Spirit-outpouring" of 2:4 and Peter's speech at 2:14 as a *fait accompli*. He reasons that the reader is not surprised by this since he has been prepared for it beforehand (Luke 24:49; Acts 1:5; 2:4) (*Missionreden*, 56). The following scholars, several of whom explicitly link *apophthengomai* with the earlier aspect of the Pentecost event (2:4), also contend that the term indicates that Peter's address is indeed inspired utterance. Lake and Cadbury, *Beginnings of Christianity: Acts*, 21; Haenchen, *Acts*, 178; Marshall, *Acts*, 72–73; Bruce, *Acts: Greek*, 88; Neil, *Acts*, 75; R. Zehnle, *Peter's Pentecost Discourse: Tradition and Lukan Reinterpretation in Peter's Speeches of Acts 2 and 3*, SBLMS 15, ed. R. A. Kraft (Nashville: Abingdon, 1971), 37, 117.

44. "We are probably meant to understand that in receiving the gift of the Holy Spirit, Paul experienced the Pentecostal ecstasy," so Neil, *Acts*, 131; but note also Ervin, *These Are Not Drunken*, 56, 61. Others simply note that reception of the Spirit, i.e., conversion, is meant, e.g., Dunn, *Jesus and the Spirit*, 193; idem, *Baptism*, 78; Conzelmann, *Acts*, 66; D. Guthrie, *New Testament Theology* (Leicester: InterVarsity, 1981), 543. (Inevitably discussion arises as to whether the laying on of hands or baptism causes the reception of the Holy Spirit, but it is doubtful that Luke makes any fixed connection between the Spirit and these events.)

45. The reference to the filling with the Holy Spirit refers to "the prophetic gift." "Paul was to bear witness before the Gentile Emperors and the Sons of Israel, and therefore he must receive the Spirit for 'the testimony of Jesus is the spirit of prophecy' (cf. also Mk. xiii. 11)" (Lake and Cadbury, *Beginnings of Christianity: Acts*, 104). Bruce links the phrase with the preaching as well: "Such filling was necessary for the prophetic service indicated in v. 15" (*Acts: Greek*, 202; cf. also Barrett, *Holy Spirit*, 1, and Dunn, *Baptism*, 71). Paul's experience in Damascus parallels the order of events in Stephen's ministry. Paul's conversion and subsequent preaching parallel Luke's presentation of Stephen's ministry in which he describes Stephen in terms of the fullness of the Holy Spirit before presenting his speaking ministry. There Luke uses the selection of the deacons as an opportunity to note that even prior to Stephen's speech before the council, he spoke under the direction of the Holy

Spirit (6:10). Perhaps the observation that Saul was present at Stephen's martyrdom (7:58) is part of Luke's effort to parallel the two ministries. As a result of Paul's preaching in Damascus the parallel misses completion when the new convert narrowly escapes martyrdom in the short term, while in the long term it seems that it is only delayed.

46. Note that John, filled with the Spirit, experiences joy (*agalliasei*) while Luke says that Jesus rejoiced (*ēgalliasato*) in the Holy Spirit in 10:21.

47. By presenting John as "filled" here, Luke seems to be going against the usual pattern in Acts of repentance/conversion preceding empowerment by the Holy Spirit.

48. It may be argued that 6:3 and 6:5 should not be included in the data. They should indeed be included as in context they do refer to empowering to speak, but a significant tendency in Lucan phraseology can be demonstrated without them. If for the moment 6:3 and 6:5 are eliminated from the inspired speaking category and Luke 4:1 is treated as referring solely to reception, then there are nine instances referring to speaking without reference to initial reception and four instances occurring in the context indicating initial reception (67% and 33% respectively). So even with the minimal amount of data in the first category, the differences are significant and are not likely due to chance.

Acts 6:3 and 6:5 should *not* be excluded from the first category; furthermore, "full of the Holy Spirit" in Luke 4:1, though it constitutes a Lucan commentary on the baptism of Jesus, should be seen primarily in terms of inspired speaking since it prefaces Jesus' victory over the temptation in which his principal weapon was inspired speaking. But putting Luke 4:1 aside, there are eleven instances of fullness with reference to reception and three of fullness without reference to initial reception which yield 79% and 21% respectively. This leaves Luke 1:15, Acts 2:4, and 9:17 as the three incidents of fullness and initial reception. If the reference to Paul at Damascus (9:17) is included in the first category, then there are twelve instances relating to speaking and two to reception, which is 86% and 14% respectively. But as we have already seen, even these three passages do not necessarily refer to conversion.

There is reason to consider even Luke 1:15 as primarily in a speaking category, which would leave only Acts 2:4 in the category of reception. Some may contend that Acts 6:3, 5 and Luke 4:1 should be included in group "B" in the chart. But even if this is done the resulting ratio of 7 to 5 is significantly different from 2 to 26. Therefore, the thesis still stands. In insisting on conversion, however, the overriding contextual use of "fullness" for speaking must be largely ignored.

49. The x^2 contingency score expresses the possibility that a given sample could randomly occur. Alone it cannot automatically be used to determine if chance or premeditated selection is responsible for a sample group. But *with* the theological tendency already noted it becomes a very strong indicator of Luke's redactional activity. See Shelton, "Filled with the Spirit," 91–93. Luke reserves *pimplēmi* (filled) to be used with the Holy Spirit. Only once does he use *plēroō* to express "filled with the Holy Spirit" (Acts 13:52). In each case, both *pimplēmi* and *plēroō* effect witness regardless of the tense used. Pace Ervin, *Spirit-Baptism*, 59.

50. Haenchen, *Acts*, 187, 216; Marshall, *Acts*, 69, 100. Marshall argues that Luke considers it possible "that a person already filled with the Spirit can receive a fresh filling for a specific task or a continuous filling." E. Schweizer presents a similar view in *The Holy Spirit* (London: SCM Press, 1980), 75. Cf. also Dunn, *Baptism*, 71; Bruce, *Acts: Greek*, 120. Ervin insists that repetitive references to infilling with the Spirit involving the same person merely remind the reader that the person in question had already been filled (*Spirit-Baptism*, 53).

51. Pace Ervin, *Spirit-Baptism*, 53, 59.

52. Cf. Lake and Cadbury, *Beginnings of Christianity: Acts*, 47, who link *parrēsias*, "boldness," in 4:31 with the same word used in v. 13 which is related to Peter's address before the rulers (vv. 8–12). In both cases fullness of the Spirit provides the courage to witness; see also Marshall, *Acts*, 107; Haenchen, *Acts*, 228; Dunn, *Baptism*, 70; Schweizer, *Holy Spirit*, 76.

53. Harnack, *Acts*, 183.

54. Pace Ervin, *These Are Not Drunken, as Ye Suppose*, 62–67; idem, *Spirit-Baptism*, 69.

55. Dunn, *Baptism*, 70–71.

56. As Dunn observes, "As for the formula *plēstheis pneumatos hagiou eipen*, when an aorist participle is used with *eipen* it always describes an action or event which takes place immediately prior to or which leads into the act of speaking" (*Baptism*, 71; see also Zehlne, *Peter's Pentecost Discourse*, 37, 117).

57. For more on the syntax of this passage see Shelton, "Filled with the Spirit," 95–98.

58. Shelton, "Filled with the Spirit," 97ff. The structure of both the passage about Stephen and the one about Paul certainly appears to be Lucan when the participial forms are noted, and when one realizes that *atenizō* and filled with/full of the Holy Spirit (*pimplēmi* and *plērēs*) are preferred expressions of Luke. (*Atenizō* is used 12x in Luke–Acts, nearly always as a participle; twice elsewhere in NT, 2 Cor 3:7, 13. *Pimplēmi* is almost exclusively used in Luke–Acts, 22 out of 24 total in the NT. *Plērēs* is dominated by Luke–Acts in contrast to the other Gospels. Furthermore, Luke often connects *plērēs*, *plētheis*, and the aorist of *pimplēmi* plus a genitival form of the Holy Spirit with *kai eipen* or similar expressions indicating speech.)

59. Which Luke might intend to be linked with the corporate witness given in 4:31.

60. This is the preferred reading over Jesus "chose his disciples by the Holy Spirit." The phrase, "through the Holy Spirit," is juxtaposed with the phrase, "had given commandment to the apostles." If Luke had intended it to modify the phrase, "whom he had chosen," why does he place it before the relative *hous* and outside of the relative clause? It cannot be that Luke placed it forward for emphasis since it is out of the relative clause altogether. See Bruce, *Acts*, 29. Rackham (*Acts*, 4), says that commandment "given through the Holy Ghost . . . is another keynote of the Acts." Pace Marshall, *Acts*, 57; and Haenchen, *Acts*, 139. Lake and Cadbury claim that the passage is obscure (*Beginnings of Christianity: Acts*, 3).

12 "Filled With the Holy Spirit ... To Speak the Word with Boldness"

*T*HROUGHOUT HIS Gospel and Acts, Luke's predominant interest in the Holy Spirit is in empowerment for witness. Under the power of the Holy Spirit, believers were "mighty in deed and word" just as Jesus was (Luke 24:19). Luke also links the Holy Spirit with miracles that are manifested in the kingdom of God beginning with the miraculous conception of Jesus in Luke 1:35 and continuing with signs and wonders throughout his Gospel and Acts. This theme, of course, is not a Lucan creation, for the OT contains many references to the Holy Spirit and miracles. Furthermore, this association may well be the oldest view of the Holy Spirit in the OT.[1] It is not surprising then that Luke presents Jesus as the wonder-worker, the new Elijah. In fact, both Jesus and his followers perform wonders through the power of the Holy Spirit.

The Holy Spirit also inspires prayer, praise, and rejoicing. Inspired prayer frequently occurs in Luke–Acts before momentous events. Spirit-directed praise and rejoicing also fit well into Luke's emphasis on celebration. Yet, first and foremost, the Holy Spirit inspired witness to take place in the ministry of Jesus and the church.

Another important aspect of Luke's pneumatology is that he sees the experiences of Jesus with the Holy Spirit as archetypical for believers. Jesus, like his witnesses in the infancy narratives (Luke 1–2) and his subsequent followers, relied on the fullness of the Spirit to accomplish his ministry. Although his experience with the Holy Spirit was unique in his conception (Luke 1:35), much of his experience with the Holy Spirit mirrored that of the disciples: Jesus was led by the Spirit (4:1) and empowered by the Spirit to perform wonders (Luke 4:14, 18; Acts 10:38), to pray and praise (Luke 10:21), and to speak (Luke 4:1, 14, 18; Acts 1:2). Luke describes Jesus in the same pneumatological terms as he describes others who minister by the power of the Spirit. The

Holy Spirit who empowered Jesus is the same one that Jesus poured out on his followers (Acts 2:33).

Luke underscores the role of the Holy Spirit in witness in several ways. Through redaction critical studies we have been to able to identify them. First, Luke often superimposes his own distinctive observations on the Gospel material in the form of his favorite phrases and unique vocabulary. Second, he often adjusts the placement of the synoptic material to provide an emphasis on inspired speech. Third, he supplements the Marcan and Q Gospel traditions with vast tracts of L material (exclusively Lucan material which comprises one-third of Luke's Gospel) to support his unique theological agenda. Finally, in Acts where he no longer has to defer to his synoptic sources, Luke frequently presents the Holy Spirit as the originator of inspired witness.

The Unique Messages of the Pneumatologies of Luke, Paul, and John

Luke has a distinctive agenda for his discussion of the Holy Spirit that must be respected in its own right. The same holds true for the pneumatologies of Paul and John. Although at points these pneumatologies have similar themes, they cannot be indiscriminately blended together. It is specifically this error that has caused so much confusion in issues concerning the Holy Spirit. Paul's pneumatology is very broad in scope, covering many areas. In the crucial passage of Romans 8, the dominant theme of Paul's pneumatology is ontology (which as we have already discussed is the study of what role the Holy Spirit has in our being Christians), although he also notes the relationship between the Spirit and prayer (8:26). But even the reference to Spirit and prayer is linked to the Holy Spirit "bearing witness" to the sonship of the Christian (8:15, 16, 23). Here, Paul's references to the Holy Spirit clarify who believers are in Christ and what comprises Christian lifestyle: "Any one who does not have the Spirit of Christ does not belong to him" (8:9).

To assume, then, that references to "receiving the Spirit," being "baptized in the Holy Spirit," or "filled with the Holy Spirit" in Luke–Acts are indicators of conversion or ontology is to miss the unique message of Luke's pneumatology and is the result of trying to force Luke's message concerning the Holy Spirit into a Pauline mold.[2] This is not to say that Luke's pneumatology says nothing of Christian lifestyle or ontology, but as we have demonstrated, Luke's dominant interest in the Holy Spirit involves Christian witness and empowerment for mission. Furthermore, we must not force Luke to say more than he wishes. We must not read our own ideas into the text. The unique context of each NT writer must be revered.

The unique context of Luke–Acts is violated when it is asserted that believers in Luke–Acts are not Christians in the fullest sense until they are filled with the Holy Spirit. One could as easily use Paul's theology to argue that Luke assumed that the disciples at Pentecost were in a full sense believers *before* they were empowered by the Holy Spirit. Paul says, "If you confess with your lips that Jesus is Lord and believe in your heart that God raised him from the dead, you will be saved" (Rom 10:9). In light of this, it seems incredible that the disciples saw Jesus crucified, die, buried, resurrected, and ascend to heaven, heard the resurrected Jesus expound the scriptures concerning himself, received his divine commission, and, according to John's Gospel, confessed him as Lord (John 20:28), and yet are not considered Christians because they had not yet received the Holy Spirit at Pentecost! It is not necessary to bring Paul or John into the discussion to see that Luke does not intend the Pentecost experience to connote conversion but rather intended it to effect empowerment. "Filled with the Holy Spirit" or "full of the Holy Spirit" does not indicate conversion in Luke–Acts so much as it indicates empowerment for mission. Similarly, the Spirit-filled experiences of Jesus and his witnesses at his birth demonstrate that they are not being converted so much as being empowered to minister and witness.

It is also incorrect to assume that Luke's concept of fullness of the Holy Spirit holds the key to Paul's pneumatology, as some believe. Classical Pentecostals generally assume that speaking in tongues always accompanies Spirit-reception or the infilling of the Holy Spirit, an assumption which they make on the basis of accounts of tongues accompanying reception of the Holy Spirit in Acts. Some more radical Pentecostals reason that if tongues always accompanies Spirit-reception, then Paul's statement that only those who have the Spirit belong to Christ (Rom 8:9) would mean that only people who have experienced glossolalia have been converted. Obviously, this is not Paul's intent or Luke's. Of course, the counter-argument is that Christians who have not experienced tongues have the Holy Spirit but not to the degree of being filled or baptized in the Holy Spirit. But is such a distinction ever made by Luke or Paul or any other NT writer for that matter? Paul lists many evidences of the presence of the Holy Spirit in his letters (e.g., Gal 5:22–23). Luke mentions tongues in relation to fullness of the Spirit and Spirit-reception, but he does not do so consistently; so even the classical Pentecostal position of tongues always being the "initial" evidence of Spirit infilling is called into question. Most often the fullness and activities of the Spirit in Luke result in inspired witness in the native tongue of both the speakers and the hearers.

Luke does not define the relationship of conversion and the Holy Spirit as clearly as Paul does. His attention is usually upon the relationship of the Holy Spirit and witness, a subject on which he is much clearer. We must not go far beyond what Luke says in our effort to interpret him. Where he is clear, we can be emphatic. Where he is unclear or silent, we must say "Amen" to his unique interest and to his silence.

Also precarious are the attempts to construe the pre-Pentecost reception of the Holy Spirit in the upper room in John's Gospel as conversion. "He breathed on them, and said to them, 'Receive the Holy Spirit'" (20:22). Often an attempt is made here to interpret John through Paul, for some assume that this is the moment the disciples became Christians. Yet the context does not indicate that conversion resulted from the reception of the Holy Spirit; instead the Spirit was given to empower for mission. In the verse immediately preceding, Jesus said, "Peace be with you. As the Father has sent me, even so I send you" (20:21). The following verse explains the nature of the commission that the irenic Spirit underwrites: "If you forgive the sins of any, they are forgiven; if you retain the sins of any, they are retained" (20:23). Here the work of the Spirit is not to convert the disciples, but to empower them, presumably to proclaim God's forgiveness to the repentant and to refrain from approving the insincere.[3] Clearly, the major pneumatological systems in the NT are not intended to be indiscriminately interchangeable.

Ramifications and Applications

Applications to Academics

This study demonstrates the validity of much of the redaction critical method. When properly applied, the method respects the Gospels as valid witnesses of Jesus and the early church and not just the works of maverick theologues superimposing alien themes on the records of the early Christian communities. At the same time it also respects the unique witness of each writer while using a less subjective and more scientific method than the older form criticism school. In contrast to form criticism, redaction criticism portrays in stark relief the distinctive agendas of the canonical writers. Controls like vocabulary preference, arrangement and adjustment of Gospel sources, inclusion of "new" material into the earlier sources, and avoidance of material in sources prevent the interpreter from extended eisegetical flights of fancy. These also provide measurable accountability both to the intent of the writers and to the Spirit who motivated them to take up the pen. Redaction criticism has rescued the NT from the tendency to indiscriminately homogenize its unique and diverse messages. Many important messages are lost when they are garbled into one, resulting in more noise than understanding. Unity cannot be achieved at the expense of diversity. Both unity and diversity characterize the NT and are hallmarks of the Christian view of inspiration.

Under the lens of redaction criticism the pneumatology of Luke can be seen for what it is, apart from assumptions of what it should look like in the light of Paul. For Luke, the dominant function of the Spirit is empowerment for mission, especially in relation to effective witness. Both Luke and Paul are not doing some novel thing when they emphasize different roles of the Holy Spirit; for even the OT writers to whom they are indebted emphasize the role of the Holy Spirit in regeneration and in power to witness (e.g., Num 11:17, 25–26, 29; 1 Sam 10:1–6; 16:13; Isa 44:3; 61:1–2; Ezek 11:19–20; 18:31; 37:1–14).[4]

This study has also demonstrated that when it comes to pneumatology, Luke has ignored the so-called three epochs that he allegedly superimposed upon the synoptic tradition. The post-Pentecost disciples, the infant John, the other witnesses of the infancy narratives, and Jesus himself all witness, empowered by the Holy Spirit. Furthermore, Luke uses the same terms to describe experiences of witnessing in the power of the Holy Spirit in each epoch. Luke blurs the distinctions between any epochs that might exist in the synoptic tradition. This calls into question Conzelmann's suggestion that Luke is responsible for their creation. It is not surprising then that Luke does not maintain neat epochal divisions in salvation history when he alludes to possible links between the Holy Spirit and conversion. He is primarily interested in how inspired witness occurs in *any* era. Thus for Luke, Pentecost is primarily an empowering event: any difference between people's experience with the Spirit before Pentecost and after is basically quantitative, not qualitative (Acts 2:17–18).

Ramifications for the Church

Non-Pentecostals/Non-Charismatics. To non-Pentecostals/non-charismatics the message of Luke is that he expects special endowments of power to occur subsequent to conversion. Inspired witness, with or without glossolalia, appears to be a repeatable pattern in salvation history; therefore, one should be open and receptive to such occurrences in the church. To argue that the "didactic" material in Paul is to be preferred as normative over the accounts of the early church in Acts ignores the nature of salvation history. It is true that one cannot expect every supernatural event of the past to be repeated on demand; yet to reject the possibility, and yes, the inevitability that events are repeated with regularity in salvation history negates the very nature of Christian revelation. Without such parallel repetition, historical events cannot be called salvific with a Saving Intelligence orchestrating them; furthermore, Christian prophecy and typology would then be called into question as well. (Note that the doctrine of Gentiles being candidates for the kingdom of God was based on historical precedent in Acts 10–11.) Salvation history and the events that it relates are not a mere addendum to the systemized message of the church; it is the message.

Furthermore, if one persists in understanding Luke's pneumatology primarily in terms of conversion, one misses the prime question Luke addresses in Luke–Acts: how does effective witness take place? Attempts to harmonize completely Paul's and Luke's material on the Holy Spirit without acknowledging the different questions they raise will only further confuse and divide the church.

Pentecostals and Charismatics. To the Pentecostal or charismatic Luke's message affirms that one should expect special occasions of empowerment. Luke indeed portrays the church as a people empowered by the Holy Spirit. Luke, however, affirms only that tongues often accompany the reception of the Holy Spirit; he does not say that tongues will always accompany it. Luke is only peripherally interested in tongues in relation to the fullness of the Holy Spirit; for him, inspired witness is the essential issue. Many Christians who have not experienced the typical charismatic manifestation may well speak, as Luke puts it, "filled with the Holy Spirit."

Luke's discussion of the Holy Spirit also includes another potential corrective for Pentecostals and charismatics. Just as some Christians minimize power and the possibility of supernatural manifestations, so too, some might be enamored with the power. Jesus himself advised his disciples after the Seventy returned from a successful ministry of preaching, healing, and exorcism: "Nevertheless do not rejoice in this, that the spirits are subject to you: but rejoice that your names are written in heaven" (Luke 10:20). Only Luke preserves this saying of Jesus. In the next breath, however, Jesus "rejoiced in the Holy Spirit" over the powerful advancement of the kingdom of God over the power of the enemy (10:21). For example, Luke records the sin of Simon the magician who tried to buy the power of the Holy Spirit

(Acts 8:9–24). He was seeking the power and not the Person, the authority and not the kingdom. Luke does not reject the power, he just rejects the worship of it.

Luke strikes a balance when he describes the Christian community's response to the Sanhedrin's threats. They did not pray for power for themselves, but simply asked, "And now, Lord . . . grant that Thy bond-servants may speak Thy word with all confidence, while *Thou* does extend Thy hand to heal, and signs and wonders take place through the name of Thy holy servant Jesus" (Acts 4:29–30, NASB, my ital.). As a result "they were all filled with the Holy Spirit, and began to speak the word of God with boldness" (4:31, NASB). The power was ultimately God's; the role of the church was obedient witness.

Sacramentalists. To the sacramentalist, Luke's message affirms that special empowerment occurs after conversion such as during the laying on of hands at confirmation. The church should be seen as a normative locus and instrument for reception of the Spirit. But initiation into the church and empowerment to minister may well occur before baptism. For example, Luke affirms that John was filled with the Holy Spirit while yet in his mother's womb before any baptism of repentance was administered (1:15).[5] Thus baptism and confirmation do not always precede regeneration and empowerment. Certainly Acts makes a case for expecting special empowerment after baptism, but the pattern is not cut in stone.

This is not an assertion that all non-Pentecostals, Pentecostals, charismatics, and sacramentalists have not heard Luke aright, but we believe that we have identified some patterns in these groups that muffle the clear voice of Luke concerning the Holy Spirit. The hope is that when the major emphasis of Lucan pneumatology is recognized, a better understanding of the diversity of the NT witness concerning the Holy Spirit will be maintained and even celebrated. Then divisions and misunderstandings that are unnecessary will cease, and all participants in the present dialogue will speak on the issue, "filled with the Holy Spirit." The Holy Spirit in Luke–Acts calls the church to prayer, praise, celebration, witness, and mission. It is a calling that needs to be heard.

Notes to Chapter 12

1. Montague, *Holy Spirit*, 11–15.
2. For example, F. D. Bruner asks, "How, then, may one be filled with the Holy Spirit? I can paraphrase Paul's answer to the Philippian jailer's

similar question about salvation and give the correct answer: 'Believe in the Lord Jesus, and you will be filled with the Holy Spirit, you and your whole house' (cf. Acts 16:31)"; see F. D. Bruner and W. Hordern, *The Holy Spirit—Shy Member of the Trinity* (Minneapolis: Augsburg, 1984), 20. Notice Luke did *not* say "filled with the Holy Spirit" but "be saved" in 16:31. Luke uses "filled" to mean primarily empowerment for mission and not conversion; *therefore, he did not use the term in Acts 16:31.* This imposition of "filled with the Holy Spirit" into the text in Acts does not respect the redactional integrity of Luke–Acts. It would appear to be an attempt to superimpose Pauline meaning upon Lucan pneumatology and soteriology.

3. Note that Thomas was absent when the Holy Spirit was dispersed by Jesus in John 20:19–23, yet later he acknowledged Jesus as Lord (John 20:24–29), even though Jesus had not breathed the Spirit on him. Obviously John does not intend the Spirit passage in vv. 19–23 to effect conversion.

4. The Old Testament writers do not intend to say that the Holy Spirit's work of grace and transformation would occur only in a later age under a completely different covenant. Salvation came in the old age as it does in the new age: through God's grace and power. O.T. references to Spirit and conversion are not so much calling for a novel experience with God as they are calling for a restoration of the gracious relationship of God's people with God. Even the law presupposed God's grace and his Spirit.

5. This passage would certainly support a case for infant baptism in acknowledgment of the work of the Holy Spirit which potentially has already occurred prenatally.

Appendix: Jesus, John, the Spirit, and the New Age

W HEN DOES THE OLD age—the old covenant—end and when does the new age—the new covenant—begin? Is there one point or event that we can identify as a turning point? How does John the Baptist fit into the picture? Was he part of the new age or was he part of the old? What about Jesus? Did the new age arrive at a precise moment in his life? These are some of the questions that many have asked in the study of Luke–Acts. It appears, however, that Luke himself was not as concerned with these points as some have thought. His concern is not so much in distinguishing when the old age ended and when the new age began as in portraying the new age as the age of the Spirit. His major interest is to show that the same Spirit who filled John and empowered Jesus is the same Spirit who filled and empowered Jesus' followers.

The Descent of the Dove:
The Beginning of the New Age?

Dunn says that it is incorrect to identify the experience of Jesus with that of believers, since the experience of Jesus at the Jordan has primary significance as a "pivotal point" in salvation history and not as divine empowering. For Dunn, the experience of Jesus at the Jordan[1] is "the beginning, albeit in a restricted sense, of the End-time, the messianic age, the new covenant."[2] Dunn considers it a pivot point upon which "the whole of salvation history swings round into a new course,"[3] the beginning of the new covenant. Therefore, according to Dunn, Luke considers John a definite part of the old epoch of the Law and Prophets.

Dunn cites Luke 16:16 and Acts 10:37 as evidence of John's exclusive role in the previous age. Because of this, he says, "Luke relates the close of the Baptist's ministry before turning to his encounter with Jesus."[4] Consequently, Dunn does not find it surprising that John's preaching was futuristic and that Jesus' preaching contained a tone of realized eschatology. John's work was of the old and was therefore of the "spirit and power of Elijah" (Luke 1:17). The post-Pentecostal works were of the "Spirit of Jesus" (Acts 16:7).[5] It follows then that "the first two chapters are entirely OT in character and even in thought and phraseology; OT ritual and piety is prominent throughout, and the Spirit is pre-eminently the Spirit of prophecy."[6]

The question arises, Is Dunn right? Is this Luke's understanding of the experience of Jesus at the Jordan? Does Luke understand the anointing of Jesus to be the pivotal point in salvation history? Granted, Dunn is summarizing the evidence of the Gospels to address contemporary questions of pneumatology; but he, like Conzelmann, relies on Lucan passages to declare John part of the old age and Jesus, anointed by the Spirit, part of the new age. It is true that Luke recognizes high points in the continuing salvation history, but it is impossible to say definitively when one age in Luke's account begins and the other ends. They often overlap and blend together. It is for this reason that the anointing of Jesus with the Holy Spirit at the Jordan cannot be considered the definitive point for the inauguration of the new age.

Dunn calls it the new covenant.[7] The use of this phrase demonstrates the ambiguity of the termination and initiation of the old and new ages. Certainly the establishment of the new covenant should be closer to the Lord's Supper, the passion, resurrection, and ascension. Only when Jesus had endured this "baptism" (Luke 12:50) was the covenant established. The ascension also played a key role in bringing in the eschaton, for as a result of it Jesus poured out the Holy Spirit (Acts 2:33) which was to occur in the last days (Acts 2:17). Surprisingly Luke does not mention the crucifixion in 9:51: "When the days drew near for him to be received up, he set his face to go to Jerusalem."

Luke does not clearly identify the day that ushered in the new age; rather, he endeavors to continue the account of salvation history by recording the coming of Jesus and the outpouring of his Spirit. Dunn notes that the events of the Jordan only initiated the eschaton "in a restricted sense."[8] But even if it was the initiation of the new covenant only in a restricted sense, does that mean that there are no parallels between the empowering of Jesus at the Jordan and the empowering of his followers?

John: New Age or Old?

It is true that John must, in some sense, be considered part of the old age, according to Luke 16:16 and Acts 10:37, as Dunn observes. The Acts passage does not necessarily refer to two mutually exclusive ages in using the phrase in reference to the Baptist, "after the baptism which John preaches." Conzelmann sees a connection between the *archesthai* ("beginning") of 10:37 and *archeō* ("beginning") in Mark 1:1 and concludes that Luke is aware of the tradition that the good news of Jesus began with John as a forerunner.[9] The material that Luke uses in 10:37 does not, according to Conzelmann, thoroughly disassociate John from the era of Jesus.

> In the pre-Lucan tradition John is understood from the standpoint of the dawn of the new eschatological age. He is more than a prophet, he is the forerunner, he is Elijah. Here Mark and Matthew use traditions which Luke himself has preserved for us, so it is all the more striking that Luke's own pronouncements point in another direction. . . . In the tradition John the Baptist stands on the dividing line between the old and the new epoch. He not only announces the imminent Kingdom of God, but is himself a sign of its arrival. . . . This is implied by the position which Mark gives him at the opening of the Gospel.[10]

Conzelmann suggests that Luke has adjusted the tradition so that John belonged to the earlier of the two epochs. "John no longer marks the arrival of the new aeon, but the division between two epochs in the one continuous story, such as is described in Luke xvi, 16."[11] Even so, Conzelmann, who believes Luke sees John as exclusively part of the old era, suspects that Acts 10:37 does not reflect this sentiment. He also acknowledges that John's preaching of repentance somehow slipped into the new epoch.[12]

Luke 16:16 appears, at first glance, to associate John with the old epoch (especially in light of 7:28); but it remains to be seen if this is a mutually exclusive association. "The law and the prophets were until John; since then the good news of the kingdom of God is preached, and every one enters it violently." "Until" (*mechri*) does not necessarily include John in the old age without access to the other; neither must it express the sense of a punctiliar transition as its use in Matthew 13:30 with the word "harvest" ($\aleph^1$, C, W, Θ) would demonstrate.

In the remaining two instances of *mechri* in Luke–Acts the word is not used to separate two events. They both occur in passages that describe the time for events as overlapping (Acts 10:30, see esp. NASB; and Acts 20:7ff.). "Since then" (*apo tote*) does not exclude John from the new age. The uses of *apo* are not always ablative, denoting separation.[13] Again, the transition must not always be viewed as punctiliar. Concerning the use of *tote*, BDF note:

> The use of *tote* as a connective particle to introduce a subsequent event, but not one taking place at a definite time ('thereupon,' not 'at that time'), is unclassical; it is particularly characteristic of Mt, but is also found in Lk (especially Acts).[14]

Blass and Debrunner immediately continue by noting that *apo tote* is one of several "equivalent circumstantial formulae." They see it introducing a "subsequent event," but the question of timing is not clearly defined.[15] Therefore, the meaning of the verse does not exclude John from activity in the new age. The "subsequent event" could be viewed as a result of the former one. Perhaps if Luke intended to exclude John from the new he would have used the combination of *apo-mechri* which would set off an era as a separate unit (Acts 10:30; Rom 5:14).[16] Jeremias identifies elements in 16:16 as traditional in character, and *apo tote* is identified as traditional as well.[17] He considers the meaning of *apo tote* to be "afterwards" or "next" (*darauf*). He apparently bases this on his opinion of the meaning of the context[18] and may be influenced by the Matthean version. Perhaps *tote* here should also carry the more classical meaning that Jeremias identifies for the thirty-five remaining uses of it in Luke–Acts,[19] "then, in those days, at that time." Luke may have appended *tote* to the *apo* he found in Q (Matt 11:12).

The identification of 16:16 as traditional raises several possibilities. First, the intent of the passage may well be from Luke's source and not be his own. If this traditional meaning excluded John from the new era, then this would not be the first time that Luke presented a traditional chronology that he modified elsewhere. Second, if he were aware of the version in Matthew, then he either created or substituted another version. (Of course two different versions of Q might have existed, and Luke might have been familiar with only one.) Matthew's reading could indicate that John was of the old era. If Luke were aware of it and understood it as such, then he may have opted for his version since in it John could be seen as part of the new era. Admittedly all of these possibilities are rather speculative for both Matthew and Luke, but Luke could well have intended the passage to mean that John initiated the preaching of the good news, and the meaning would be similar to the Matthean parallel, as understood by BAGD, that all the prophets and the law were "up to the time of John [*eōs Iōannou*]."[20] This would be in keeping with the associations of John with the good news and salvation in 1:77 and 3:18 (pace Conzelmann, who maintains that contextually

euangelizesthai means preaching in these verses).[21] Therefore, it is difficult to compartmentalize Jesus and John into two ages on the basis of
Luke 16:16, and then assume that Jesus' anointing was the inauguration
of the new age, or that the address at the Nazareth synagogue was the
new beginning. The activity of John and Jesus elsewhere in Luke make
such an interpretation unlikely.

Other elements in the immediate context also mitigate against
it. In the Matthean parallel the reference to the Prophets and the Law
prophesying until John (Matt 11:13) is linked with the promise that
though none then born of women was greater than John the Baptist, the
least in the kingdom was greater than he (Matt 11:11). Luke separates
these two; the former he places in 16:16, the latter in 7:28. Luke's
account of the latter notes that "no one of those born of women is greater
than John, but the least in the kingdom of God is greater than he is"
(my trans.). His account of the saying is axiomatic with the use of the
present; thus, this fact would not be changed in the future. Both statements co-exist. Matthew, however, notes that none had yet arisen born
of a woman (*ouk egēgertai en gennētois gynaikōn*, note the perfect tense)
that was greater than John (11:11). Matthew appears to have temporally
separated John from the kingdom age more than Luke purportedly did.
This is confirmed by Matthew's contextual linkage of this saying with
the notation of the end of the era of the prophets with John (11:13ff.).
Luke uses the version that John was greater but that the kingdom-of-
God people would be even greater to identify the penitent believers with
the kingdom (7:28). Matthew uses it to make an observation concerning
the ages.

This obviously challenges Conzelmann's suggestion that Matthew and Mark see John as the beginning of the Gospel and thus as less
of a separate age, and that Luke has superimposed the ages on the
traditions. The tendency to speak of separate times for John and the
kingdom in Matthew 11:13 has parallels in the antithetical parallelism
of the water baptism and Spirit baptism sayings of John (Matt 3:11;
Mark 1:8). Matthew also apparently sees two epochs, one for the herald
and one for Jesus who would save Israel from its sins (1:21); for in his
account of John's ministry he omits the reference to forgiveness of sins
(Matt 3:2; Mark 1:4; Luke 3:3). These instances imply epochal distinctions between John and Jesus. Implicit in the account of John's questions
to Jesus in Q is a temporal division between John and Jesus. John's
emissaries ask, "Are you he who is to come, or shall we look for another?"
(Matt 11:3). By recording this, Matthew preserves a statement contra-
dictory to the idea that John is the initiation of the eschaton. Here the
forerunner as the initiator of the new age is minimized, and Jesus is

considered the Coming One. (If this ambivalence is present in Luke's sources, one can see how he is forced to the conclusion that John and Jesus shared the office of the New Elijah.) The Petrine confession, common to the synoptic tradition, groups John with the prophets of old and distinctively sets Jesus apart from all of them. Thus it is not so easy to maintain that Mark and Q place John "on the dividing line between the old and new epoch."[22] In fact, a dynamic tension must be maintained to some degree in all of the Gospels. Perhaps it is fair to say that Q tends to place John in a separate epoch more than Mark does.[23] Yet even Mark, though he identifies the beginning of the Gospel with John, maintains a temporal distinction between John's prediction and Jesus' fulfillment of it in his preaching (Mark 1:15).

Luke also preserves material that would mitigate against the concept of John as the division between the two epochs. Conzelmann is comfortable with the presence of the purported old tradition chronology since he maintains that Luke's omissions and additions to these reveal his true motive.[24] But the question arises, Why does Luke often allow this material to stand unedited? Luke recognizes John's baptism as acceptable for signifying the forgiveness of sin (3:3). He largely incorporates the baptism of John into his accounts of the early church preaching,[25] and he feels free to superimpose Christian structures on the Baptist traditions (see chapter 3). This can hardly be the redactional activity of a writer who sees the works of Jesus and John in two different epochs. Jesus continued John's preaching of repentance, as Conzelmann notes. But it is to miss the point to say that "it is only through the proclamation of the Kingdom that John's preaching, and only through the Spirit that John's baptism, are raised to a level appropriate to the new epoch."[26] He assumes that John's denial of being Messiah precludes him from the new age.[27] Only by disallowing the infancy narrative as genuinely Lucan can Conzelmann divorce John and his work from the new age. Luke sees John's coming as the beginning of the age of the good news of salvation (Acts 10:37; 1:22; Luke 1:77–78; 3:18). If Dunn is correct that the Gospels generally consider John's preaching as futuristic, then it is most surprising that Luke records John's practical definitions for repentance in the sample sermon of chapter 3.

Furthermore, the initiation of the new covenant becomes less of a point in time and more of an era in itself with poorly defined parameters when the activity of the Holy Spirit, the hallmark of the new age, is seen so prevalent in the infancy narrative. It is inadequate to relegate John's filling with the Holy Spirit in his mother's womb (1:15) and his subsequent inspired statements in chapter 3 to the "spirit of Elijah," and then conclude that John and the other prophetic speakers in Luke 1 and 2 were operating as OT prophets.[28] First of all, the role of Elijah is shared by John *and* Jesus in Luke's estimation, as we have previously observed. This sharing cannot be seen as Luke's attempt to view Jesus as the fulfillment of the eschatological forerunner and herald belonging to Elijah's office. It is not a case of usurpation of John's role but an association of the miraculous aspects of Elijah's ministry with Jesus.[29]

It cannot be ignored that John was filled with the Holy Spirit and therefore spoke authoritatively in his ministry, just as Jesus and his followers did. The other inspired speakers and witnesses in the infancy narrative could not have spoken in the office of Elijah. They too must be seen as speaking, as Luke notes in his commentary, full of the Holy Spirit or when the Holy Spirit came upon them. It is not adequate to relegate the speaking of John, Zechariah, Simeon, and Elizabeth to the OT era.[30] The OT allusions in the infancy narrative do not demand an OT epoch. (Even the so-called epoch of the church began with references to the OT.) If this were so then Jesus' inaugural address, since it is a reading from the prophecy of Isaiah, should be seen in terms of the old age. The use of *pimplēmi* here is significant; it cannot be viewed as just OT prophecy. The Lucan stamp is too indelible for its use in the infancy narrative to be divorced from the rest of Luke–Acts. Luke's infancy narrative is correctly called a "little Pentecost." How else can one explain the increased activity of prophecy in an age when it is generally assumed to have terminated hundreds of years earlier? Luke's understanding of the salvation history, as reflected in the sermons in Acts, sees the flow of that history as continuous. The works of John, Jesus, and his church were in its mainstream. Luke does not consider the prophetic work of the Holy Spirit as a priori part of the old epoch.[31] The work of the Holy Spirit as presented in both of Luke's volumes primarily focuses on inspired speaking. Speaking is the dominant activity of the Holy Spirit in Jesus' ministry and in the believers' witness. Even in the accounts of healings and exorcisms this is the case. P. S. Minear notes that we are not dealing with "separate and specific Old Testament predictions" when we look at the prophecies of the infancy narrative, but rather "we are dealing with an outburst of the gift of prophecy, in which each interpreter of the Scriptures is himself a prophet for his own day, and for the church of Luke's day."[32] He expresses Luke's comprehensive understanding of the salvation history:

> In Luke, all the prophetic figures are servants of the same word, glad recipients of the same promise, linked together into one community by the same Spirit, giving testimonies to a single divine action. The individual prophets, who appear seriatim, have a close kinship to one another as do those whose tongues were touched at Pentecost.

All speak of the same salvation. It is God's fulfillment of his promise to which they all point. And they do more than point to the fact of fulfillment; they illustrate the communal response evoked by the fact: faith, hope, endurance, joy, expectation, exultation. Luke does not argue that the event of consummation is vindicated by its correspondence to specific predictions; rather, he joins in the full spectrum of response to the Good News, with the resurgence of the prophetic gift as one of the phenomena of the new age.[33]

Pneumatologically speaking, the ages are blurred and overlap. This is due to Luke's imposition of his pneumatology on the traditions he has received. He tries to maintain the epochal distinctions in their various forms in Mark and in Q, but he had to abandon the divisions at points or at least broaden them to accommodate his pneumatological observations. For Luke the Holy Spirit's work is the common thread of the total salvation history. If Luke emphasizes one particular age it can only be seen as the age of the fullness of the Holy Spirit. All other epochs and events must serve this goal of history and must be viewed as subunits of the whole. This is why Luke finds it necessary to express the coming of the new age in terms of the Holy Spirit; to him it is the age of the Spirit. Thus it is impossible to assign the arrival of the Holy Spirit and the commencement of the new age to one specific point in time in Luke's Gospel, especially the anointing of Jesus at the Jordan. To do so is to strain several delicate points.

For example, since Dunn believes that the anointing of Jesus at the Jordan was the initiation of the new age, he finds it necessary to consider the birth of Jesus as part of the old covenant.[34] In Luke's Gospel, we see the Holy Spirit at work not only in the witnesses to Jesus in the first three chapters but also in the very birth of Jesus himself. How can his conception by the Holy Spirit not be considered a part of the new age? His conception by the Holy Spirit coupled with his anointing with the same not only mitigates against adoptionistic Christology, but it also discourages breaking up the complete act of salvation into separate mutually exclusive epochs.[35] To separate the advent of the incarnation himself from the new age appears totally arbitrary. The empowering of Jesus is a beginning, but it cannot be divorced from his birth. Dunn notes:

> There is a sense in which Jesus is Messiah and Son of God from his birth (1.35, 43, 76; 2.11, 26, 49); but there is also a sense in which he only becomes Messiah and Son at Jordan, since he does not in fact become the Anointed One (Messiah) till then (Isa. 61.1–2; Luke 4.18; Acts 10.38), and only then does the heavenly voice hail him as Son; just as there is a sense in which he does not become Messiah and Son till his resurrection and ascension (Acts 2.36; 13.33).[36]

Jesus is considered the Son of God both on the merit of his being conceived by the Holy Spirit (1:35) and on the basis of his future anointing at the Jordan. It can also be argued that the divine voice only announced what was already a fact, the sonship and messiahship of Jesus.[37] The anointing should be seen then as a subunit of the new age whose beginning preceded the anointing at an undetermined time. G. E. Ladd's observations concerning the eschaton's having come but having not yet been fulfilled[38] fit Luke's scheme well. The kingdom came before Jesus' anointing in the events of the infancy narrative, especially the incarnation. Its fulfillment seems to have come in installments with the final act to occur in the Parousia. Thus Jesus' anointing, resurrection, and ascension, and the outpouring of the Holy Spirit upon believers all in their own right can be seen as eschatological fulfillment.

Jesus' experience at the Jordan should be considered a subsection of the new age, as should his birth and ascension. In this structure, Dunn's observation concerning the various fulfillments of Jesus' sonship would fit well as would the following observation, "At each new phase of salvation history Jesus enters upon a new and fuller phase of his messiahship and sonship."[39]

Luke's Comprehensive View of Salvation History

The "change in history" cannot be narrowed down in Luke's Gospel to one event in the life of Jesus but occurs in the whole event—the incarnation, in his announced arrival, conception, empowering, death, resurrection, and ascension. Luke's comprehensive view of salvation history minimizes such divisions, as is evident in his presentation of the salvation history in the speeches in Acts. To superimpose exacting divisions upon Luke's work is to repeat Conzelmann's mistake. The divisions are there, but they do not progress in well-defined steps. But of Conzelmann's three divisions (the old epoch, the Jesus epoch, and the church epoch), the first two are not Luke's construction.

He has inherited them from his sources and chafes at the segmented chronology superimposed upon him. He is so interested in the third epoch that he structures the other two in terms of the life of the church. Thus, sometimes, if not often, Luke sees the epochs not as separate voices but as one voice steadily increasing in volume. We should not be surprised that the overlaps occur in a work which sees the eschaton as realized in the community yet which also records the apocalyptic appearing of God which will transform the cosmos.

Minear criticizes a similar chronological structure which Conzelmann constructs as a result of rejecting a priori the Lucan character of the infancy narrative.[40] By ignoring the eschatological, soteriological, and pneumatological themes in chapters 1 and 2 and common to the rest of Luke–Acts, Conzelmann is able to divorce John the Baptist from the new age and make the beginning of the new age the day, the *sēmeron*, which Jesus read about in Isaiah 61:1 and declared fulfilled at Nazareth. In contrast Minear correctly notes that a decisive shift in history occurred when God honored his promises and the prayers of his people by sending the Savior.

> This decision is announced by Gabriel's message and by the powerful actions of the Holy Spirit. Gabriel and the angels are the first messengers who tell the good tidings (Conzelmann admits the Lucan character of *euangelizesthai* but insists upon its "non-eschatological" content [pp. 23, n. 1; 40, 222–23]).[41]

This demands that John be seen as part of the new age which in some manner commenced before Jesus' inaugural address at the Nazareth synagogue. Minear also points out the typological correspondence between Jesus and John which Conzelmann acknowledges to be present in the infancy material.[42] This comparison of John in no way denigrates him; rather, the honorable title of "prophet of the Most High" is conferred upon him (1:76). "The work of both men is seen as essential to the fulfillment of the promise, as ground for the joy of redemption."[43] Thus the two cannot be separated. If Conzelmann's interpretation of Luke 16:16 is correct, then it seems strange that Luke allows the high estimation of John in the infancy narrative to stand. Minear notes:

> In passage after passage Conzelmann interprets Luke's omissions and additions to Mark as part of a conscious intention on the redactor's part to diminish the role of John, so that he will no longer mark "the arrival of the new aeon" (p. 22–23).[44]

Conzelmann is correct in noting that after the infancy narrative, explicit references to John as Elijah diminish,[45] but implicitly the office of forerunner is still John's. Luke does not ignore John's role after the infancy narrative. Instead he more strictly defines John's role in order to present Jesus as the One empowered to do the wondrous works of the Holy Spirit and to emphasize his role as the Baptizer in the Holy Spirit, not to mark the end of John's age. If Jesus' announcement of his anointing with the Holy Spirit at Nazareth is the point at which the new era begins, then one would expect little or no association of John the Baptist and the other characters in 1:15–3:18 with the Holy Spirit. But we have exactly the opposite; these references to the activity of the

Holy Spirit carry the Lucan stamp which is so prevalent in the rest of Luke–Acts.

It therefore seems unlikely that there is a chasm that cannot be bridged between John and Jesus which would hinder viewing the experiences of the pre-baptismal witness to Jesus and the experiences of the post-ascension church as parallel to Jesus' anointing of power at the Jordan. Minear is correct in observing, "Surely the whole sequence of events from the conception of John to the arrival of Paul in Rome belongs within the orbit of Luke's testimony to the ways in which God is pouring out his Spirit 'on all flesh.' "[46]

But even if Dunn is correct and the anointing at Jordan primarily functioned as the initiation of an era, the parallels between Jesus' empowering by the Holy Spirit and the believers' endowment with power cannot be ignored or minimized. According to Luke, Jesus saw the finished role of his "baptism" (i.e., his death, resurrection, and ascension, 12:50) not in the empowering at the Jordan but in the ascension. Jesus' ministry culminated in the ascension which enabled him to pour out the Holy Spirit on his followers (Acts 2:33).

Notes to Appendix

1. Dunn avoids referring to the event as the baptism of Jesus since he wishes to avoid a causal relationship between the water baptism of Jesus and the descent of the Holy Spirit (*Baptism*, 32–33). With the possible exception of Matthew, the Gospels all make it clear that Jesus' baptism by John is not the primary interest, and thus the baptism cannot be seen as the term to express the complete significance of the divine acts at the Jordan.

2. Ibid., 24.
3. Ibid.
4. Ibid., 25.
5. Ibid., 26.
6. Ibid., 31–32.
7. Ibid., 25 and passim.
8. Ibid., 24.
9. Conzelmann, *Theology*, 22.
10. Ibid.
11. Ibid., 22–23.
12. Ibid., 23.
13. BAGD, 86–87.
14. BDF §459,2, p. 240.
15. BDF §459,3, p. 240.
16. BAGD, 86.
17. Jeremias, *Die Sprache*, 259.
18. Ibid.

19. Ibid.

20. BAGD, 335.

21. Conzelmann, *Theology,* 23.

22. Ibid., 22.

23. If Mark is inclined to emphasize the continuity of John in the new epoch and if Q emphasizes the distinctiveness of the eras of John and Jesus, then Luke can be seen as their mediator creating a blend of both.

24. Conzelmann, *Theology,* 22.

25. It may be argued that the Ephesian Pentecost of Acts 19 recorded Paul's rejection of John's baptism, but this is not the case. Paul made available to the Ephesians the Spirit baptism of Jesus which complemented their Baptist experience. The rebaptism was not for repentance unto the forgiveness of sins but to acknowledge Jesus as the Baptizer in the Holy Spirit. If Luke intended otherwise, he would have contradicted the Petrine initiatory formula of Acts 2 which he already had superimposed upon the Baptism traditions of Luke 3. At the Samaritan Pentecost (Acts 8) the baptism of John was probably assumed in the baptism in Jesus' name. Note that the baptism was not presented in terms of repentance but as an acknowledgement of Jesus as the Christ on the basis of the miraculous acts performed by Philip.

26. Conzelmann, *Theology,* 23.

27. Ibid.

28. Dunn, *Baptism,* 26.

29. Perhaps this is also due to a pneumatological analogy between Elijah calling fire down from heaven at Mt. Carmel and Jesus baptizing the people in the Holy Spirit and fire at Pentecost when he poured out the Holy Spirit from heaven.

30. Dunn, *Baptism,* 31; and Bruce, "The Holy Spirit in Acts," 167.

31. Dunn unsuccessfully attempts to dispose of P. S. Minear's criticism of Conzelmann's epochs in which Minear notes that the prophecy of the infancy narrative is hard to divorce from Jesus and his age. Minear argues that "the mood, resonance, and thrust of the birth narratives are such as to discourage the neat assignment of John and Jesus to separate epochs" ("Luke's Use of the Birth Stories," 123). Dunn argues that in the infancy narrative speakers primarily function as prophets. Therefore, they must be considered part of the OT epoch since the Spirit in the narrative "is pre-eminently the Spirit of prophecy" (*Baptism,* 31–32).

32. Minear, "Luke's Use of the Birth Stories," 119.

33. Ibid., 119–20.

34. Dunn, *Baptism,* 31.

35. Dunn does not present an adoptionistic Christology, but he does say that this is not the central issue. "It is not so much that Jesus became what he was not before, but that history became what it was not before; and Jesus as the one who effects these changes in history from within history, is himself affected by them" (*Baptism,* 29). Jesus could well have been affected by the Holy Spirit's working in history and indeed was, but this in no way demands that he could not have been affected by the Spirit's acts before his anointing at the Jordan.

36. Ibid., 28.

37. Marshall, *Luke*, 155; E. Lohmeyer, *Das Evangelium des Markus* (Göttingen: [n.p.], 1959), 23.

38. G. E. Ladd, *The Presence of the Future* (London: SPCK, 1974), 114ff.

39. Dunn, *Baptism*, 29.

40. Conzelmann, *Theology*, 118.

41. Minear, "Luke's Use of the Birth Stories," 122.

42. Conzelmann, *Theology*, 24.

43. Minear, "Luke's Use of the Birth Stories," 122.

44. Ibid., 123.

45. Note that Luke follows Mark and Q in quoting Isaiah 40 which was understood to be a reference to Elijah in his sources. Furthermore, in his eulogy of John in ch. 7 he includes Mal 3:1 which would readily be associated with Elijah. So the references diminish, but neither disappear nor contradict the associations of John with Elijah in later passages.

46. Minear, "Luke's Use of the Birth Stories," 120.

Selected Bibliography

Alexander, P. H. "Blasphemy Against the Holy Spirit." *Dictionary of Pentecostal and Charismatic Movements.* Grand Rapids: Zondervan, 1988, 87–89.

_____. "Jesus Christ and the Spirit." *Dictionary of Pentecostal and Charismatic Movements.* Grand Rapids: Zondervan, 1988, 88–91.

Allen, W. C. *A Critical and Exegetical Commentary on the Gospel According to St. Matthew.* ICC. Edinburgh: T. & T. Clark, 1901.

Anderson, H. "Broadening Horizons: The Rejection at Nazareth Pericope of Luke 4:16–30 in Light of Recent Critical Trends." *Int* 18 (3, July 1964): 259–75.

Bacon, B. W. *American Journal of Theology* (1905): 451–73.

Barrett, C. K. *The Holy Spirit and the Gospel Tradition.* 2d ed.; London: SPCK, 1966.

Beare, F. W. *The Gospel According to Matthew: A Commentary.* Oxford: Blackwell, 1981.

Bengel, J. A. *Gnomen of the New Testament.* Translated by A. R. Fausset. Edinburgh: T. & T. Clark, 1858.

Black, M. *An Aramaic Approach to the Gospels and Acts.* 3d ed.; Oxford: Clarendon Press, 1967.

Brown, C., ed. *The New International Dictionary of New Testament Theology.* 3 vols. Grand Rapids: Zondervan, 1975–1978.

Brown, R. E. *The Birth of the Messiah: A Commentary on the Infancy Narratives in Matthew and Luke.* Garden City: Image Books, 1977.

Bruce, A. B. *The Expositor's Greek Testament: The Synoptic Gospels.* Vol. 1. Edited by W. R. Nicoll. London: Hodder and Stoughton, 1897.

Bruce, F. F. *The Acts of the Apostles: The Greek Text with Introduction and Commentary.* Leicester: InterVarsity, 1952.

_____. *Commentary on the Book of the Acts: The English Text with Introduction, Exposition, and Notes.* NICNT. Grand Rapids: Eerdmans, 1954.

_____. "The Holy Spirit in the Acts of the Apostles." *Int* 27 (April 1973): 131–204.

Bruner, F. D. and W. Hordern. *The Holy Spirit—Shy Member of the Trinity.* Minneapolis: Augsburg, 1984.

Bultmann, R. "*agalliasis.*" *TDNT* (1964) 1:19–21.

_____. *The History of the Synoptic Tradition.* Translated by J. Marsh. 2d ed.; Oxford: Blackwell, 1972.

Burgess, S., and G. McGee, eds. *Dictionary of Pentecostal and Charismatic Movements.* Grand Rapids: Zondervan, 1988.

Burkitt, F. C. *Christian Beginnings.* London: London University, 1924.

Cadbury, H. J. *The Making of Luke–Acts.* London: SPCK, 1961.

_____. *The Style and Literary Method of Luke.* HTS 6. Cambridge: Harvard, 1920.

Chilton, B. D. *God in Strength: Jesus' Announcement of the Kingdom.* Studien zum Neuen Testament und seiner Umwelt. Edited by A. Fuchs and F. Linz. Freistadt: Verlag F. Plöchl, 1979.

Conzelmann, H. *A Commentary on the Acts of the Apostles.* Translated by J. Limburg, A. T. Kraabel, and D. H. Juel. Philadelphia: Fortress, 1987.

_____. *History of Primitive Christianity.* Translated by J. E. Steely. Nashville: Abingdon, 1973.

_____. *The Theology of St. Luke.* Translated by G. Buswell. New York: Harper and Row, 1961.

_____. "*charis.*" *TDNT* (1974) 9:359–415.

Cranfield, C. E. B. *The Gospel According to Saint Mark: An Introduction and Commentary.* CGTC. Edited by C. F. D. Moule. Cambridge: Cambridge University, 1959.

Creed, J. M. *The Gospel According to St. Luke: The Greek Text with Introduction, Notes, and Indices.* London: Macmillan, 1942.

Dabeck, P. "Siehe, es erschienen Moses und Elias." *Bib* 23 (1942): 175–89.

Dalman, G. *The Words of Jesus.* Vol. 1. Edinburgh: T. & T. Clark, 1902.

Dibelius, M. *From Tradition to Gospel.* Translated by B. L. Woolf. New York: Scribner's, 1965.

_____. *Studies in the Acts of the Apostles.* Translated by M. Ling. London: SCM, 1956.

Dillon, R. J. *From Eye-Witnesses to Ministers of the Word: Tradition and Composition in Luke 24.* AnBib 82. Rome: Biblical Institute, 1978.

Dodd, C. H. *The Apostolic Preaching and Its Developments.* Grand Rapids: Baker, 1936.

_____. "The Appearances of the Risen Christ: A Study in Form-Criticism of the Gospels." In *More New Testament Studies,* 102–33. Grand Rapids: Eerdmans, 1968.

Dunn, J. D. G. *Baptism in the Holy Spirit.* London: SCM, 1970.

_____. *Jesus and the Spirit.* London: SCM, 1975.

_____. "Spirit and Kingdom." *ExpT* 82 (1970–71): 36–40.

Dupont, J. *Etudes sur les Acts des Apôtres.* Lectio Divina 45. Paris: Editions due Cerf, 1967.

Ellis, E. E. *The Gospel of Luke.* NCB. Rev. ed.; London: Oliphant, 1966.

Erdmann, G. *Die Vorgeschichten des Lukas und Mättaus—Evangeliums und Vergils Vierte Ekloge.* FRLANT 47. Göttingen: Vandenhoeck, 1932.

Ervin, H. M. *Conversion-Initiation and the Baptism in the Holy Spirit.* Peabody, Mass.: Hendrickson, 1984.

_____. *Spirit-Baptism: A Biblical Investigation.* Peabody, Mass.: Hendrickson, 1987.

_____. *These Are Not Drunken, as Ye Suppose.* Plainfield, N.J.: Logos, 1968.

Esser, H.-H. "Grace, Spiritual Gifts." *NIDNTT* (1976) 2:115–24.

Faierstein, M. M. "Why Do the Scribes Say that Elijah Must Come First?" *JBL* 100 (March 1981): 75–86.

Farmer, W. R. *The Synoptic Problem: A Critical Analysis.* Dillsboro, N.C.: Western North Carolina, 1976.

Fitzmyer, J. A. "The Aramaic 'Elect of God' Text from Qumran Cave 4." In *Essays on the Semitic Background of the New Testament,* pages 127–60. Missoula, Mont.: Scholars, 1974.

_____. *The Gospel According to Luke.* 2 vols. AB 28, 28A. New York: Doubleday, 1981, 1985.

_____. "The Priority of Mark and the 'Q' Source in Acts." In *To Advance the Gospel: New Testament Studies,* pages 3–40. New York: Crossroad, 1981.

Flender, H. *St. Luke: Theologian of Redemptive History.* Translated by R. H. and I. Fuller. London: SPCK, 1967.

Franklin, E. *Christ the Lord: A Study in the Purpose and Theology of Luke–Acts.* London: SPCK, 1975.

Freudenberger, R. "Zum Text der zweier Vaterunserbitte." *NTS* 15 (1968–69): 419–32.

Fuller, R. H. *The Formation of the Resurrection Narratives.* New York: Macmillan, 1971.

Gärtner, B. "Suffer." *NIDNTT* (1978) 3:719–26.

Gasque, W. W. *A History of the Criticism of the Acts of the Apostles.* Grand Rapids: Eerdmans, 1975.

Gils, F. *Jésus Prophète d'Après Les Evangiles Synoptiques.* Louvain: Université de Louvain Institut Orientaliste, 1957.

Godet, F. *A Commentary on the Gospel of St. Luke.* Translated by E. W. Shalders. Edinburgh: T. & T. Clark, 1879.

Grässer, E. *Das Problem der Parusieverzögerung in den Synoptischen Evangelium und in der Apostelgeschichte.* Berlin: A. Töpelmann, 1957.

Green, M. *I Believe in the Holy Spirit.* Grand Rapids: Eerdmans, 1975.

Gundry, R. H. *Matthew: A Commentary on His Literary and Theological Art.* Grand Rapids: Eerdmans, 1982.

Guthrie, D. *New Testament Theology.* Leicester: InterVarsity, 1981.

Haenchen, E. *The Acts of the Apostles: A Commentary.* Translated by B. Noble, et al. Oxford: Basil Blackwell, 1971.

Harnack, A. *The Acts of the Apostles.* Crown Theological Library 27. Translated by J. R. Wilkinson. London: Williams and Norgate, 1909.

_____. *The Sayings of Jesus.* London: [n.p.], 1908.

Harris, R. W., ed. *The New Testament Study Bible.* 16 vols. Springfield, Mo.: The Complete Biblical Library, 1986.

Hinnebusch, P. *Jesus the New Elijah.* Ann Arbor, Mich.: Servant Books, 1978.

Hoffman, P. *Studien zur Theologie der Logienquelle.* Munich: C. H. Beck, 1924.

Jeremias, J. *Die Sprache des Lukasevangeliums: Redaktion und Tradition im Nicht-Markusstoff des dreitten Evangeliums.* Göttingen: Vandenhoeck and Ruprecht, 1980.

_____. "*ēlias.*" *TDNT* (1976) 2:928–1041.

_____. *Jesus' Promise to the Nations.* Translated by S. H. Hooke. London: SPCK, 1958.

_____. "*kleis.*" *TDNT* (1965) 3:744–53.

_____. *New Testament Theology: The Proclamation of Jesus.* Vol. 1. London: SCM, 1967.

_____. *The Parables of Jesus.* 2d rev. ed.; New York: Charles Scribner's Sons, 1924.

_____. *The Prayers of Jesus.* London: SCM, 1967.

Käsemann, E. "The Disciples of John the Baptist in Ephesus." In *Essays on New Testament Themes,* pages 136–48. London: SCM, 1964.

Kealy, J. P. *Luke's Gospel Today.* Denville, N.J.: Dimension Books, 1979.

Keck, L. "Jesus' Entrance upon His Mission." *RevExp* 64 (1967): 465–83.

Kilgallen, J. *The Stephen Speech: A Literary and Redactional Study of Acts 7, 2–53.* AnBib 67. Rome: Pontifical Biblical Institute, 1976.

Kilpatrick, G. D. *The Origins of the Gospel According to St. Matthew.* Oxford: Blackwell, 1946.

Kittel, G. and G. Friedrich, eds. *Theological Dictionary of the New Testament.* 10 vols. Translated by G. Bromiley. Grand Rapids: Eerdmans, ET 1964–1976.

Klausner, J. *The Messianic Idea in Israel.* New York: Macmillan, 1955.

Klostermann, E. *Das Lukasevangelium.* Handkommentar zum Neuen Testament 5. Tübingen: Mohr [Paul Siebeck], 1929.

Ladd, G. E. *The Presence of the Future: The Eschatology of Biblical Realism.* London: SPCK, 1974.

Lagrange, M.-J. *Evangile selon Saint Luc.* 3d ed.; Paris: Victor Lecoffre, 1927,

Lake, K. and H. J. Cadbury. *The Beginnings of Christianity: The Acts of the Apostles, Part 1.* Vol. 4. Edited by F. J. Foakes Jackson and K. Lake. London: Macmillan, 1933.

Lampe, G. W. H. "The Holy Spirit in the Writings of St. Luke." In *Studies in the Gospels: Essays in Memory of R. H. Lightfoot.* Edited by D. E. Nineham, pages 159–200. Oxford: Blackwell, 1955.

_____. *The Seal of the Spirit: A Study in the Doctrine of Baptism and Confirmation.* London: SPCK, 1967.

Leaney, A. R. C. *A Commentary on the Gospel According to St. Luke.* BNTC. Edited by H. Chadwick. London: Adam and Charles Black, 1966.

Lee, S. H. "John the Baptist and Elijah in Lucan Theology." Ph.D. diss., Boston University, Boston, 1972.

Lienhard, J. T. "Acts 6:1–6: A Redactional View." *CBQ* 3 (April 1975): 228–36.

Lindsey, R. L. "A New Approach to the Synoptic Gospels: A Modified Two-Document Theory of the Synoptic Dependence and Inter-dependence." *NovT* 6 (1963): 239–69.

Lohmeyer, E. *Das Evangelium des Markus.* Göttingen [n.p.], 1959.

_____. *The Lord's Prayer.* London: SCM, 1965.

Luce, H. K. *The Gospel According to St. Luke.* CGTC. Cambridge: Cambridge University, 1933.

Lyonnet, S. "*chaire, kecharitōmenē.*" *Bib* 20 (1939): 131–41.

McConnell, D. *A Different Gospel.* Peabody, Mass.: Hendrickson, 1988.

McNamara, M. *Targum and Testament.* Grand Rapids: Eerdmans, 1972.

McNeile, A. H. *The Gospel According to St. Matthew.* London: Macmillan, 1961.

Maneck, J. "The New Exodus in the Books of Luke." *NovT* 2 (1955): 8–23.

Manson, T. W. *The Sayings of Jesus.* London: SCM, 1949.

Marshall, I. H. *The Acts of the Apostles: An Introduction and Commentary.* TNTC. Leicester: InterVarsity, 1980.

————. *The Gospel of Luke: A Commentary on the Greek Text.* NIGTC. Exeter: Paternoster, 1978.

————. *Luke: Historian and Theologian.* Grand Rapids: Zondervan, 1970.

————. "The Resurrection of Jesus in Luke." *TynB* 24 (1973): 55–98.

Metzger, B. *A Textual Commentary on the Greek New Testament.* New York: UBS, 1971.

Minear, P. S. "Luke's Use of the Birth Stories." In *Studies in Luke–Acts.* Edited by L. E. Keck and J. L. Martyn, pages 111–30. London: SPCK, 1966.

————. *To Heal and to Reveal: Prophetic Vocation According to Luke.* New York: Seabury, 1976.

Miyoshi, M. *Der Anfang des Reiseberichts, Lk. 9, 51–10, 24: Eine redaktionsgeschichtliche Untersuchung.* AnBib 60. Rome: Biblical Institute, 1974.

Montague, G. T. *The Holy Spirit: Growth of a Biblical Tradition.* New York: Paulist, 1976.

Moore, G. F. *Judaism in the First Centuries of the Christian Era.* 2 vols. Cambridge, Mass.: Harvard University, 1928.

Mowinckel, S. *He That Cometh.* Nashville: Abingdon, 1954.

Navone, J. *Themes of St. Luke.* Rome: Gregorian University, 1970.

Neil, W. *The Acts of the Apostles.* Century Bible Commentary. Edited by R. Clements and M. Black. London: Morgan, Marshall, and Scott, 1973.

Neyrey, J. *The Passion According to Luke: A Redactional Study of Luke's Soteriology.* New York: Paulist, 1985.

Norden, E. *Agnostos Theos: Untersuchungen zur Formengeschichte religiöser Rede.* Leipzig: Teubner, 1913.

O'Connor, E. D. *Pope Paul and the Spirit: Charisms and Church Renewal in the Teachings of Paul VI.* Notre Dame: Ave Maria, 1978.

Oepke, A. "*kalyptō.*" *TDNT* (1965) 3:556–92.

Oliver, H. H. "The Lucan Birth Stories and the Purpose of Luke–Acts." *NTS* 10 (1964): 202–26.

Orchard, B. *Matthew, Luke and Mark: The Griesbach Solution to the Synoptic Question.* Vol. 1. Manchester: Koinonia, 1976.

Orchard, B. and T. R. W. Longstaff, eds. *J. J. Griesbach: Synoptic and Text-Critical Studies 1776–1976.* SNTSMS 34. Cambridge: Cambridge University, 1978.

Osborne, G. *The Resurrection Narratives: A Redactional Study.* Grand Rapids: Baker, 1984.

Ott, W. *Gebet und Heil: Die Bedeutung der Gebetsparanese in der Lukanische Theologie.* Munich: [n.p.], 1965.

Peisker, C. H. and C. Brown. "Open." *NIDNTT* (1976) 2:726–29.

Plummer. A. *A Critical and Exegetical Commentary on the Gospel According to St. Luke.* ICC. Edinburgh: T. & T. Clark, 1901.

Rackham, R. B. *The Acts of the Apostles: An Exposition.* London: Methuen, 1930.

Robertson, A. T. *Word Pictures in the New Testament: The Acts of the Apostles.* Vol. 3. Grand Rapids: Baker, 1930.

Robinson, J. A. T. "Elijah, John, and Jesus." *Twelve New Testament Studies.* London: SCM, 1962.

Rodd, C. S. "Spirit or Finger?" *ExpT* 72 (1960–61): 157–58.

Scharlemann, M. H. *Stephen: A Singular Saint.* AnBib 34. Rome: Pontifical Biblical Institute, 1968.

Schulz, S. *Q-Die Spruchquelle der Evangelisten.* Zurich: Theologischer Verlag, 1972.

Schürmann, H. " 'Bericht vom Anfang,' Ein Rekonstruktionsversuch auf Grund von Lk 4, 14–16." In *Traditionsgeschichtliche Untersuchungen zu der synoptischen Evangelien.* Düsseldorf: Patmos, 1968.

————. *Das Lukasevangelium.* Herders theologischer Kommentar zum Neuen Testament. Freiburg: Herder, 1969.

Schweizer, E. *The Holy Spirit.* Translated by R. H. and I. Fuller. London: SCM, 1980.

————. *The Good News According to Luke.* Atlanta: John Knox, 1984.

————. *"pneuma."* *TDNT* (1968) 6:332–455.

Shelton, J. B. " 'Filled with the Holy Spirit' and 'Full of the Holy Spirit': Lucan Redactional Phrases." In *Faces of Renewal: Studies in Honor of Stanley H. Horton.* Edited by P. Elbert, 80–107. Peabody, Mass.: Hendrickson, 1988.

————. "Luke 2:18–4:13." In *The New Testament Study Bible: Luke.* Edited by R. Harris, pages 69–119. Springfield, Mo.: The Complete Biblical Library, 1988.

Smalley, S. S. "Spirit, Kingdom, and Prayer in Luke–Acts." *NovT* 15 (1, 1973): 59–71.

Stanton, G. "Stephen in Lucan Perspective." In *Studia Biblica 1978: Papers on Paul and Other New Testament Authors.* JSNT 3. Edited by E. Livingstone, pages 345–60. Sheffield: JSOT, 1980.

Starcky, J. "Les Quatre Etapes du Messianisme à Qumrân." *RB* 70 (1963): 489–505.

Streeter, B. H. *The Four Gospels: A Study of Origins Treating of the Manuscript Tradition, Sources, Authorship and Dates.* London: Macmillan, 1924.

Stronstad, R. *The Charismatic Theology of St. Luke.* Peabody, Mass.: Hendrickson, 1984.

Talbert, C. H. "An Anti-Gnostic Tendency in Lucan Christology." *NTS* 14 (1968–69): 259–71.

_____. *Literary Patterns, Theological Themes, and the Genre of Luke–Acts.* SBLMS 20. Missoula, Mont.: Scholars, 1974.

_____. *Luke and the Gnostics: An Examination of the Lucan Purpose.* Nashville: Abingdon, 1966.

_____, ed. *Perspectives on Luke–Acts.* Edinburgh: T. & T. Clark, 1978.

_____. *Reading Luke: A Literary and Theological Commentary on the Third Gospel.* New York: Crossroad, 1986.

_____. "Shifting Sands: The Recent Study of the Gospel of Luke." *Int* 30 (1976): 381–95.

Tannehill, R. *The Narrative Unity of Luke–Acts.* Philadelphia: Fortress, 1986.

Taylor, V. *Behind the Third Gospel: A Study of the Proto-Luke Hypothesis.* Oxford: Clarendon, 1926.

_____. *The Gospel According to St. Mark.* London: Macmillan, 1966.

Tödt, H. E. *The Son of Man in the Synoptic Tradition.* Translated by D. M. Barton. Philadelphia: Westminster, 1965.

Trites, A. A. "The Prayer Motif in Luke–Acts." In *Perspectives on Luke–Acts.* Edited by C. H. Talbert, pages 168–86. Edinburgh: T. & T. Clark, 1978.

Turner, M. "Spirit Endowment in Luke–Acts: Some Linguistic Considerations." *VoxEv* 12 (1981): 45–63.

Tyson, J. B. "Source Criticism of the Gospel of Luke." In *Perspectives on Luke–Acts.* Edited by C. H. Talbert, pages 24–39. Edinburgh: T. & T. Clark, 1978.

Vermes, G. *Jesus the Jew.* New York: Macmillan, 1973.

Violet, B. "Zum rechten Verständnis der Nazareth-Perikope, Lc 4:16–30." *ZNW* 37 (1938): 251–71.

Wellhausen, J. *Das Evangelium Lucae.* Berlin: Georg Reimer, 1904.

Wilckens, U. *Die Missionreden der Apostelgeschichte: Form und traditions-geschichtliche Untersuchungen.* WMANT 5. 2. Neukirchen: Neu-kirchener Verlag, 1962.

_____. *"sophia."* *TDNT* (1972) 8:465–526.

Wilson, S. G. "Lucan Eschatology." *NTS* 15 (1970): 330–47.

Wink, W. *John the Baptist in the Gospel Tradition.* Cambridge: Cambridge University, 1968.

Winter, P. "On Luke and Lucan Sources." *ZNW* 47 (1956): 217–42.

Zahn, T. *Das Evangelium des Lucas.* Leipzig: A. Deichert, 1913.

Zehnle, R. F. *Peter's Pentecost Discourse: Tradition and Lukan Reinterpretation in Peter's Speeches of Acts 2 and 3.* SBLMS 15. Edited by R. A. Kraft. Nashville: Abingdon, 1971.

Index of Authors

Index of Ancient Sources